325/415

NEW GUESTS OF THE IRISH NATION

NEW GUESTS
OF THE
IRISH NATION

BRYAN FANNING
University College Dublin

IRISH ACADEMIC PRESS
DUBLIN • PORTLAND, OR

First published in 2009 by Irish Academic Press

2 Brookside,
Dundrum Road,
Dublin 14, Ireland

920 NE 58th Avenue, Suite 300
Portland, Oregon,
97213-3786, USA

www.iap.ie

British Library Cataloguing in Publication Data
An entry can be found on request

978 0 7165 2966 8 (cloth)
978 0 7165 2967 5 (paper)

Library of Congress Cataloging-in-Publication Data
An entry can be found on request

Printed by the MPG Books Group in the UK

Contents

Acknowledgements

A large number of people deserve thanks for their help and support. In particular I wish to acknowledge Neltah Chadamayo, Dr Roland Erne, Dr Alice Feldman, Professor Tom Garvin, Pat Guerin, Dr Deborah Hayes, Dr Kevin Howard, Dr Beth Humphries, Lisa Hyde, Dr Daniel Jewesbury, Dr Patricia Kennedy, Sr Breege Keenan, Professor Gabriel Kiely, Fidele Mutwarasibo, Dr Pat Nugent, Dawn O'Connor, Fergus O'Donoghue S.J., Professor Michel Prum, Piaras Mac Éinrí, Dr Ronnie Moore, Professor Willie Nolan, Joan Roddy, Professor Jo Shaw, James Stapleton, Dier Tong and Dr Angela Veale.

Many of the chapters have earlier published incarnations and are reproduced here by permission. These have been edited to avoid unnecessary repetitions but not so as to interfere with their individual coherence. In a few cases postscripts have been added. The urge to impose twenty-twenty hindsight has been resisted. As the book developed, the need to place the changes of the last decade in a historical context became apparent, hence the inclusion of Chapter 2. It seemed difficult to consider the integration of immigrants without first addressing the question: integration into what? Chapters 13 and 14, along with Chapter 2, address this question. The origins of other chapters are as follows. Chapter 3: 'Go move shift in twentieth-century Clare', in M. Lynch and P. Nugent (eds), *Clare: History and Society. Interdisciplinary Essays on the History of an Irish County* (Dublin: Geography Publications, 2008); Chapter 4: 'The "violent Irish" and anti-Traveller violence', in M. Prum, B. Deschamps and M.C. Barbier (eds), *Killing the Other: Racial, Ethnic, Religious and Homophobic Violence in the English-Speaking World* (London: Cavendish, 2007): Chapter 5: 'The political currency of Irish racism: 1997–2002, *Studies*, 91, 364 (2002); Chapter 6: 'Asylum-seeker and migrant children in Ireland: Racism, institutional racism and social work', in D. Hayes and B. Humphries (eds), *Social Work, Immigration and Asylum: Debates, Dilemmas and Ethical Issues for Social Work and Social Care Practice* (London: Jessica Kingsley Press, 2004); Chapter 7: B. Fanning, 'Internal Exiles', *Asyland*, no. 5 (summer 2003), 'On beasts of burden (and their children)', *Asyland*, no. 10 (winter 2004) and 'New guests of the nation', *Studies*, 93, 369 (2004); Chapter 8 (with Fidele Mutwarasibo): 'Nationals/non-nationals: immigration, citizenship and politics in the Republic of Ireland', *Ethnic and Racial Studies*, 30, 3 (2007), pp.439–60; Chapter 9: 'Irish connections: Immigration and the politics of belonging', *Variant*, 26 (2006), pp.6–8; Chapter 10: 'Seamus Deane and Edmund Burke', *Studies*, no. 374 (2005), pp.300–7; Chapter 11: 'Against the racial state', *Studies*, 96, 381 (2007), pp.7–16; Chapter 12 (with Roland Erne): 'Social partnership and the politics of immigrant worker protection', 'The Unprotected Migrant: Mobility, Social Policy and Labour Rights in Europe' conference, Tampere, Finland, May 2006; Chapter 13: 'The new Irish: Cosmopolitanism and adaptive nation-building', Keynote address at 'The New Irish?' conference, Centre for the Study of Culture and Society, Dundalk Institute of Technology, 27 September 2007; Chapter 14: extract published as 'The protocols of the tribe', *Translocations*, 3, 1 (2008). This book is dedicated to the memory of Zhao Liu Tao, John Ward, Michael Doherty, Mariusz Szwajkos and Pavel Palite.

List of Abbreviations

AFRI	Action from Ireland
AkiDwa	Akina Dada wa Africa
AMCSS	Association of Management of Catholic Secondary Schools
ASC	Africa Solidarity Centre
CDP	Community Development Project
CERD	Committee on the Elimination of Racial Discrimination
DPP	Director of Public Prosecutions
EEA	European Economic Area
ECRE	European Council on Refugees and Exiles
GAA	Gaelic Athletic Association
HSE	Health Services Executive (HSE)
IBEC	Irish Business and Employers Confederation
ICTU	Irish Congress of Trade Unions (ICTU)
IOM	International Organisation on Migration
JMB	Joint Management Body for Secondary Schools (JMB)
NAPS	National Anti-Poverty Strategy (NAPS)
NCCRI	National Consultative Committee on Racism and Interculturalism
UN	United Nations
UNESCO	United Nations Educational, Scientific and Cultural Organisation
VFI	Vintners' Federation of Ireland (VFI)

CHAPTER ONE

Introduction

At the 2006 McGill Summer School Brian Cowen (hardly a man to use flowery language; he was reflecting on the title of the conference) proclaimed that the soul of Ireland was in good shape. It had become 'a significantly better place than it was twenty, forty or eighty years ago'. The challenge now was to make the most of historic opportunities. He insisted that neither Irish culture nor identity was under threat:

> It is possible to take a snapshot in time, idealise it and call it national culture. I reject this approach because it misses the essentially dynamic nature of a strong culture. Circumstances change, and in our case we should all be thankful for this. National identity and culture should evolve, not stay rooted in the past.[1]

In Irish politics the culture question is now only beginning to rear its head after a decade when the business case for mass immigration found ready acceptance. *New Guests of the Irish Nation* takes stock of Irish responses to immigration within a broader analysis of the politics of nation-building and Irish identity. The title is borrowed from a 1931 short story by Frank O'Connor, 'Guests of the Nation', which poignantly explores the limits and complexities of nationalist solidarity. As with O'Connor's story the focus here is on hosts at least as much as upon immigrant 'guests'. The book brings together essays written between 2001 and 2008 about Travellers and asylum seekers, racism and politics, institutional discrimination and social policy, the Citizenship Referendum, distinctions between 'nationals' and 'non-nationals', the exploitation of immigrant workers and the 'new Irish'. These case studies are book-ended by explorations of the historical, political and ideological settings of debates about twenty-first-century Irish identity and the rules of belonging.

This book builds on two earlier volumes, *Racism and Social Change in the Republic of Ireland* (2002) and *Immigration and Social Change in the Republic of Ireland* (2007). It proposes a broader conceptual focus than either on rights, politics, culture, history, ethics, empathy and the limits of solidarity as a necessary toolkit for making sense of present and future Irish responses to immigrants. Considerable emphasis is placed on what is termed the mechanics of exclusion, how barriers and discriminations become manifested in specific contexts and on the problems these potentially set up for the successful integration of immigrants. The focus of a number of chapters is upon the cognitive, normative, administrative, political and constitutional barriers that, for all that these are presented as commonsense responses to immigration, may also serve to undermine future social cohesion.

Many chapters address limits to empathy and solidarity that need to be treated realistically in debates about integration. Ireland has acquired its own immigration politics at a time when many Western countries are pessimistically reassessing theirs; Dutch, Danish, French and British debates about immigration are often reported in Ireland and so inform Irish debates as much as specific Irish experiences; an example here is the received wisdom that multiculturalism does not work. Yet here there is a disjuncture between ideology and experience. Experiences elsewhere suggest that receiving countries tend to make mistakes in their responses to immigrants; they do too little to be inclusive; there is ready political capital to be gained from imposing restrictions on vulnerable groups of migrants; there is not enough to be gained from taking the long-term view. The Irish experiences documented here suggest the same. Irish society faces an uncertain future (as all futures are) where the temptation will be towards 'ethnic nepotism', an ongoing solidarity with fellow citizens, the 'nationals', that works to exclude the 'non-nationals' with whom they now share an interdependent future.

At the turn of the new century Ireland suddenly acquired a large immigrant population. As things stand many of these are unlikely to become Irish citizens. Their Irish-born children are no longer granted Irish nationality as a birthright. In 2004 the Irish nation as a political entity retreated into a nineteenth-century definition of nationality as a defensive response to immigration. The nation-states that emerged out of the nineteenth century presumed that there would be a common national culture. Twentieth-century immigrants to these countries were in the main allowed to become citizens; Germany was a notable exception. It was presumed that migrants from former colonies could be folded into the host nation. In such cases citizenship was constituted as the starting place for integration. By contrast the United States constituted itself as an immigrant nation where at any one time a large proportion of the population were born abroad but were encouraged to become American citizens from the moment of arrival. Ireland has become an immigrant society at a time when globalisation has radically changed patterns of migration. Except for the retuned Irish of the Diaspora who instantly rejoined the Irish ethnic-nation, immigrants remain guests of the nation. Since 2004 this holds also for their Irish-born children.

Chapter 2 examines an ongoing modernisation of Irish identity that has left some Irish behind even as it proposes rules of belonging that accept large numbers of immigrants. This modernisation has in many respects been a generic modernisation. Just as the same corporations, shops and brand names are found everywhere, so too have work and lifestyles become somewhat generic. It is this surface-sameness that makes large-sale immigration feasible. But there is much more to 'fitting in' and being accepted than economists presume. If the Irish nation-state is to have a viable twenty-first century it will need to invest heavily in future social cohesion. Most multiethnic countries can point to failures in securing the integration of some groups; these generally had easy access to citizenship. The stock obituary for multiculturalism gives as cause-of-death the failure of policies that allowed migrant communities to pull away from mainstream society. The evidence is stronger, however, that what occurred in many instances was that minorities were pushed away by racism, discrimination and inflexible rules of belonging. Ireland does not have to look abroad for examples here. Chapters 3 and 4 examine the experiences of Travellers as an object lesson in the failures of the politics of rejection. Chapter 5 locates these experiences in a broader analysis of political populism.

This book argues that the primary goal of any viable integration project should be to close gaps between 'nationals' and 'non-nationals' for the sake of future social cohesion. Unless Irish nationality comes to reflect more accurately the diversity of Irish society, 'nationals' will be tempted towards ongoing acts of ethnic nepotism which, for all that these seem to make immigration acceptable to existing citizens, actually make integration more difficult. The value of a realistic conception of the limits of solidarity is emphasised in a number of chapters; the analysis emphasised draws on observations by Hannah Arendt (drawn in turn from Edmund Burke) about the absence of a right to rights for stateless persons; who gets rights and on what terms very much depends on the actions of nation-states.[2] The concept of ethnic nepotism as used in a number of chapters is addressed in an endnote (Chapter 15). Many Irish people might be attracted by the frequently cited aspiration in the 1916 Proclamation (and Article 2 of the 1937

Constitution) of cherishing all the children of the nation equally as part of an inclusive republicanism. Crucially this is not the same as cherishing all children equally. The elephant in the corner is a widespread willingness among nation-states to remove rights from some non-citizens as a response to new waves of migration. Societies that have been schooled to find racial apartheid abhorrent now see nothing unnatural with introducing administrative apartheid between citizens and some non-citizens. Racism might result in a person being discriminated against in the receipt of education or some other public service. Yet crucially under such circumstances, a person is being denied something to which she is deemed to have a right. Migrants excluded from citizenship – the 'non-nationals' – face some matter-of-fact discrimination, especially if they come from outside the European Union and are exempt from EU-wide reciprocal entitlements. Chapter 6 examines ways in which such administrative exclusions reinforce broader cognitive barriers to empathy and solidarity.

Chapter 7 documents the build-up of cognitive distinctions between citizens and non-citizens in the run up to the 2004 Referendum on Citizenship, while Chapter 8 analyses the politics of the referendum. It examines efforts to mobilise racism in support of the 'commonsense citizenship' proposed by the government. Yet, for the most part, the referendum encouraged ethnic nepotism rather than racism; it pitted 'nationals' against 'non-nationals'. At one level the referendum was clearly pragmatic; it arguably anticipated widespread anxiety about immigration. Some 80 per cent of voters supported it after all, but at the same time regrettably undermined a constitutional mechanism for automatically folding immigrants into the Irish nation. An influential justification for the referendum was that most Western states, including the EU countries within the common travel area, did not grant citizenship as a birthright. The Irish citizenship birthright constituted a pull factor for EU migrants who, once regularised, could access other EU states also. It could be viewed as undermining the sovereignty of the Irish nation-state, a factor that accounts for Department of Justice, Equality and Law Reform aggression towards asylum seekers with Irish-born children. Restoration of the citizenship birthright might be politically unfeasible. However, the Irish case for a liberal naturalisation process – proactively turning immigrants and their children into citizens – is one in danger of being lost in a context where (see Chapter 15) ethnic nepotism is presented as an intellectually credible response to immigration.

For the sake of its future social cohesion the Irish nation-state can ill afford a status quo that reinforces a nineteenth-century essentialist definition of Irish identity. Because 'nationals' have the power of veto there is a need to engage intellectually with various strands of Irish nationalism and to examine the capacity of the specific conceptions of solidarity these emphasise to include also the new guests of the nation. Here especially there is a need to disentangle the complex intellectual politics that shape or blinker, depending on one's vantage point, Irish academic perspectives. Chapters 9, 10 and 11 address the shortcomings of influential Irish post-colonial perspectives on the politics of Irish identity as tools for addressing Irish ethnic chauvinism, racism and the broader mechanics of exclusion that impede integration. These tend to emphasise colonial legacies of racism and generic racial state models while sidestepping questions about nationalism and majority group ethnic nepotism.[3] However, Chapter 10 acknowledges the intellectual importance of the post-colonial critique of Irish modernity as a vantage point for thinking about immigration. When it comes to many of the exclusions experienced by marginal groups in post-independent Ireland 'revisionist' historians and liberal political scientists tend to have little to say. Post-9/11 Western liberalism seems intellectually and politically dominated by illiberal liberals and ethnocentric liberals. There is huge scope for a revitalised Irish studies project that takes immigrant-Irish cultures seriously. This would offer a vital intellectual corrective to an Irish developmental liberalism seemingly uninterested in anything other than the market as the basis of social cohesion.

The focus of the final three chapters is on the broader political and institutional contexts that are likely to define adaptive nation-building responses to mass immigration. Various contexts where crude distinctions between 'nationals' and 'non-nationals' break down are considered here. Chapter 12 examines the responses of trade unions to migrant workers. In 2006 union resistance to a 'race to the bottom' translated into opposition to the exploitation of migrant workers. Union membership is not bounded by citizenship yet is represented in the social partnership processes that shape public policy. Here there is important scope for the recognition of immigrants. Chapter 13 considers the cosmopolitan extension of rights and entitlements beyond citizenship by means of trans-national conventions, EU-wide reciprocal norms and through rights offered by the nation-state to non-citizens. Ireland is one of a number of EU countries that allows non-citizens to vote and stand in local government elections.[4] The symbolic and practical value of the positive politics this allows for cannot be overstated.

Chapter 14 emphasises that the nation-state is likely to remain *the* crucial vehicle of future social cohesion, albeit one open to change from below. It examines the ongoing appeal of chauvinistic nationalism within a broader analysis of the cultural politics of integration. It faces up to the need to engage with different shades of Irish nationalism. In doing so it examines the legacy of essentialist nationalism, the viability of civic republicanism and of civic nationalism in the Irish case. Clearly the equation that came to define the Irish nation (Irish Nation=Irish Citizen=Ethnic-Irish) needs to be recalculated to take account of the empirical reality of a diverse twenty-first-century Ireland. Chapter 14 emphasises the role of cultural recognition in the politics of integration. It identifies the most likely contours of the 'Irish solution' to the challenge of integration, one that straddles civic republicanism and formal recognition of Irish and immigrant culture in the crucial nation-building domain of education. It is perhaps too soon to give a name to the twenty-first-century adaptive nation-building project that must build on the legacies of post-independence 'Irish-Ireland' and post-1950s developmental nation-building. By necessity it must promote a broader conception of social cohesion than can be provided by the economy. What is worth striving for is easy enough to articulate. The twenty-first-century Irish nation-state must recognise, reflect and invest in the diverse composition of Irish society. Here it must reckon with the historical legacies that are the subject of the next chapter and the mechanics of exclusion explored in a number of subsequent chapters.

CHAPTER TWO

After the End of Irish History

And so everything changed just like that! A society with a long aptitude for squeezing out surplus family members and even, it seemed during the 1950s and 1980s, entire generations threw open its doors unequivocally to four hundred million fellow Europeans and conditionally to cherry-picked migrants from elsewhere. No Statue of Liberty or Ellis Island was needed. No grand proclamations of an Irish Dream were issued. A commitment to immigration-fuelled economic growth was blandly inserted into a national development plan. Globetrotting employment fairs were sponsored by the state. The internet and cheap air travel handled the human traffic. In less than a decade Irish society experienced its greatest transformation since the 1846 Famine. That triggered a population collapse, mass emigration, massive changes in social mores and several generations of population decline; trends still resonant in the 1980s when the generation of emigrants that I belonged to were inclined to mutter, 'last one out turn off the lights'.[1]

The changes that have taken place in the last decade are profound. A nation-state used to depicting itself at the centre of its own self-contained universe, intensely preoccupied by local affairs, a backwater where the Second World War was called the Emergency, where change proceeded at a snail's pace now pressed hard on the fast forward button. A country whose main minorities – Travellers, Jews and Protestants – experienced marginalisation, one where the arrival of a few thousand asylum seekers in the late 1990s was portrayed as a dangerous flood somehow put the GNP pedal to the floor with mass immigration as fuel. What transpired, especially since 2004 when the state decided to open its borders to the ten new EU countries, was maybe the largest act of social engineering since the Plantations.

In the driving seat was a system of government and social partnership wedded to a developmental nation-building ideology, one that emerged in fits and bursts since the 1950s. In January 1988 *The Economist* portrayed Ireland as the 'poorest of the rich'. Almost a decade later it struggled to make sense of an 'economic miracle'. Specifically, joining the EU levered in structural funds and gave Ireland access to markets that enabled it to attract multinationals and charge them rent. New technologies meant that Ireland was no longer a periphery when it came to investment. The expansion of education since the 1960s bore fruit. The Irish were suddenly somehow in the right place at the right time. Or as summarised by Ray MacSharry and Pádraic White in *The Making of the Celtic Tiger*, a combination of good luck, good timing and good policies allowed Ireland to catch a wave.[2] Labour market expansion and economic growth went hand in hand. The Celtic Tiger fed first on Irish women, with returned emigrants as a second course and immigrants for dessert. Saskia Sassen's observation that it is far better, economically, to be an importer of labour than an exporter was borne out spectacularly in the Irish case. Ireland's history of shedding so many of its people brought emigrant remittances but had no conferred macroeconomic advantage.[3]

The 1980s saw what many commentators regard as the end of a distinct phase of nation-building in the West. Neo-liberalism flourished in response to globalisation. The end of the decade saw the collapse of state socialism, what Francis Fukuyama described as the end of history. Fukuyama's *The End of History and the Last Man* is one of those books more talked about than read. As generally presented it offers a colour-by-numbers scenario that allows exposition in a single sentence; the fall of the Berlin Wall in 1989 marked the triumph of liberal democracy and free markets. Triumphal accounts of the Celtic Tiger seemed to slot easily into this narrative of ideological progress.[4] And of course many of those labelled the 'new Irish' have been displaced by the impact of free markets on eastern Europe.

One effort to impose Fukuyama's thesis onto the Irish case was Alvin Jackson's inference that the Belfast Agreement might amount to the end of Irish history insofar as the sectarian conflicts that gave the recent Irish past its prominent contours had run out of steam.[5] Tom Garvin suggests that Irish nationalism was affected by the late twentieth-century erosion of historicist thought, accelerated by the collapse of the Soviet bloc and the demise of Marxism. What ended was not history but historicist nationalism:

> No one speaks seriously of Ireland's national destiny any more. Perhaps we are seeing not the death of history, as suggested by

Fukuyama, but rather its return after two centuries of being enserfed by the purposes of nationalists and nation-states. Modern political theory offers us a powerful image of the political process as being an endless voyage on a world that is all ocean. The helmsman of the ship may dream of landfall, but that is all it is; a dream. He may even promise landfall to his crew and demand they accept his claim, but there is no land; the parable denies bluntly the validity of any attempt to organise political life around some dream of perfect virtue or authenticity, whether nationalist or socialist.[6]

Ernest Gellner and Benedict Anderson emphasise how nineteenth-century nationalisms expressed modern forms of mass identity that only became possible with mass literacy and education. In Gellner's account identity became rationalised and codified. The dominant sense of what it was to be an Irishman drew heavily on a nationalist cultural revival but the histories of this new 'imagined community', to use Anderson's term, painted the past in primary colours. In the Irish case this first essentialist phase of political nation-building persisted for several decades after independence. For many nationalists the primary archetypical goal of nation-building, the unification of the nation within the nation-state, was not achieved with the creation of a twenty-six-county free state. From the 1930s onwards, Irish historians fought a battle over the Irish past within which 'revisionists' challenged the earlier greening of Irish history. Revisionism, Conor McCarthy suggests, was a trace variable for a wider modernisation of belonging. It was not just an argument among scholars but the 'historiographic outrider' of modernity as it has come to be experienced in Ireland.[7] However, nineteenth-century essentialist ideas of Irishness remained influential. They were sustained by the persistence of sectarian conflict in the North. For example, the concept of an Irish mind – an atavistic collective consciousness in need of therapy – was emphasised within *The Crane Bag*, a prominent intellectual journal launched in 1977.[8] The narrow gauge national identity produced by the early phase of Irish nation-building, sometimes referred to as Irish-Ireland, remained a force to be reckoned with. However, its influence had already begun to wane during the 1950s when a new developmental nation-building was championed, among others, by Seán Lemass. The new path of generic Western modernisation could not but (it seems in hindsight) undermine the Irish-Ireland theology of national identity.

Much of *The End of History* questions the validity of universal histories and claims about the nature of progress in Hegelian tradition.

Hegel, among other things, provided the intellectual scaffolding for romantic nationalism with its metaphysical claims that nations have destinies, that there exists a national spirit or *Geist*, more important than the fate of individuals, that can be conjured up and presented as real. Various strands of romantic nationalism proclaimed that Ireland had a destiny to fulfil. However, as Fukuyama observed, claims about national destinies found expression alongside efforts to present universal histories of human progress, the most potent of which is modernisation theory. Marx in *Das Kapital* wrote that industrially developed countries reveal to less developed countries the image of their own future.[9] The modernisation thesis permeates discussions on the needs of the developing world, past portrayals of Irish underdevelopment and, more recently, the developmental ideology of Celtic Tiger Ireland. Economic nationalism now takes the form of anti-isolationist competitive corporatism where once cultural isolationism fostered protectionism. A new mercantile education paradigm emerged which challenged the emphasis on religious reproduction and cultural nationalism within the education system.[10] In essence, a new modernising nation-building project emerged.

THE ONCE AND FUTURE IRISH NATION

Modernisation theory is extremely influential in the academic literature on nationalism and nation-building that inform a number of chapters of this book. Gellner's prerequisites for nationalism as a basis of social cohesion include mass literacy and school-inculcated culture.[11] The ideal of a common culture shared by people who might never meet was central to intellectual and political nation-building projects of the nineteenth and twentieth centuries. In 1843 *The Nation*, a Young Irelander periodical, proposed history, story and song as the 'weapons' and 'materials of nationalisation':

> *National* books, and lectures and music – *national* painting and busts and costume – *national* songs, and tracts, and maps – *historical* plays for the stage – *historical* novels for the closet – *historical* ballads for the drawing room – we want all these, and many other things illustrating the *history*, the resources and the genius of our country, and honouring her illustrious children, living and dead. These are the seeds of permanent nationality and we must sow them deeply in the People's hearts.[12]

Historians became midwives to modern ideals of belonging through the narratives they imposed on the past. Romantic nationalisms were historicist insofar as history was projected onto the future. But modern nations also needed venerable histories if they were to acquire political legitimacy. They required a discernable trajectory, a narrative of unfolding and a sense of inevitable or deserved destiny. They needed a shared sense of authentic culture. What they had little use for, according to Gellner, were the 'often baroque structures' and the plethora of 'nuances and ambiguities and overlaps' that served the functional needs of pre-modern society. In Gellner's account cultures became streamlined and homogenised:

> Not all the old cultures, let alone all the subtleties and shading, can conceivably survive into the modern world. There were too many of them. Only some survive and acquire a new literate underpinning, and become more demanding and clearly defined. The new primary ethnic colours, few in number and sharply outlined against each other, are often *chosen* by those who adhere to them, and who then proceed to internalise them deeply.[13]

Efforts to colonise the Irish past became central to the intellectual politics of nation-building. Millions of dead inhabitants of the island of Ireland, real and imaginary tribes of ancestors, were pressed into the service of the nascent nation-state. My own journey through the distant Irish past began with a book acquired by my grandfather in New York during the 1920s. Martin Haverty's 1867 *The History of Modern Ireland from the Earliest Period to the Present Time* ended with an essay that promoted the Fenian cause.[14] It began, using a synthesis of then-accepted scholarship, with an account of the early Irish past that employed the creationist timeline of the Annals of the Four Masters.[15]Here Ireland's first identifiable inhabitants were a colony from Migdonia, supposed to be in Macedonia, in Greece, under a leader called Parthalon, 'about 300 years after the Deluge, or according to the chronology adopted by the Four Masters in the year of the world (Anno Mundi (AM)) 2520'.[16] This immigrant community supposedly lasted three hundred years until all 9,000 were killed by a pestilence that left the country unpopulated. Thirty years later the next wave arrived, this time from south-eastern Europe. The Nemedians reputedly lasted two hundred years. Most were killed by pestilence, others by Fomorian pirates in AM 3066. The survivors became Ireland's first emigrants. Again, the Four Masters maintained, Ireland was effectively uninhabited. Next to arrive were the Firbolgs in AM 3266 who, according to Haverty's best information, may have been Belgae Celts or of Teutonic or Gothic origin; migrants from Britain and Europe in any case. At this stage Haverty's reliance on pure fable gives way to legends, he maintained, that could not be set aside lightly 'because there is sufficient reason for believing them to be historic truth'.[17] These recorded that the next arrivals, the Tuatha de Dannan, held sway from AM 3303 to AM 3500; some 1,700 years before the birth of Christ. From here Haverty dated the birth of Irish history.

Haverty, in common with many later 'primordialist' nationalist histories, identified an early Christian golden age of Irish civilisation that provided lineage and legitimacy to modern nation-building endeavour.[18] These emphasised how Ireland, the land of saints and scholars, colonised and re-Christianised barbarian Europe. They promoted, in Elizabeth Crooke's summary, 'the glory of the Golden Age, the degenerate impact of the English and the potential for regeneration'.[19] They adhered to the template of Herder and Fichte with their assertion that nationality is one of the great truths about human nature.[20] Seamus McCall's 1931 contribution to the genre *And So Began the Irish Nation* insisted that the Irish nation was as old as the human presence on the island of Ireland, a story that 'begins with Ireland as the empty cradle of an unborn nation'.[21] McCall presented 'the evolution of the Irish nation as complete' with the arrival of the Christian Golden Age of saints and scholars and a high king at Tara.[22]

McCall presented the post-Golden Age history of Ireland as a bitter interregnum. Ireland was 'brutalised that she might be coerced', her 'national culture' effaced and 'all memory of the past eradicated'.[23] But he also implied, as did many others, that there existed a primordial and inviolable Irish spirit. In a more recent example, Thomas Cahill's 1995 *How the Irish Saved Civilisation* depicts innate Irish character as essentially fixed from the time of Saint Patrick.[24] Almost 120 years earlier Haverty maintained that the faith planted in Erin by St Patrick had never faltered.[25] Cahill claimed that in Ireland's history nothing had trumped the Golden Age; it had known neither 'Renaissance nor Enlightenment'.[26] Or to put it otherwise, Ireland may have been brutalised but had never been infected by the intellectual legacy of the Reformation. Through such assertions both Irish exceptionalism and manifest destiny could be implied. As claimed by Haverty: 'Ireland has been exempt from the changes which so many other countries have undergone; and a large and interesting portion of our history will relate to the struggles which her steadfastness entailed upon her.'[27]

This claim was influentially asserted in Daniel Corkery's *The Hidden Ireland* in 1925 which fixated on the sixteenth century as the basis for a Catholic and Gaelic cultural restoration.[28] *The Hidden Ireland* was part of a larger project of opposition to the influence of Reformation and Enlightenment ideas. Critics such as Seán O'Faoláin and Frank O'Connor argued that *The Hidden Ireland* promoted cultural isolationism and a climate of censorship that rendered many of the real problems of modern Irish society invisible.[19] A number of prominent Irish intellectuals in the post-independence era emphasised the need for a combined Catholic and Gaelic restoration to counter, as Michael Tierney put it in 1938, 'the great heresies of the last three hundred years'. Tierney's own recipe sought to combine elements of Catholic anti-modernism with the idealised Gaelic medievalism of Corkery. However, these ideals were mobilised within an astute analysis of the politics of nation-building that understood its workings in much the same way as did Gellner. The nation-state, Tierney emphasised, was a nineteenth-century invention that 'coincided with the decay and gradual disappearance of the native ways of thought, life and expression'. Tierney's reconstruction of Ireland would exorcise the alien secular ideas of the Enlightenment that, he admitted, had been the very building blocks of Irish independence. A modern Irish culture, he argued, could be built on the old Gaelic culture but a viable political system could not.[30]

While many of Tierney's essays promoted an anti-utilitarian and high-culture Irish restoration, he is mostly remembered now as a moderniser. His lasting legacy is the vast 1960s modern concrete Belfield campus of University College Dublin, of which he was president from 1947 to 1964. Here then was the dilemma of modern cultural nationalism. It fostered new forms of social cohesion while promoting yearnings for tradition. It attracted conservatives while underwriting social change. Nationalist movements championed folk culture but what they in fact created was a codified version of this expressed through literacy and mediated through mass education. As put by Gellner, nationalism fostered 'the phenomenon of *Gesellschaft* using the idiom of *Gemeinschaft*', modern societies with complex interdependencies simulating a closed community.[31] But newly minted national identities also discarded their roots in locality and folklore. These placed considerable emphasis on cultural revival but were in fact made possible, Gellner insists, by mass amnesia.[32] Old cultural layers became smoothed out to fit the requirements of the present. The shared memories of a mass culture had first to be written down, codified, published and disseminated.

The ways in which whole peoples were written in and out of existence are of concrete interest to a society now on the cusp of a new nation-building project of integrating immigrants. In 1988, not long before Fukuyama proclaimed the end of history, BBC Northern Ireland aired a series of broadcasts that presented the history of Ireland in terms of the impact of different waves of settlers from prehistoric times. The broadcasts, with their accompanying book *The People of Ireland*, were clearly lessons aimed at then prevalent sectarianism, the subsequent unravelling of which has been called the end of Irish history. Their thesis was that sectarian presentations of Irish history did no justice to the pluralism of ten thousand years or so of disparate human settlement.[33]

Hubert Butler's *Ten Thousand Saints* depicted an early Ireland peopled by branches of European tribes who lost their histories as they migrated, fought and merged. Only through their ancestral pedigrees – long lists of obviously invented ancestors – could they hang onto their identities within oral cultures.[34] The cultural legacy of early Christianity included sanctified genealogies. Each parish could claim its own saints within local folklore.[35] Some, who bore the names of pagan gods and sacred places, had been Christianised alongside pagan festivals. Folklore preceded history that was often no more than the former written down generations after the presumed events. The early Christian rebranding of Ireland was no less an act of cultural reinvention than that attempted by modern nationalists. The early Church superimposed saints on existing folk culture. These saints archetypically had fantastic powers and grotesque attributes borrowed from those of the legendary ancestors who stood in for real ones in pre-Christian oral folk culture. Fr Ryan's 1931 book *Irish Monasticism* exemplified how the Irish saints could be 'tidied up for history' so as to satisfy the requirements of religious orthodoxy and nationalism.[36] What Ryan did, according to Butler, was to strip the saints of any folklore that got in the way of portraying them as exemplars of real Irish monasticism. This removed the only thing that might be real about some of these. Butler's account suggested several degrees of separation from the real past. Legendary ancestors stood as a proxy for real ones within oral culture. Their attributes were used to mass produce Irish saints. These were then modernised and presented as real historical figures.[37]

AMNESIA AND MODERNITY

Gellner suggests that the early official histories of nation-states selectively sift the past, writing past peoples in or out of existence. But it is not just the distant past that becomes codified. The treatment of

Travellers within the histories of modern Ireland suggests that the condition of amnesia diagnosed by Gellner also includes ongoing cognitive filtering. Travellers encountered spatial and other forms of material exclusion in modern Ireland that can be understood as a modernisation effect. But their invisibility as a still-oral culture within a society that built its social cohesion on literacy contributed to their marginality within the Irish nation-state. Travellers became the focus of linguistic scholarship in the later nineteenth century.[38] But they remained, to use Eric Wolf's phrase, a people without history.[39]

Yet they were present within the folklore written down during the Celtic Literary Revival. Some of J.M. Synge's plays, including *The Tinker's Wedding* (not performed on an Irish stage until 1970) and *The Shadow of the Glen* (1910), had Tinker protagonists. Travellers were written into the literature of the Irish revival as 'the embodiment of freedom, wildness and danger'. Fintan O'Toole suggests what made *The Tinker's Wedding* unpalatable to the Irish audiences of its day was that 'Synge was letting them down in front of strangers by showing drink, sex and violence.'[40] The exposure of the unruly Irish either here or in the better-known *Playboy of the Western World* presented a problem for a nation intent on sprucing up its past.

Folklore sought to justify the marginality of Travellers. Lady Gregory collected a story in which St Patrick punished a 'tinker' for deceiving him. The punishment was to forever have every man's face against them.[41] Such stories had much in common with justifications for racism that cited Scripture.[42] But by inverting such folklore Travellers could weave their own primordial folk history. As put by Nan Joyce, in a fair précis of the literature on Traveller origins:

> Some of my ancestors went on the road in the Famine but more of them have been travelling for hundreds of years – we're not dropouts like some people think. The Travellers have been in Ireland since St Patrick's times, there's a lot of history behind them though there's not much written down.[43]

The question of Traveller origins remains contested. In their own folklore Travellers depicted themselves as true Irish who experienced the major cataclysms of Irish history, be it those wrought by Oliver Cromwell or the Famine. There are indications that Travellers existed as a distinct group within Irish society before Elizabethan times.[44] Accounts of pre-Famine Ireland collected by the Whately Commission describe a society where large numbers of people were seasonally forced onto the road and many were displaced from their small holdings. These accounts suggest that Travellers were part of this larger population. Catriona Clear's 2007 *Social Change and Everyday Life in Ireland, 1850–1922* distinguishes Travellers from vagrants. She argues that 'it is unlikely that the antecedents of the people we now know as "Travellers" were those steadily persecuted as vagrants'. Unlike these, Travellers went about in family groups and did not leave their children to be a burden to others ('always one of the primary objections to homeless men'). Insofar as they practised trades or carried goods to sell they were not 'wandering around without visible means of support'. Furthermore, 'Travellers usually had strong identification with some particular part of the country and, crucially, they were *known*; it was the unknown homeless who were feared.'[45]

The second half of the twentieth century witnessed a good cop/bad cop official focus on the Travelling people. In 1951 the Irish Folklore Commission distributed a 'tinker questionnaire' that generated considerable material on 'tinker' society, languages and customs. Here, the elegiac focus was on documenting a vanishing way of life 'before it was too late'.[46] By contrast the focus of the 1960 Commission on Itinerancy was upon the obliteration of this way of life. Its terms of reference were to 'promote their absorption into the general community', and 'pending such absorption, to reduce to a minimum the disadvantages to themselves and to the community resulting from their itinerant habits'. Travellers came to officially exist during the second half of the twentieth century as a problem for a modernising Ireland.[47]

But unlike Protestant and Jewish minorities, Travellers were not rejected by the majority ethnic nationalism. The new state became monolithically Catholic, but Travellers were also Catholic. The Irish Jewish community encountered sporadic anti-Semitism that portrayed it as an enemy of both faith and fatherland. Fr Creagh, instigator of the 1904 Limerick 'pogrom', urged his congregation 'not to be false to Ireland, false to your country and false to your religion, by continuing to deal with the Jews'.[48] That same year, an editorial in the *United Irishman* by Arthur Griffith presented the Jews as enemies of the nation, exploiters of Irish workers and farmers, whose connivances might even drive the latter to emigration:

> No thoughtful Irishman or woman can view without apprehension the continuous influx of Jews into Ireland ... strange people, alien to us in thought, alien to us in sympathy, from Russia, Poland, Germany and Austria – people who come to live amongst us, but who never become of us ... Our sympathy – insular as it

may be – goes wholly to our countryman the artisan whom the Jew deprives of the means of livelihood, to our countryman the trader whom he ruins in business by unscrupulous methods, to our countryman the farmer whom he draws into his usurer's toils and drives to the workhouse across the water.[49]

Travellers were not depicted as enemies of the 'Irish-Ireland' nation in such terms. However, they came to be despised by the subsequent developmental one. Travellers remain caught in a double bind. They became conspicuous when displaced as Ireland developed from a rural to an urban society. Their increased distinctiveness over time emanated in no small part from their growing social distance from the mainstream. Their culture remained rooted in a real forgotten pre-modern Ireland. To modern perceptions (first Irish-Ireland and then developmental Ireland) they were anarchic and increasingly out of step. They are now despised for much the same reasons the Abbey audience rioted in response to *The Playboy of the Western World*. The mirror Synge held up in 1907 revealed an Ireland at odds with the one then under construction. Travellers were not displaced by nationalism *per se* but by the modernisation that gathered pace as cultural nationalism gave way to its developmental successor. Of course these changes did not just affect Travellers but they affected them more than most.

At the same time Travellers remained outside official Irish history even when their existence became well documented. In the case of history books published before 1960 (when the Traveller issue became explicitly politicised) their absence is easy enough to understand. But in the decades since, even highly regarded histories of modern Ireland that seek to contest narrow conceptions of Irish society manage to disregard Travellers altogether or are incurious about their history.

By way of example, Roy Foster's 1988 *Modern Ireland 1600–1972* makes no mention of Travellers.[50] Another 1988 volume, *The People of Ireland*, notwithstanding its project of emphasising historical and present social diversity, made no reference to Travellers. The book included a captioned photograph of a nameless Traveller woman and child connected to nothing in the main text.[51] Travellers got one mention in Dermot Keogh's 1994 *Twentieth-Century Ireland* where they pop up, as if by magic, as the subject of an unexplained 1960 Commission on Itinerancy.[52] In Diarmaid Ferriter's 2005 *The Transformation of Ireland 1900–2000*, praised for its focus on social history, prejudice against Travellers is discussed on two occasions. However, no clues to *their* history are offered.[53] Foster's *Luck and the Irish: A Brief History of Change*

1970–2000, an addendum to his 1988 book, again makes no reference to them.[54] There is no mention of Travellers in Terence Brown's *Ireland: A Social and Cultural History 1922–2002*, nor are they referred to in Joe Lee's *Ireland: Politics and Society 1912–1986*.[55] Historians reflected the normatively marginal status of Travellers in other fields. Even books with stated objectives of examining the role of ethnicity and social diversity ignored Travellers. Two examples from 1997 and 1998 respectively were *In Search of Ireland: A Cultural Geography* and *Ireland and the Politics of Change*.[56]

A big part of the problem has been the weakness of Irish social history; in its absence the study of literature has emerged as its main proxy. Declan Kiberd's *Inventing Ireland: The Literature of the Modern Nation* exemplifies how the Irish nation-state was written into existence and how a fictive past has been mined by a later post-colonial generation. The Irish historians and literary critics who sought to make sense of the emergence of the Irish nation-state are primarily engaged in, to use Roy Foster's term, 'the study of mentalities'.[57] In the main, historians have interpreted pluralism as relating to the 'national question'. Irish cultural histories tended to focus on writers, artists and their reception within a broader literature. Culture so understood excluded most of what anthropologists defined it as. Indeed, anthropologists have contributed much to understandings of Travellers in recent decades.[58] So too have Travellers themselves. But memoirs like Nan Joyce's 1985 *Traveller* and Nan Donohoe's 1986 *The Life of an Irish Travelling Woman* fell far below the cultural radar when compared to similar earlier endeavours by the Blasket Islanders that found their way onto the national curriculum and into the literary canon.[59]

Nomenclature is always important in the politics of identity. The term 'Traveller' was embraced as a necessary alternative to the usually pejorative ones employed by the wider population. Attitudinal studies documented a deepening of anti-Traveller prejudice in Irish society between the early 1970s and late 1980s, particularly among the middle classes. These concluded that the majority viewed Travellers 'as almost an untouchable caste'.[60] The 1990s saw the case being made for Travellers' ethnic status as a means of contesting prejudice. It is worth noting that academic definitions as to what constitutes a caste to some extent mirror those of ethnicity. The markers of stigma that cut a group out from a wider society can in turn be asserted as ethnic markers.[61] Definitions of caste emphasise forced cultural delineation, social stratification and apartheid, all conditions that came to apply to Travellers. Better then, the anthropologists who took up their cause counselled, to seek ethnic status.[62]

An ethnic group is generally defined as a socially distinct community of people who share a common history and culture and often share a distinct language and religion. As generally used in the social sciences, the concept of ethnicity is taken to refer to 'subjectively shared culture'. Emphasis is placed upon self-identification or 'bottom-up' conceptions of identity. Ethnicity is also taken to refer to current rather than essentialist forms of identity. Past identities are seen as important only insofar as they shape *currently* shared cultures.[63] In 1983 the United Kingdom Law Lords ruled that such a definition applied to Travellers.[64] It was ultimately unsurprising that the 1995 *Report of the Task Force on the Travelling People* fudged the question of ethnic status. Some members – three councillors and one local authority official – authored a minority report that portrayed Travellers as a deviant underclass.[65] They reflected a constituency where hostility to Travellers was a political fact of life. Traveller ethnicity has become normalised within the policies and practices of the Equality Authority and the likeminded National Consultative Committee on Racism and Interculturalism (NCCRI) whose key officials had previously worked for Traveller organisations.[66] However, Traveller ethnicity continues to be vociferously denied by other state actors.[67] Even the 2004 Irish government submission to the Committee on the Elimination of Racial Discrimination (CERD) reflected this ambivalence by denying ethnic status while effectively admitting ethnic distinctness:

> Some of the bodies representing Travellers claim that members of the community constitute a distinct ethnic group. The exact basis for this claim is unclear. However, the Government of Ireland accept the rights of Travellers to their cultural identity, regardless of whether the Traveller community may be properly regarded as an ethnic group. The Government is committed to applying all the protections afforded to ethnic minorities by the CERD equally to Travellers.[68]

The case for ethnicity was hardly unclear. The unmentioned roadblock was one of political *realpolitik* in the face of widespread anti-Traveller prejudice.

IDENTITY AND THE NATION-STATE

Gellner suggested a number of phases of nation-building that might, as related to the Irish case, be summarised as follows. First, the emergence of the modern nation-state required much rationalisation of past identities. Amnesia within the dominant nation went hand in hand with the rejection of difference within the boundaries of the nation-state. Protestants had been integral to the development of nineteenth-century cultural and political nationalism but became marginalised as narrower Catholic ethnic conceptions of Irishness came to dominate. By the 1990s, evidence of a separate Protestant ethnic identity in the Republic was no longer politically evident.[69] A number of factors contributed to this. Post-independence and intermarriage contributed to their numerical decline. Irishness became de-hyphenated. The Protestant-Irish could not sustain a political identity in the new state. The Ascendancy became, in Hubert Butler's term, 'the descendancy'.[70] A number of studies of the Protestant minority emphasised how its members felt that they had to keep their heads down, not to exhibit signs of outward cultural distinctiveness.[71]

Second, internal minority groups may be subordinated to a dominant national ideal of belonging. A third phase, evident in a number of countries, has been the emergence of multiculturalism; the assertion by minorities within the nation-state of their cultural distinctiveness as a means of combating racism and discrimination. Modern Travellers have inevitably streamlined their own past folk culture. Traveller pamphlets, periodicals, documentaries and websites emphasise the distinctness of Traveller culture.[72] Travellers pioneered the use of ethnicity and multiculturalism in a polity wedded to a nineteenth-century concept of nation. This was a significant public intellectual contribution given how the predominant understanding of pluralism was a reactive one limited to the problem of sectarianism. Traveller organisations advocated a model of 'interculturalism' subsequently taken up by the state with the establishment of the NCCRI in 1998.[73]

However, the intercultural project has stalled and seems likely to be abandoned as a model for future integration policy. Official antipathy toward ethnicity has not been restricted to Travellers. In 2007 the state refused a Sikh member of the Garda Síochána the right to wear a turban, an accepted practice in United Kingdom police forces.[74] Collectively these issues suggest an implicit leaning towards a republican ideal of civic inclusion, an antipathy to multiculturalism that draws on post-Pym Fortune European norms as well as good old-fashioned Irish monoculturalism. The latter was exemplified by the justification for the ban on turbans offered by the Minister for Integration: 'If we are to take integration seriously, people who come here must understand our ways of doing things.'[75]

In the current era of 'globalisation', when identities are often best described as hybrid or multiple, the nation-state remains a crucial entity. Tom Garvin suggests that for all the efforts of nationalists to lay claim to primordial or modernist theories of origin, the success of nationalism as a unifying social principle owes much to its ideological agnosticism and 'intellectual emptiness'. In Garvin's summary, Irish nationalism is a cocktail of tribal identity, religious sectarianism, democracy, egalitarianism, populism and liberalism. The magpie nature of nationalism allows the jumbling of new and old loyalties. Older ones can find themselves disregarded or at least treated as no more than trace elements. Nationalism, he suggests, will persist as a dominant principle of political organisation for mechanical and practical reasons, even where the historicist ideals originally underpinning it are decreasingly popular or even believable.[76]

As Irish society begins a debate on integration, the question of defining what exactly it is that immigrants are to be integrated into has proved difficult to nail down. In the era of *Riverdance* few Irish people get worked up by whether Ireland has ten thousand saints or none at all. Nationalist historians wove a mythic past and a Golden Age into the story of the Irish nation. Celtic Tiger Ireland had commodified primordial histories of the Irish race with Michael Flatley's *Lord of the Dance*. Economic prosperity (Ireland had the fourth highest per capita income in the world in 2007) however fleeting has done much to bury even recent memories of economic and social trauma.[77] Arguably this latest bout of amnesia makes possible the acceptance of large-scale immigration and a new phase of nation-building. The old cultural politics have had little influence upon decisions to admit hundreds of thousands of people. Integration was understood as integration into the economy. That neither social nor cultural consequences had to be debated arguably illustrates the extent to which the developmental nation-building project has become one of generic Western modernisation.

However, even à la carte Irishness has its rules of belonging. In the Irish case, as in the French, an implicit cultural identity underscores the dominant taken-for-granted neutral cultural ideal. This finds expression in a multitude of norms, attitudes and forms of knowledge that the French sociologist Pierre Bourdieu defines as cultural capital.[78] Generally the losers in the cultural capital stakes are understood as those from lower socio-economic groups. In France the ideological denial of ethnicity has led to an unreal climate of public and political debate that hides the systematic marginalisation of French-born citizens of minority ethnic background. In the Irish case, Travellers are still often represented as a deviant sub-group of the dominant 'normal' culture. In this context

Travellers are further outside the dominant imagined community than are many immigrants. Yet, as the 2004 Referendum on Citizenship indicates, the ethnicity of the dominant group cannot be ignored. A tribal cognitive distinction between 'nationals' and 'non-nationals' can exert considerable political power when it is still the case that most citizens are unhyphenated Irish. If their sense of being Irish seems lightly worn compared to the essentialist identities of yore it is also the case that 'nationals' may come to define themselves anew – 'a nation once again' – in opposition to the new guests of the nation.

CHAPTER THREE

The Remaindered People

In 1963 District Court Judge Barra O'Brian likened the nature and extent of exclusion faced by Travellers in County Clare to that of apartheid.[1] As the judge put it, they 'were booted from town to town and place to place and got little chance to live from the people'. This chapter examines their experiences during the last four decades of the twentieth century. It draws considerably on accounts that appeared in the main county newspaper, the *Clare Champion*, on a weekly basis, between 1963 and the end of 1999. Most of the newspaper articles detailed the proceedings of meetings of Clare County Council and the Ennis Urban District Council. Other articles related to court proceedings, accounts of residents' campaigns, meetings of voluntary groups and letters to the newspaper.[2] For the most part this was a one-sided conversation that excluded Traveller voices. A key source of alternative perspectives was a report entitled *Young Travellers: Many Voices, One Community* published by the Ennis Traveller Training Centre in 1984.[3] This consisted of 101 pages of writings and transcripts by mostly young people about their lives and hopes for the future. *Young Travellers* addressed experiences of settlement, tradition and change, religious practice, education, prejudice and discrimination. It noted optimistically that: 'By writing freely on a variety of issues, Travellers are evolving ... (into) articulate, confident spokesmen and women who can take their rightful place at the negotiating tables where agencies make decisions which affect their community.'

However, by the 1980s the political exploitation of anti-Traveller prejudice in Clare had become routine. A small number of councilors were consumed with anti-Traveller hostility throughout long careers in local politics. Others felt the need, for electoral purposes, to establish anti-Traveller credentials or, at least, not be seen as supporters of Travellers.[4] Few local authority debates on Traveller issues were reported between 1963 and 1999 without central prominence given to vehement anti-Traveller statements. But this had not always been the case. As noted in *Young Travellers: Many Voices, One Community*:

> Up to the 1950s Travellers had a role in the rural economy. They made and repaired tinware, dealt in horses, cleaned chimneys and peddled lino ... many were seasonal labourers. They also recycled scrap metal and materials. Begging was an economic necessity, children had to be fed. Before the turn of the century they slept in hay barns or in hedgerows. Then the shelter tent became the norm. After the First World War, the barrel-wagon was introduced and adopted while shelter tents were retained as additional accommodation for large families.

Prior to the 1960s they had a place within Clare rural society. As put by John Sherlock: 'Most of the time there was an open door and a kettle put down for tea. The farmers were glad to see us. We were needed.' Older people whose stories were collected in *Young Travellers* described the satisfaction as well as the hardship of the travelling life. As evoked by Julie McDonagh:

> The morning I had my second child the nearest town was eight miles away and there was no hospital. The children that were born on the side of the road were never sick, but the later ones born in hospital had many a sick day.
>
> I'd take the two year old and do maybe ten miles of a country road in the teems of rain and carry back a few spuds and an old turnip and a bit of boiled meat. I'd want to eat it myself but I'd think of my husband and children and have to bring it back. I used to bake bread on the griddle with the rain hopping off my shoulders. I'd go to bed in wet clothes and get up and try to dry my rug over the fire before going off again. There was great flavour in the food in those days. We made griddle bread and oven cakes. You'd put the oven cake in a metal tin and put coals on the lid. We shared our food. My mother used to always say: 'Ah, you don't know who might come, put down enough.' After the meal the women used to sit around the fire and the men played cards. Children were never allowed to listen.

What Julie McDonagh described was by no means a bucolic existence. The food might have tasted good but had to be cooked in the rain by a woman who then had to sleep in wet clothes. Fond memories of such experiences may seem a triumph of the human spirit. Yet Traveller accounts of their way of life as human stand in sharp contrast to the dehumanising stereotypes that have prevailed in the decades since they were economically displaced from the Irish countryside.

As recalled by Mary McDonagh: 'People started buying plastic buckets and this knocked out the sale of the galvanised. They were cheaper. We drifted away from the land into town.' One result of economic change was an increased social distance between Travellers and settled communities. Traditional contacts and relationships between both were eroded. In an increasingly urban Ireland Travellers were stigmatised as a deviant sub-group. The terms of reference of the Commission on Itinerancy set up in 1960 were 'to promote their absorption into the general community' and 'pending such absorption, to reduce to a minimum the disadvantages to themselves and the community resulting from their itinerant habits'.[5]

OFFICIAL RESPONSES

Initial discussion by councillors that emerged as a response to the *Report of the Commission on Itinerancy* (1963) was fixated on achieving a once and for all solution. The main focus was on the possibility of using the army camp at Knocknalisheen, which had been utilised as a refugee camp some years earlier, to accommodate all the Travellers in the region.[6] Clare County Council, in conjunction with the local authorities in neighbouring counties, sought to develop the camp as accommodation for all Travellers living within a twenty- or thirty-mile radius of Limerick city.[7] Here, they could be educated, in one place, about how 'the settled way of life was better than the nomadic one':

> The chairman said that the regional camp would be an experiment. It was a first step. He felt that there was not much point in talking about the elderly itinerants. They would have to concentrate on the children and see that they were educated. He felt that education was the kernel of the problem and they would have a far better chance of educating the children if they were in a central camp.[8]

The second advantage, in the view of some councillors, was that it would remove the need to provide 'camping sites' around the county. As put by one councillor: 'If they provide camps in other places they would have people objecting.'[9] However, proposals to develop the camp were found to be impractical. As put by one councillor, who was also a senator and had served on the Commission on Itinerancy, they 'could set up a regional camp but there would be no question of herding the itinerants into it. The itinerants had to get a living where they could find it and it would be unrealistic putting them into a big camp unless they were provided for.'[10] He advocated, instead, the development of a number of small camping sites at places frequented by Travellers on an ongoing basis. The Knocknalisheen proposal proved unworkable, not least because it would have required an unprecedented level of co-operation between local authorities, and the army would have had to agree to release it.

The local political debate on the 'itinerant problem' remained somewhat abstract for much of the 1960s. Plans to settle the Travellers first emerged through the voluntary sector. The Ennis Itinerant Settlement Committee, established in 1967, began to work on plans to find a site where the 'large number of itinerants who frequent this area and in many instances make it their headquarters can be trained to become citizens able to live in a community'.[11] Committee members were strongly motivated by a desire to alleviate the chronic poverty experienced by Travellers who lived on the roadsides of Clare and to stop what was seen to be the terrible consequences of hounding them from place to place.[12] The committee initially worked to provide new tents and caravans for those who were living in ramshackle tents or under upturned carts covered with tarpaulin. Their efforts principally focused upon a group of almost one hundred Travellers who were permanently camped on the Lees Road on the outskirts of Ennis. Their living conditions were described as 'worse than those of animals'.[13]

By 1969 the committee had devised a specific proposal for a 'camping site'. The site was to include grazing land for Traveller horses and to meet the needs of the community living on the Lees Road as a group.[14] However, the proposal was thwarted by the emergence of a political unwillingness to provide sites. The political barriers on this occasion remained pretty much the same in the case of almost all proposals to provide sites for Travellers in the years and decades that followed.[15] Those advanced by local authorities from the 1970s onwards were designed primarily to take account of the objections of residents rather than to meet the needs of Travellers. This resulted in a significant proportion of the local Traveller population having no option but to remain on the roadside in the decades which followed.

Much of the initial impetus to develop designated sites for Travellers in Clare emerged from the voluntary sector rather than the local authorities. The settlement committee had a few isolated successes in settling Travellers in rural areas.[16] However, plans to develop a large-scale site for Travellers in the vicinity of Ennis failed as a result of objections from residents of the area in which the site was to be located.[17] In 1969 the county council considered an ambitious proposal for a large-scale site at Lees Road to accommodate fifteen families. The county council agreed to acquire the land for such a site but objections from local farmers, which were supported by some councillors, were sufficient to undermine support for the proposal. Within a very short period the possibilities for such a site receded and not one member of the council expressed support for the proposal.[18] Some councillors had earlier supported an alternative location in a move to prevent a motion to develop the Lees Road site from being put forward. However, the proposal to develop this site, on convent-owned land within the town, was never considered seriously. The *Clare Champion* reported that the proposal provoked laughter from councillors.[19] The council had, according to the settlement committee, 'passed the buck'.[20]

This effectively ended any real hope of settling the Traveller community as a whole. A brief attempt to develop an alternative large scheme, on land offered by the Catholic bishop, Dr Harty, for the entire community camped at Lees Road was abandoned at a very early stage in the face of a well-organised residents' campaign.[21] Subsequently, proposals were devised for the development of four small sites, which would accommodate four families each in caravans, with a paddock for horses on a fifth site.[22] Horses would not be allowed, under any circumstances, on the residential sites even though the paddock was several miles from some of these. Places on the sites were to be offered to families who had lived in the Ennis area for a number of years. The council maintained from the outset that these were to be temporary sites.

Residents, in each case, either sought to prevent the sites being established or to reduce the number of Travellers allowed. As put by a spokesman for the various residents groups, they wanted 'time to discuss the matter between themselves and come up with a final solution'. The 'right' of residents to veto plans to accommodate Travellers became a factor in these and subsequent negotiations. A number of the proposed 'temporary' sites were eventually developed. These were, in some cases, reduced in scale, in response to objections by residents about the number of families to be accommodated. They were ill-equipped to meet the needs of the Travellers; a number had to be subsequently rebuilt because of the temporary and unsuitable nature of the facilities that were put in place.[23]

Insufficient levels of accommodation resulted in the ongoing presence of Travellers on roadsides in the Ennis area. The miserable conditions they faced on the Lees Road were replicated elsewhere when they were displaced because of residents' protests to the 'aptly named Watery Road'.[24] The settlement committee subsequently campaigned vigorously for the development of a comprehensive site on the Watery Road. They publicised the 'sub-human' living conditions experienced by Travellers,[25] and lobbied the government to put pressure upon the local authorities.[26] Subsequently, the county council proposed a scheme along the lines envisaged by the settlement committee. However, objections from residents of nearby housing estates led to these proposals for twelve houses, a community centre and a paddock being pared back to just six houses with no ancillary facilities.[27]

By 1970 there was a clear separation between the understandings and approaches of local authorities and the itinerant settlement movement in relation to the Traveller issue. Both understood 'itinerancy' itself as the problem. Assimilationism, as a solution to this problem, seemed hegemonic. For example, in 1970 the Catholic hierarchy issued a statement calling for prayers for the welfare of the Travellers. It concluded: 'On next Sunday let us pray that we may be generous in our acceptance of the travelling people and untiring in our efforts to help them settle.'[28] However, commitments to pursue the assimilation of Travellers unravelled in the face of political opposition to all attempts at settlement. Councillors saw the settlement committee as 'a bunch of fanatics' and an unrepresentative clique, while members of the committee criticised council inaction as unjust.[29]

After an initial burst of activity in the late 1960s and early 1970s little new specific accommodation for Travellers was developed until the mid 1980s. In 1972 there were forty-two families in the Ennis area. Proposals had been developed for sites at Doora, Gaurus, Drumcliffe and Cahercalla to provide Traveller-specific accommodation that could cater for, at most, just twenty-two of these.[30] There was a political unwillingness to commit to accommodating the rest of the Travellers. As put by one councillor: 'It would be too much for any town to house forty-two itinerant families.'[31] As put earlier by a spokesman for Gaurus and Roslevan residents, there was a willingness to accept one family.[32] However, residents did not always get their way. Subsequently, four housing units were constructed at Gaurus.[33] The approach of the local authorities was summed up succinctly in a statement by the Ennis Itinerant Settlement Committee:

1. The council never plans for all of the families.
2. Each proposal to help the Travellers is balanced by a restricting promise to the objectors.
3. Decisions are deferred and deferred and deferred.[34]

The local authorities pursued a minimalist policy of maintaining exist-ing sites and, at the same time, sought to evict unsettled Travellers. A pattern of 'go move shift' had been set by the early 1970s that persisted into the twenty-first century.

SPATIAL CONFLICT

Efforts to settle Travellers living on the outskirts of Ennis in the late 1960s were thwarted, among other things, by the competing pressures of suburban development. Where suburban residential development had yet to occur it was argued that Traveller accommodation should not be allowed because it would lead to a potential loss of future rates to the local authorities.[35] Rural areas on the outskirts of the town that had been longstanding unofficial halting sites became suburbanised and the new settlers were quick to cast the Travellers as interlopers. This can be seen from the changing nature of opposition between 1969 and 1978 to sites for Travellers that emerged in the Lees Road area. The objections that emerged to the initial proposed development principally came from farmers. Objections by farmers to a second proposal, just a few years later in 1971, were accompanied by those of a residents asso-ciation. The solicitor representing the residents described the people in the area as middle class and expressed concern that the value of their bungalows would fall if itinerant families were settled there.[36]

From the early 1970s the local authorities increasingly prosecuted Travellers living in the town under public health legislation and for illegal parking. Those living in or around the town were fined and evicted on an ongoing basis throughout the 1970s and 1980s.[37] Plans to develop accom-modation went hand in hand with efforts to fine and evict even those des-ignated to receive accommodation. For example, in 1971 six Traveller families awaiting accommodation on the Watery Road were fined two pounds each for obstruction. Their fines were paid by the Ennis Itinerant Settlement Committee, who considered that they had been put in an invidious position through inaction by the local authorities in developing the site for their use.[38] Unaccommodated Travellers on the roadsides near Ennis lived precarious lives. A storm in January 1974 destroyed or dam-aged most of their homes.[39] A group of thirty families consisting of fifty-four adults and forty-two children had been living in ten huts, six cara-vans, six barrel-wagons and seven canvas or plastic shelters. A second storm later that month caused further damage to their homes.

Opposition by residents to Travellers who halted took a number of forms. It usually emerged through residents groups that lobbied councillors or took legal proceedings. Most of such activism was bound up with efforts to exclude Travellers from a locality. Sometimes the actions of such groups took the form of boycotting or harassment. For example, some councillors argued that Travellers on unofficial sites should be deprived of all basic amenities, including water.[40] In some cases Travellers were physically prevented from halting. For example, in 1982 three councillors confronted Travellers attempting to halt at Drumbiggle in Ennis and 'informed them that further parking in the area would simply not be tolerated'.[41] The Travellers moved on. A more usual form of spatial exclusion took the form of trenching lay-bys and using boulders to block off these and other unofficial sites used habitually by Travellers so as to prevent their return.

By the 1980s many of the unaccommodated Travellers living in the Ennis area had been born or had grown up in the town.[42] The size of this 'indigenous' community grew from an estimated fifteen families and some single people in 1976 to twenty families in 1984.[43] From time to time they were displaced by the local authorities following protests by residents and councillors but the use of the courts for such purposes became increasingly recognised as ineffective. Once evicted, they moved elsewhere in the town, 'playing' what one councillor referred to as 'musical chairs with the council, Gardaí and the public at large'.[44] Yet, the use of such orders to placate anti-Traveller feeling persisted.[45] In 1970 residents of the market area objected to the construction of a public toilet on the grounds that Travellers might make use of it.[46] In 1977 a group of Ennis residents threatened a rent strike unless the urban district council agreed to 'rid their area of itinerants'.[47] In 1982 businesses at the Ennis shopping centre similarly threatened to withhold their rates.[48] These and a number of other protests against Travellers resulted in an ongoing political impetus to exclude Travellers from the town.

Councillors spoke in terms of making a stand against the Travellers. This became increasingly seen as the need to oppose not just roadside halting but their presence in the town. By 1974 eighteen families lived in council houses in Ennis; councillors increasingly spoke of not allowing any more to be housed.[49] During the 1980s the main emphasis of halting site policy was, effectively, to prevent Travellers from accessing housing in the town. Two forms of exclusion were envisaged with the construction of a large halting site well outside the town at Drumcliffe. The first was to seek to compel Travellers living on the roadsides in Ennis to move away from town. The second was to prevent such Travellers obtaining housing in the town.

The Drumcliffe development had been opposed from the outset by

Travellers as well as by local residents. Ennis Travellers had a deep-rooted antipathy to the site because of its proximity to a cemetery where many of their dead were buried.[50] They also considered that the site was too far from the town. Those who lived on the roadsides in and around Ennis by that time were the children and relatives of those living in houses in the town. Many had grown up in houses but became homeless when they married and had children of their own. In a survey conducted by the committee in November 1984 of twenty-eight families living on the roadside and in Beechpark, an overcrowded site in Ennis, twenty-four families stated that they would not move to Drumcliffe under any circumstances.[51] Only one family was prepared to use the site but this was conditional on it being occupied by other local families. Officials were unwilling to meet with members of the committee to discuss the proposal in advance of it being approved by the council.[52] Travellers refusing to move onto the site were threatened with prosecution for unauthorised parking.[53] At the same time motions were put before the local authorities that no housing applications from Travellers be accepted unless they first moved onto the Drumcliffe site.[54]

Some Ennis Travellers eventually moved onto the site to join some transient Travellers who lived there. Efforts to manage the site were minimal.[55] In 1996 a violent incident involving about fifty Travellers occurred on the site.[56] This resulted in considerable damage to the site, a number of Traveller families being made immediately homeless and a High Court ruling that the site should be closed. The Drumcliffe site was closed in February 1997 and sixteen families were consigned to the roadsides around Ennis.[57] The High Court decision had ordered the provision of an alternative site.[58] Subsequent plans by the local authorities to develop a number of replacement halting sites some miles outside Ennis, against the long-expressed wishes of the Ennis Travellers, met with considerable opposition from residents groups.[59] These plans were by and large unsuccessful in the face of High Court actions by these groups.[60] A lack of alternative accommodation was combined with overcrowding and poor conditions on existing approved sites in the county.[61] For example, a site at Beechpark in Ennis had opened in 1973 as a temporary site for eight families. In 1981 Travellers living on the site complained that council workers had refused to collect refuse from the site for over two years and that all the families on the site had to share one tap and one broken flush toilet.[62] By 1998 it was occupied by eleven families. The local authorities had agreed that the number of families living on the site should be reduced to six but in the absence of alternatives the site remained overcrowded and improvements had been deferred for many years.[63]

HOUSING DISCRIMINATION

Many Travellers in Clare expressed a preference for standard housing
or group housing schemes rather than halting sites. By 1976 it was estimated that half the Traveller population in the Republic of Ireland had
been 'settled' even if a considerable number still wanted to travel.[64]
Ironically, claims that Travellers did not want housing were used to justify discrimination by local authorities seeking to exclude Travellers
from Ennis. Some urban district councillors argued that the local
authorities had fulfilled their obligations to Travellers. They put forward a motion in 1982 that no more Travellers be housed other than
those already on housing waiting lists.[65] During the 1980s Ennis
Travellers contested what they described as discrimination in the allocation of council housing on a number of occasions. Many of these
were of a generation that had grown up in such housing in the town.
As put by a spokesman of the Ennis Committee for Travelling People in
1987:

> Since the late 1960s, up to thirty families had been provided for
> in either standard or group housing schemes. No provision has
> been made for the children of Travellers who had been housed.
> These young people ... had been born in or near Ennis, had
> attended school and the travellers training centre and had lived
> happily with their settled neighbours.
>   Inevitably, they have grown up and married, thereby creating
> new families. Of necessity, they are then forced to go back on the
> roadside ... From then on they were subjected to harassment,
> forced to pay fines and legal fees for illegal parking and were con-
> stantly living with the threat of being moved. Unfortunately they
> had no choice other than moving onto another illegal parking
> place.[66]

In 1987 the local authorities in Ennis came under considerable criticism
for discriminating against Travellers. Claims by the authorities that there
was no demand for housing among Travellers were disputed. It was
argued that eight out of the fifteen local families on the side of the road
at the time wanted houses.[67] The Ennis Committee for Travelling People
accused the county council of, in effect, maintaining separate housing
waiting lists for Travellers and settled people. The local authorities
argued that there were no plans to construct houses at the time because
of an overall lack of demand. They discounted claims that Travellers
wanted standard housing and argued that there was a significant

demand for halting site accommodation.[68] These arguments masked an unwillingness to house Travellers in the town.[69] The argument that Travellers did not want housing and, as such, that there was no demand for such housing replaced more blatant statements made at the time the Drumcliffe proposal was being considered, that Travellers would not be allowed onto waiting lists unless they moved onto the Drumcliffe site. As detailed by the National Council for Travelling People:

> The Assistant County Manager states that Clare County Council cannot accommodate the fifteen local travellers presently on the roadside or the average eleven new marriages each year. At the same time he states that the Council have cut back on their housing programme because of a reduction in demand from settled people. In other words, if settled people need houses they can be built, if Travellers need them, forget it. Where citizenship is concerned some are more equal than others are.
>
> During the course of a meeting with our committee, Mr Ó Ceallaigh, the Assistant County Manager, made an even more astonishing statement that no Traveller family would be considered in the imminent allocation of vacant houses. Five local Traveller families have applied for those houses, filled in the forms and have been visited by the health inspector who recorded the number of their children, their living conditions and how long they had been applying for a house. All five are married couples with from three to six children. All want a local authority house, not group housing or a site. All are local to the Ennis area. Some have lived in houses here as children and teenagers for up to fourteen years. They are very together couples with no problems their neighbours might object to. None has ever been in trouble with the law. Yet the council can deprive them of their constitutional rights to be considered for a home.[70]

But there was no constitutional right to housing. Complaints by local authority tenants about the allocation of two houses to Traveller families in 1987 resulted in demands from Ennis councillors to be consulted on all future letting decisions.[71] Two of these councillors were on record as opposing the allocation of any houses to Travellers,[72] while another two had argued that no more Travellers should be allowed to live on some estates.[73] The county manager acceded to this request in part, and it was agreed that the councillors would be informed of any proposed letting decision in advance. Pressure to discriminate against Travellers persisted during the years that followed. In 1991 a deputation of 150 residents from Clancy Park objected to the allocation of a further house to a Traveller family on top of the existing five occupied by Travellers on the estate.[74] In 1994 a deputation of residents from Clarecastle protested against what they understood as the abandonment of a promise not to house any more Traveller families in the area.[75] These complaints might be understood, to some extent, as a response to the curtailment of earlier discriminatory letting policies.

THE PERSISTENCE OF 'GO, MOVE, SHIFT'

The Travellers evicted from Drumcliffe in 1997 were subsequently evicted from land adjacent to Ennis industrial estate following a High Court action by tenants.[76] They subsequently moved to open spaces around the town and to areas adjacent to existing Traveller sites.[78] This met with opposition from resident groups. For example, the arrival of five families on land adjacent to Traveller houses on the Watery Road prompted local residents associations to raise funds for a possible High Court action against the local authorities.[78] As put by one Traveller representative: 'We have been treated like dogs since the Drumcliffe site was closed in December, being run from place to place around Ennis.'[79] The Ennis town manager, according to an article in the *Clare Champion*, 'vowed to go to every court in the land' to have Travellers removed from the vicinity of one Ennis site, following claims that they were causing problems for local residents.[80] As put by the chairman of Ennis Urban District Council at the time: 'The Travellers cannot be allowed to rule the roost.'[81] Some of the displaced Travellers sought to counter this dominant perspective, however. As explained by one Traveller woman:

> We don't want to be illegally parked but have no option because the council hasn't provided any temporary halting site. We want to stay in Ennis because we are from the town and our children are going to school here. We understand that the car parks are not suitable but we have nowhere to go. Some Travellers looking for houses have been on the housing list for ten years and if they obtained houses this would help the situation considerably.[82]

In 1997 the Catholic bishop, Dr Walsh, who was also chairperson of the Travellers Accommodation Advisory Committee, permitted four local Traveller families to halt on his lawn in a gesture 'aimed at encouraging a more positive response by the local authorities'.[83] However, this evoked considerable hostility from councillors who opposed the presence of

Travellers in the town. One demanded that Dr Walsh be prosecuted for being in breach of planning regulations.[84]

A Traveller Accommodation Advisory Committee had been established in 1997 to prepare to meet the statutory requirements of the 1998 Housing (Travellers) Accommodation Act to produce a Traveller accommodation plan for the county. It was agreed that the advisory committee would be made up of councillors, council officials and a representative of the Travelling community. A request for more than one Traveller representative on the committee resulted in a threat by the councillor who was to chair the committee that he would resign;[85] a decision to allow a second Traveller member to represent Travellers at Shannon resulted in his resignation.[86] Prior to the establishment of the advisory committee by the county council in 1997, Travellers in Clare had never been formally consulted about accommodation proposals. The advisory committee quickly produced a report which set out the accommodation requirements of Travellers living in the county. It proposed seven group housing schemes, five single rural houses, seven serviced sites and twelve units of local authority housing all to be located near the main towns in the county – Ennis, Shannon and Ennistymon – with, in the case of group housing or sites, less than six families in any one scheme. The report also stated the need for a number of transient sites in the county, to accommodate newly formed families awaiting permanent accommodation and to make provision for visiting Traveller families with a limit of eight families and twelve mobile homes or caravans on any one site. The report, as such, stated that most Travellers wanted housing and a minority wanted to be accommodated on halting sites and that such sites should accommodate small numbers.

The county council received the report in October 1997. It was opposed by a number of councillors but was formally accepted, on the advice of officials that not to do so would potentially result in the matter being taken out of their hands by the Minister for the Environment.[87] The plan had little impact upon the proposals that emerged to provide accommodation for Travellers in the late 1990s. The council constructed a halting site near Shannon, whose design paid no heed to the recommendations of the advisory committee and ignored the consultation undertaken with Travellers. Against their wishes it consisted of a number of caravan pitches adjacent to small *tigíns*. The county council pursued plans to develop halting sites in a number of areas some miles from Ennis even though the Travellers stated a desire to live in Ennis and the other towns in the county.

Officials had stated that an accommodation blueprint would be published in early 1999 but this was deferred in the face of potential public hostility pending the 1999 local government elections.[88] A report in the *Clare Champion* in September 1999 stated that councillors had 'trenchantly refused to allow a draft plan to confront the problem of accommodating Travellers to go on public display'.[89] This resistance brought yet another warning from the county manager that unless they 'got their house in order' they faced the prospect of having the final say on the make-up of the Travellers accommodation plan being taken away from them by the Minister for the Environment and Local Government.[90] In the absence of measures to address the accommodation needs of Travellers the local authorities persisted in seeking to move Travellers on from unauthorised sites through the courts. However, the courts were increasingly reluctant to find in favour of the local authorities given that they had failed in their obligations to provide accommodation.[91]

A census of Travellers undertaken in Clare by the local authorities in November 1998 noted that fifty Traveller families were accommodated in standard housing and Traveller-only group housing schemes.[92] Twenty families were living on serviced halting sites, with thirty-seven living on unauthorised sites; a further three families were living on private accommodation. Although councillors and officials often gave the impression that many of the unaccommodated families were transient outsiders, the Traveller Accommodation Sub-Committee had identified the need for an accommodation programme to cater for fifty-three 'indigenous' families in immediate need of permanent accommodation as well as eight transient families. The committee emphasised the need to take account of projected population increases and new household formations (an estimated five families) by 2004. However, as expressed by a spokesperson for a residents association in October 1999:

> By my reading of the plan, it will not be until 2002 to 2005 before halting sites are provided. It is not easy on the community but there is sympathy for the travellers who are living in those conditions without running water, sanitation or refuse collection. There is a fire and health hazard in an area where there are between 12 and 15 caravans on a site just big enough to accommodate a bungalow ... People living in Kosovo would not put up with the living conditions that the travellers are enduring.

A judge during the proceedings of an illegal parking case had expressed an even more pessimistic analysis two years previously. In reply to a statement by a Traveller woman that her sixty-six-year-old father would be seventy by the time the council provided a halting site for her family the judge replied: 'You'll be seventy yourself by the time they provide a site.'[93]

TRAVELLER VOICES

By the 1980s, independent Traveller voices began to emerge. However, these tended to be ignored by councillors and officials. In 1987 a senior local authority official castigated the local voluntary sector for fomenting discontent among Travellers. As reported in the *Clare Champion*: 'It was clear his remarks were aimed at what he called do-gooders allegedly concerned with the issue and he told them in no uncertain terms that if they followed the Christian example set by the local authority – instead of trying to undermine public confidence in the council – the issue would be nigh solved at this stage.'[94] On another occasion, at a local government conference, these 'unChristian do-gooders' were identified by a councillor as the 'clergy, nuns and social services working with Travellers in Ennis'.[95]

In 1981 Travellers who complained about refuse collection at a local authority meeting were praised by councillors and officials who noted that this was the first time that Travellers had participated in a local authority discussion of Traveller issues.[96] Ann Mongan explained that her site had become a health hazard because the council had not collected refuse for some time even though a refuse lorry passed her site every week. Such participation was very infrequent for a number of reasons. One of these was that local authority meetings were routinely characterised by overt expressions of hostility against Travellers. Most accounts of anti-Traveller hostility from 1963 to 1999 recorded in the *Clare Champion* were drawn from the proceedings of such meetings. Travellers, as a small minority, lacked political power.[97] However, they increasingly became involved in community development work, organising training projects, arts projects and youth clubs.[98] In 1984 *Young Travellers: Many Voices, One Community* was published by the Ennis Traveller Training Centre, located in the industrial estate on the Galway Road. The centre, which opened in 1982, was set up as part of a national network of training centres for Travellers. The code of practice adopted by the centre noted that not all Travellers sought full integration within the settled community. It emphasised the right of Travellers to retain their culture and identity. The centre, which was envisaged as a catalyst for community development and a forum for debate,[99] organised events aimed at highlighting Traveller homelessness. For example, in 1987 Ennis Young Travellers undertook a survey of homelessness in their own area and submitted the results, along with those from other parts of the country, to the Minister for the Environment.

From the mid-1980s Travellers contested housing discrimination in a number of ways. *Young Travellers: Many Voices, One Community* gave accounts of prejudice and discrimination in the Ennis area. In particular, it emphasised the feelings of embarrassment on being turned away from shops, public houses, cinemas and dances. Bernie McDonagh described how Travellers were not welcome in most pubs and could never be sure of admittance to local dances. Jimmy McCarthy described the shock of his first experience of discrimination:

> I went to a dance. There was a friend with me and as we were going in the door we were stopped by a big man who said:
> 'You're not coming in.'
> I turned and walked away. I felt real bad, so I went home. I sat there thinking about it, and I couldn't get over it. I was saying why are we different from others? Why are travellers treated like dirt? It's very embarrassing when you are turned away like that. A Traveller is treated like dirt because hardly any buffer will speak to Travellers. You'd get more guards talking to Travellers than you would buffer people.[100] I didn't even know I was a Traveller when I was small because I was in the school in Tralee. I was an altar boy. I went to Mass every day. I was very religious. It was only years later I left school and lived in the site at Ashline in Ennis that I knew I was a Traveller, when I learnt the way of Travellers. I didn't know we were different from townspeople but I soon found out.

Following other such experiences Jimmy McCarthy wrote a letter of complaint to the manager of a hotel that discriminated against him. A number of young Travellers emphasised their constitutional rights to be treated the same as other citizens. John McDonagh described how a woman in another Ennis McDonagh family was refused service in a supermarket in the town. When this sort of thing happened Travellers tended to go elsewhere, even to another town, but now – speaking, he felt, for most Travellers – they would fight for their rights. Such arguments in *Young Travellers: Many Voices, One Community* were reported positively in a number of articles in the *Clare Champion* about Traveller community development.[101] One article in 1985 noted that a musical group of young Travellers from Ennis would be 'making their mark' in an appearance on the 'Late Late Show'.[102] This offered a rare media platform which was used by Ennis Travellers in the audience to criticise plans for the Drumcliffe site and the actions of the official in charge of Traveller accommodation. Councillors and officials in Clare were angered by the criticisms and they subsequently passed a resolution to write to the 'Late Late Show' to demand that the allegations of the Travellers be retracted. Gay Byrne, in reply, advised them against over-reaction. He wrote of a 'danger that the council members may over-react and in demanding official corrections may be seen to be anti-itin-erant or generally hostile or may indeed be using an elephant gun to shoot gnats'.[103] The Travellers who appeared on the show were accused by councillors of mounting a conspiracy against the use of the 'magnif-icent halting site in Drumcliffe'.[104]

Individual Travellers on occasion contested prejudicial statements by councillors.[105] For example, in 1991 the *Clare Champion* reported the responses of a man 'whose address is a caravan somewhere in Ennis' to allegations that there was an influx of non-indigenous Travellers into the town. He stated that indigenous families who were forced to move by Ennis Urban District Council and Clare County Council to other towns and cities and to England had returned with the hope that the house or site for which they had waited many years would at last be available. He told the *Clare Champion* 'that he and his wife lived in houses with their parents prior to their marriage and he said they were currently in need of a home in the Ennis area'. As he put it:

> Why should my family and I have to go to an unsuitable site or to any other town or foreign country? All Ennis Urban Council have done so far for us is to take me to court for illegal parking, have me fined and then put me in prison when I could not pay. This carry on is very annoying to say the least. Our oldest child should be at school every day but it is not possible in our present circum-stances.[106]

In 1997 another man who had lived in Ennis for twenty-two years suc-cessfully sued a publican who had refused to serve him. When he asked why he was refused the publican had replied 'the citizens', which he took to mean he was being refused because the other customers would object.[107] Judge Albert O'Dea also delivered a strong criticism of the local bar. Local solicitors had refused to represent the Traveller in the case and he had to go to Gort to obtain legal representation.[108] The solic-itor who took the case was congratulated for 'his brave public spirit'.

CONCLUSION

For the most part the role of councillors on Traveller issues was one of opposition rather than leadership. Councillors played a central role in articulating anti-Traveller feeling and in opposing efforts to provide accommodation for Travellers even though they were the elected members of the local authorities with responsibility for providing such accommodation. Since the 1960s local authorities could avail of central government funding to provide accommodation for Travellers but they were not required by law to do so prior to the 1997 Housing (Traveller Accommodation) Act. In this context councillors could disassociate themselves from plans to provide accommodation and engage themselves in populist anti-Traveller protest. However, at the same time councillors were expected to deal with the problem of Travellers. Travellers lived on the roadside because local authorities were unwilling to provide accommodation for them. Such unwillingness was in turn caused by opposition to sites for Travellers. The response of some councillors to this seemingly insoluble problem was to press for the exclusion of Travellers, to denigrate them as a deviant group and make arguments for discriminating against them.

By the early 1970s the effort to provide accommodation for Travellers had run out of steam. Local authorities and councillors became the focus of criticism from the voluntary sector for failing to provide accommodation and from residents for not having prevented Travellers from halting in their localities. During the 1980s many councillors advocated excluding Travellers from the town of Ennis. Statements by councillors and officials often emphasised past generosity towards the Travellers. In a number of statements during the 1980s and 1990s Ennis and Clare were depicted as having done more than any other town or county for Travellers.[109] Ennis Urban District Council was described as having 'one of the most enviable records of housing Travellers'. Such statements emerged as a defence against accusations by organisations and the local clergy of neglect and discrimination by the local authorities against Travellers.[110] Travellers were depicted as ungrateful when they made complaints or whenever complaints were made on their behalf. The persistence of a Traveller problem was represented as one that was caused by past and present generosity.[111]

The language used by some councillors in debates about Travellers was often heated. *Clare Champion* headlines such as 'Fifteen houses for itinerants amid angry objections by residents', 'Itinerant problem heading for explosive situation', 'Outrage over plans for halting site' and

'Halting site to spark residents' revolt' illustrate a sense of licence that allowed unguarded expressions of hostility towards Travellers that would be criticised if expressed towards other groups.[112] However, the 1990s saw unprecedented official acknowledgement of the problems caused by allowing discrimination against Travellers to drive public policy. The 1995 *Report of the Task Force on the Travelling People* made some 400 recommendations aimed at redressing discrimination in areas such as health, education and accommodation. The 1997 Housing Accommodation Act introduced a statutory obligation upon local authorities to draw up and implement plans to accommodate Travellers, while the 2000 Equal Status Act prohibited discrimination against Travellers in the provision of goods and services. It covered the kinds of situation described in 1984 by Jimmy McCarthy and other young Travellers.

Yet, in Clare as elsewhere, there was considered resistance by councillors and local officials to the recommendations of the 1995 report. Political pressure to displace Travellers was unrelenting. The 2002 Housing (Miscellaneous Provisions) Act allowed for the impounding of Traveller caravans even where the obligations towards them under the 1997 Act to have somewhere to live were not met. The effect of the 2002 Act was described by Ennis Community Development Project (CDP) in the following terms:

- Families given 48 hours by the Gardaí to move caravan
- Due to the extensive placing of boulders on open areas and trenching of ditches and lay-bys outside the town only options left open to the families were illegal ones
- Families moved on average 40 to 60 times during 2003
- Impounding of caravans
- €100.00 to remove caravans from the Garda pound
- No option but to sign form to say they would not park illegally
- The circle continued
- Damage to caravans while being impounded.[113]

As put by Ennis CDP those affected were 'very upset if not traumatised by the untenable situations they found themselves in'. 'When', the report concluded, 'you are confronted with families who are exhausted from the cycle of moving on, impoundment, humiliation, criminalisation, homelessness, dealing with sick children and trying to manage money under difficult circumstances ... the absurdity really hits home; that is to use the law and our own police force to make people homeless without providing an appropriate safety net to support such families.'

The last four decades of the twentieth century witnessed a climate of ongoing discrimination. Spatial conflict between urban and suburban residents and Travellers drip-fed an ongoing political impetus to discriminate against them. The councillors whose utterances at public meetings were usually reported verbatim in the local media represented the visible part of a broader prejudice against Travellers in the county. To some extent this increased over time and broke significantly from earlier relationships between Travellers and other Clare people before the 1960s. Before then, Travellers had a distinct if precarious place in Clare society characterised by some communal solidarity with what they called the 'country people'. As Ireland modernised and urbanised there proved to be less space for Traveller ways of life. In the Ireland of the late twentieth and early twenty-first centuries relationships between Travellers and settled people became mediated through laws and public policies rather than custom and tradition. The pattern of prejudice and the politics of social exclusion that emerged four decades ago have persisted to a considerable extent.

CHAPTER FOUR

A History of Violence

In 2001 I went into a shop in Ennis, County Clare where I lived at the time. I overheard the shopkeeper discuss with some customers a family of Travellers who had parked their caravan nearby in a local car park. He said that he felt like going there with a shotgun and giving them 'both barrels'. The customers nodded in agreement and chuckled. All were put out when I objected to them advocating violence in the presence of my children who were with me in the shop. What the shopkeeper had said echoed the remarks of a Wexford councillor reported in the *Sunday Independent* in 1996:

> The sooner the shotguns are at the ready and these travelling people are put out of our county the better. They are not our people, they aren't natives.[1]

All through my life in Ireland I have heard expressions of hostility and intolerance towards Travellers in shops, in pubs, from some relatives, friends and academic colleagues. Hostility towards Travellers is frequently uncritically reported in the local and national press yet has rarely been the subject of academic research. Media coverage generally relates to opposition by residents and politicians to the provision of accommodation of Travellers, to court cases against Travellers and to pejorative accounts of deviance among Travellers. Claims that Travellers are intrinsically violent have become central to a politics of ethnic exclusion in Ireland. This has been reflected in media coverage of Travellers,[2] which has focused, in particular, upon accounts of feuds between Traveller families and unruly behaviour at weddings and funerals. It is arguably the case that the racialisation of Travellers as a violent out-group in Irish society has intensified in recent years in response to the introduction of legislation against discrimination and social policies aimed at promoting the social inclusion of Travellers.[3]

There is a profound disjuncture between official policies promoting the integration of Travellers, which to some extent acknowledge Traveller ethnicity, and a trenchant opposition by many residents groups and local politicians to the very presence of Travellers in their communities. For example, in 2002 the Vintners' Federation of Ireland (VFI) marshalled accusations of Traveller violence to campaign for the exemption of Travellers from the 2000 Equal Status Act.[4] This Act specifically outlawed discrimination against Travellers in the provision of goods and services. As a result of this campaign the state's Equality Authority lost its powers to directly investigate allegations of discrimination against Travellers by owners of hotels and public houses.

The case study addressed in this chapter focuses on anti-Traveller racism in County Clare between the beginning of 2000 and the end of 2002. It develops a previous analysis of the politics of Traveller exclusion in Clare from the 1960s to the end of 1999.[5] From the 1960s opposition to the provision of halting sites for Travellers and discrimination against Travellers in the provision of public housing was frequently justified by claims that the dominant community lived in fear of Travellers. Anti-Traveller hostility was sometimes expressed in terms of spurious claims about Traveller violence.

Opposition to Traveller accommodation was justified on an ongoing basis by allegations of violence by Travellers against settled people. Emotionally charged, hyperbolic or even apocalyptic language was a feature of most discussions on Travellers at local authority meetings. Newspaper accounts of discussions about Travellers frequently described residents and councillors as angry. Residents were often said by councillors and spokespersons to be living in fear of Travellers, being 'terrorised' by Travellers or harassed, abused and assaulted by them. Allegations often focused on how elderly settled people or women at home during the day lived in 'a constant state of fear' of Travellers. These often combined with allegations that Travellers posed a threat to the health of settled people. Similarly, allegations that Travellers deposited excrement on the doorsteps of vulnerable 'old people' were made from time to time. However, allegations of these kinds were always vague. No specific instance of violence or harassment by a Traveller against any member of the settled community was identified by councillors, local authority officials or residents groups from 1963 to 1999 in Clare to support the various allegations which were made.[6] Travellers in Clare lived under a microscope where any real or imaginary transgressions were subject to intense scrutiny. The general lack of evidence of Traveller violence against settled people did not prevent such allegations acquiring the status of 'truth'. Over the last two decades councillors have from time to time predicted outbreaks of violence.[7] Most recently, in 2001, this took the form of warnings about the potential emergence of vigilante groups. In effect, the threat under discussion was often one of potential violence against Travellers that might transpire if Travellers were not excluded. The very presence of Travellers was portrayed as fuel upon the fires of community anger.[8] In other words, Travellers constituted a danger to the social order because of the violence and hostility that they inspired in the dominant community.

MODERNISATION AND COLONISATION

A number of studies have emphasised the role of modernisation in the exclusion of Travellers.[9] In particular, accounts from an anthropological perspective emphasise their economic displacement from the rural economy from the 1950s and their transformation into an urban poor.[10] This modernisation thesis draws upon accounts of, and justifications for, the displacement of less advanced societies by more advanced ones. In essence, it is a 'structuralist functionalist' thesis that posits that the social structures of societies converge as they become more advanced.[11] Convergence theorists imply that modern societies by virtue of their use of similar technologies will develop similar social structures and similar norms. In this context social control and socialisation are understood as expressions of an underlying social consensus. Deviance is understood in terms of distance from dominant norms. Groups out of step with or at a considerable 'social distance' from the dominant social consensus can be stigmatised as part of a process of social rationalisation. From this perspective the expulsion of Travellers can be deemed reasonable.

MacLaughlin relates anti-Traveller racism to a hegemonic modernisation thesis, exemplified in the thought of John Locke and Adam Smith, which perceived a 'social Darwinist' conception of social progress that hierarchically ranked societies according to their ways of utilising resources. Each 'stage' of the evolution of society was characterised by a different mode of production. The destruction of ineffective societies could be justified in the name of progress.[12] Specifically, he notes the institutionalisation of a form of social Darwinist ideology in Irish society following the Famine that ideologically justified the displacement of the rural poor. Emigration can be understood as an aspect of the post-Famine rationalisation of Irish society. So too can the subsequent stigmatisation of 'out-groups' within the Irish nation such as

Travellers. They did not become objects of state policies of assimilation until they had been displaced from the rural economy.

The general movement of Travellers to urban centres was part of broader demographic changes in Irish society. However, the urbanisation of Travellers rendered them extremely vulnerable to hostility from the dominant community as the spaces within Irish society for non-sedentary ways of life diminished.[13] In this context, Travellers were constructed as a social problem experienced by sedentary people. Assimilationist policies to address the Traveller problem emerged but, for the most part, assimilation was vigorously rejected. Residents groups and local politicians sought to displace rather than settle Travellers.[14] This took the form of a 'spontaneous and organised enmity' towards Travellers. As explained by Sinéad Ni Shuinear:

> We need to look no further than our daily papers for examples of this: from the more dramatic manifestations like pickets, marches and mob attacks on Traveller camps, to the institutionalised harassment of evictions and the deliberate blocking off of and destruction of any and all possible camp sites by boulders (officially termed 'landscaping') to the de facto apartheid of barring Travellers from pubs, schools and dances on the (all too justified) grounds that their presence would lead to trouble.[15]

The terms of reference of the Commission on Itinerancy set up in 1960 were 'to promote their absorption into the general community' and 'pending such absorption, to reduce to a minimum the disadvantages to themselves and the community resulting from their itinerant habits'.[16] The problem was formulated as the problem of the existence of Travellers. Depictions of Travellers as a sub-culture of poverty predominated within official discourse until the 1990s when a degree of acceptance of their ethnic distinctiveness emerged alongside an emphasis on the role of discrimination in explaining intergenerational poverty among some Travellers.[17] By contrast with the modernisation convergence thesis, a conflict thesis of social order emphasises the exploitative nature of power relations. Dominant or hegemonic ideologies and norms are seen to maintain social inequalities.[18] From this perspective their displacement is explained in terms of class conflict and colonisation.

Present-day depictions of Travellers as an 'underclass' and a corresponding state emphasis on punitive policies of social control strikingly resemble anti-Irish racism during the Victorian era to the extent that racist discourses in both cases often seem interchangeable. Engels, writing in 1844 in *The Condition of the Working Class in England*, described Irish immigration to Britain as the product of long centuries of colonial injustice. However, Engels also viewed the Irish firmly through the lens of colonial stereotypes. He depicted them as a danger to the English nation in viewing them as corruptors of the moral character of the English working classes. The Irish were 'rough, intemperate and improvident' and were to blame for degrading the English working classes with their 'brutal habits'. For Engels, the solution was, where possible, to turn them into Englishmen:

> For work which requires long training or regular pertinacious application, the dissolute, unsteady drunken Irishman is on too low a place. To become a mechanic, a mill-hand, he would have to adopt the English civilisation, the English customs, become in the main, an Englishman ... And even if the Irish, who have forced their way into other occupations, should become more civilised, enough of the old habits would cling to them to have a strong degrading influence on their English companions in toil, especially in view of the general effect of being surrounded by the Irish. For when, in almost every great city, a fifth or a quarter of the workers are Irish, or children of Irish parents, who have grown up amongst Irish filth, no one can wonder if the life, habits, intelligence, moral status – in short the whole character of the working-class – assimilates a great part of the Irish characteristics.[19]

A number of accounts of anti-Irish racism cite nineteenth-century depictions of the Irish as physically brutish and biologically inferior.[20] Engels, in common with Victorian 'race' thinking, oscillated between an environmental (and hence malleable) and a biological (and hence immutable) conception of the Irish character.[21] In the post-Famine era the Irish in Britain were racialised as harbingers of crime and disorder. Such stereotypes predominantly drew on the poorest Irish immigrants absorbed into the urban 'underclass'. Irish 'ghettos' became a specific focus of police and media scrutiny and to some extent the Irish became over-represented in crime statistics and contemporary accounts of disorder.[22] These were also, to some extent, an aspect of a spatial politics of exclusion insofar as accommodation discrimination was frequent and remained common more than a century later.[23]

The social control of Travellers in modern Ireland can be seen to partly reflect an internalisation of colonial preoccupations with race and hygiene. Welfare and philanthropy debates in nineteenth-century Ireland were influenced by racialised stereotypes of the Irish poor. On the one hand Irish philanthropy reflected determinist Victorian notions of the poor as a race apart; on the other hand the social control of the Irish 'underclass' in Ireland was guided by dominant colonial ideals of social membership. Protestant and Catholic charities alike promoted the notion that the Irish poor were morally and intellectually inferior to such ideals.[24] Twentieth-century Catholic welfare institutions such as the Magdalene laundries perpetuated mid-nineteenth century Poor Law conceptions of the poor as immoral and indolent.[25]

MacLaughlin identifies two of the 'principal setbacks' encountered by displaced Travellers in Ireland in recent decades. Firstly he emphasises the rise of a virulent anti-Traveller racism characterised by violence and intimidation.[26] This is seen as a manifestation of their rejection by the dominant community. Generally this rejection is expressed in the use of stereotypes of Traveller deviance from contemporary social norms. One much-quoted 1996 article in the *Sunday Independent* erroneously claimed that Travellers were responsible for over 90 per cent of violent crimes against the rural elderly.[27] It employed stereotypes that evoked the most histrionic Victorian constructions of the poor as a 'race' apart:

> It is a life worse than the life of beasts, for beasts are at least guided by wholesome instinct. Traveller life is without the ennobling intellect of man and the steadying instinct of animals. This tinker 'culture' is without achievement, discipline, reason or intellectual ambition. It is a morass. And one of the surprising things about it is that not every individual bred in this swamp turns out bad. Some individuals amongst the tinkers find the will not to become evil.[28]

According to O'Connell, anti-Traveller racism builds on 'fantasies related to dirt, danger, deviance and crime'. It invokes a pariah syndrome that is employed to legitimate prejudice and to deny that such prejudice is racism. Its central theme is a depiction of Traveller nomadism 'as an atavistic aberration which has to be eliminated by modernisation or, failing that, coercion'.[29] Anti-Traveller racism can therefore be represented as the ideological expression of an increase in 'social distance' between the dominant community and Travellers over the last number of decades. Mac Gréil concluded from attitudinal surveys undertaken in 1977 and 1988–9, and the majority negative responses contained therein to questions about willingness to be friends with Travellers, avoiding them in social situations, or buying a house next door to them, that Travellers had the status of a lower caste in Irish society. His findings indicated that a majority of Irish people were hostile to Travellers.[30]

The findings of a 1999 survey indicate that this hostility has increased rather than diminished.[31]

MacLaughlin argues that a second important setback has been the gradual internalisation of feelings of social inferiority among Travellers themselves: 'Having been oppressed and demoralised for so long, a growing body of evidence suggests that many Travellers are beginning to internalise feelings of racial inferiority and taking to alcohol abuse and petty crime as outlets for the frustration they experience in their day-to-day lives.'[32] Similar arguments have been made by other writers who seek to come to terms with the overwhelming negativity of stereotypes of Travellers:

> It is worth noting that settled perceptions of Travellers are so overpoweringly negative that if the individual Traveller demonstrates that he or she clearly does not conform to the negative stereotypes, he or she is suddenly redeemed from Traveller status: they become 'a former itinerant', a 'housed Traveller', a 'settled Traveller', 'of Traveller stock' or whatever. [33]

Franz Fanon's argument that colonialism is predicated on the negation of the colonised subject, the notion that at every level the colonised subject is induced to reject his or her own culture and internalise the values of the colonial power, has previously been applied in analyses of anti-Irish racism.[34] According to this argument colonisation is expressed through ideological stereotypes through which those experiencing colonisation recognise that 's/he is an object of fear, an unpredictable and violent natural force, in the eyes of the colonist'.[35] Fanon's argument can similarly be applied to Travellers in Ireland. The choices for those experiencing colonisation are stark. They can opt for an identity created by the colonialist 'other' or internalise the pathological projections of the colonialist's fears and risk further alienation from their own experience.

BARKING AND BITING

Stereotypes of the 'violent Irish' and the 'violent Traveller' have both served to ideologically justify assimilation and coercive social control measures. Assimilation implies an effort to subordinate groups perceived as deviant *within* the presumed civilisation of the dominant group. However, the coexistence of racism and xenophobia alongside assimilationist ideologies more often than not justifies the rejection and exclusion of groups deemed not to meet the criteria for admission into the dominant social order. In this context the relationship between racist ideology and acts of coercion and violence needs to be explored. The experiences of Travellers highlight a number of ways in which the rejection of out-groups can be attained. They have been the subject of acts of hate speech, acts of discrimination, acts of intimidation and acts of violence aimed at achieving spatial exclusion and a form of social 'apartheid'.[36] Allport identifies five categories of behaviour associated with the rejection of out-groups:

(1) antilocution or verbal rejection: the use of speech to articulate antagonism;
(2) avoidance: withdrawal from the disliked;
(3) discrimination: denial of treatment accorded to the dominant group;
(4) physical attack: various forms of violence including intimidation; and
(5) extermination.

He argues that violence (the last two categories) is always the result of milder forms of rejection.[37] As he puts it: 'Most barking (antilocution) does not lead to biting, yet there is never a bite without previous barking.'[38] According to Taguieff, this suggests that speech acts are always capable of engendering physical attack. Verbal rejection is not a substitute for violence but a potential cause of violence: 'The penchant for racist murder is present in each of us; the genocidal drive is natural in humanity, as it is already at work in prejudices (hate-prejudices) which arise spontaneously in the world of humanity's common experience.'[39] The ever-present lure of violence then is something that must be consciously overcome. The question of the relationship between racism and violence has been central to academic debates on the causes of the Holocaust, of colonial genocide and, more recently, of ethnic cleansing.[40] Bauman, in the case of the former, offers a functionalist account of the relationship between racist ideology and racist violence that can be seen to explain the resort to violence in terms of a failure of actions within Allport's first three categories to achieve such ideological goals. If verbal rejection does not work, if withdrawal from the disliked is unfeasible and if discrimination does not secure their displacement then the lure of violence may beckon.

As noted in Chapter 2, Travellers remain invisible in most academic histories of Ireland. However, there are indications that a disproportionately high number of Travellers were murdered during the Irish Civil War.[41] In 1940 the Minister for Justice noted that the Gardaí (police) were under ongoing pressure at a community level to shift Travellers from their campsites.[42] Such intimidation has persisted to the present time. A history of anti-Traveller intimidation and violence in Clare can be identified from local media records. For example, there have been ongoing efforts by residents groups and councillors to deprive Travellers of water and other basic amenities.[43] There have also been some mob actions against Travellers; in 1985, in Sixmilebridge, a group was surrounded by 'a crowd of about 100 drunk and aggressive locals chanting for blood'.[44] They attempted to burn a van containing six Travellers and then to push it into a river. A Traveller woman was chased by a group of twelve or thirteen people armed with sticks, planks and hurleys. She fell through a glass window, extracted herself from the glass and continued to flee. In 1986 a large crowd of about 100 gathered outside the local authority house of a Traveller family chanting 'burn them out'.[45] Some councillors used the latter incident to argue that no local authority housing should be allocated to Travellers in future.[46] The response of the Gardaí in such cases was to arrest Travellers, both to protect them and to placate mobs of settled people. The Gardaí tended to view 'friction' between settled communities and Travellers as a problem to be addressed through the prosecution and criminalisation of Travellers.[47] In 1992 residents who lived near an unofficial halting site outside Shannon hired a mechanical digger to make it uninhabitable while many of its occupants were on a pilgrimage to Croagh Patrick. They physically prevented the Travellers from accessing the site on their return.[48]

Anti-Traveller racism was exploited by the main political parties in the run-up to the 2002 general election. One of the opposition parties, Fine Gael, introduced a bill which sought to criminalise Travellers who halted on unofficial sites. This was endorsed by the government and became the 2002 Housing (Miscellaneous Provisions) Act. It was passed by an overwhelming cross-party majority. On 16 July 2002 the caravans of four Traveller families in Ennis were confiscated by the Gardaí; other seizures followed. Traveller families who lived on the roadside in and around the town had been periodically brought to court by the local authorities. However, prior to the 2002 Act, prosecutions were generally overturned by the courts because the local authorities were deemed to have failed in their statutory obligations to provide accommodation under the 1997 Travellers (Housing Accommodation) Act. The 2002 Act allowed Travellers to be evicted and to have their caravans seized even where their statutory accommodation entitlements had not been met. Objections to the 2002 Act by members of Citizen Traveller, a state-funded anti-racism body, led to the withdrawal of its government funding.[49] State intimidation arguably reflects political hostility towards Travellers.

At present, legal remedies to the politics of verbal rejection – what Allport describes as the use of speech to articulate antagonism – are weak. The 1989 Prohibition of Incitement to Hatred Act has had little or no impact on anti-Traveller racism. The Act made it an offence to incite hatred against any group of persons on account of their 'race, colour, nationality, religion, age, sexuality, ethnic or national origins, or membership of the Travelling Community'. Just one case relating to Travellers has been referred to the Director of Public Prosecutions (DPP); the defendant was acquitted. In September 2000 the Minister for Justice, Equality and Law Reform acknowledged that the Act was ineffective and stated that new legislation was necessary. The Act was ineffective, in part, due to the extensive burden of causal proof required to demonstrate that racist acts had been incited.[50]

Although the Gardaí have begun to document allegations of racist assaults, they do not yet disaggregate these so that offences against Travellers are identifiable. There is some evidence that Travellers are subject to over-policing. Traveller and Garda respondents in a recent study of the policing of Traveller wedding and funeral rituals described the approach of the Gardaí as 'heavy handed'. One Traveller respondent described how the Gardaí 'establish roadblocks and prosecute a captive audience. They create an impression that everyone who is attending the funeral is a potential trouble maker.' Another described how Gardaí used the occasion of funerals to 'target Travellers' vehicles for tax, insurance and tyre inspections and encouraged shop, café and pub owners to close their premises temporarily and as such endorse discrimination against Travellers'.[51] Indications of over-policing and undue criminalisation of Travellers combined with an apparent lack of emphasis on them as potential victims of crime suggests some commonalities to the forms of institutional bias revealed by the Macpherson Inquiry into the London Metropolitan Police.[52] This identified the simultaneous criminalisation of black people and the under-protection of black communities from crime and racist violence. Again some similarities with the past experiences of the criminalisation of the Irish in Britain can be noted.[53]

DISCRIMINATION AND VIOLENCE IN CLARE 2000–2002

In October 2001 a statement by an Ennis councillor, reported under the front-page headline 'Vigilante uprising against Travellers' in the *Clare*

Champion, provoked a degree of national controversy. As stated by the councillor:

> Vigilantes will be in this town in the near future. People out there are not prepared to put up with what is going on anymore. They are going to stand up. You are going to have people organising themselves against what is happening at the moment. They are going to get together to win back our town. They are going to fight back.[54]

To some extent the statement itself was typical of claims made by councillors in Ennis over the years that the presence of Travellers might provoke violence. The specific context of the statement was, as often before, a campaign to displace 'indigenous' Ennis Travellers with no access to an authorised site from an unauthorised one. The novel element here was the implied threat of vigilante action against Travellers. The vigilante claim was subsequently reiterated by the councillor in a media briefing organised to press for the removal of eight Traveller caravans from a housing estate in the town. On that occasion a residents' spokesperson stated: 'We are law-abiding citizens but unless something happens soon we may be forced to take action.'[55] The threat emerged in a context where the courts and the Gardaí were unable to evict the Travellers because the local authorities and local councillors had demonstrably failed to provide the Travellers with an alternative option.

The previous year another councillor had claimed, again at an urban district council meeting, that vigilante groups could emerge in response to a growing drugs crisis in the county.[56] During the 1990s in some urban areas there had been vigilante expulsions of suspected drug dealers and users from their homes and a high-profile political debate on the issue. Populist protest against drug users was, to a considerable extent, protest against perceived inaction by the Gardaí and the government. Some forms of such anti-drug activism, such as punishment beatings, echoed paramilitary communitarianism against 'anti-social behaviour' in Northern Ireland and in themselves constituted a law and order problem. The response of the government was to instigate proactive police actions against suspected drugs dealers.[57] In May 2002 the Minister for Justice, Equality and Law Reform criticised the statements of the Ennis councillor on vigilantism and insisted that law and order was solely a matter for the Gardaí.[58] The vigilante discourse portrayed Travellers as perpetrators of anti-social behaviour which was not being addressed by the state. Typically, anti-Traveller activists claimed that the

Gardaí 'did nothing'.[59] This behaviour was seen to legitimise a violent community response. From the vigilante perspective this violence could only be avoided if the government and the Gardaí took action against Travellers. This generally took the form of prosecutions aimed at securing the eviction of Travellers from unauthorised halting sites. However, with the passing of the 1997 Travellers (Housing Accommodation) Act local authorities had a statutory duty to provide accommodation for Travellers, and the courts were often unwilling to evict Travellers in the absence of designated halting sites or other accommodation options.[60]

In 2002 there were a total of 258 'indigenous' Travellers, including 101 children, living on unauthorised sites in Clare. These constituted over 40 per cent of the county's Traveller population. Clare had the joint-highest proportion of unaccommodated Travellers of any county in the Republic of Ireland.[61] In April 2000 the High Court permitted the Gaelic Athletic Association (GAA) to evict a number of families who were halted outside the Cusack Park sports ground in Ennis.[62] These families had been periodically displaced from one unauthorised site to another since 1997 when a large official halting site outside the town was closed down due to political pressure from residents and councillors. A number of these relocated, by necessity and as an act of protest, to two local authority office car parks. This time the courts rejected an application from the council to evict them 'because the council had no designated site'. An editorial in the *Clare Champion* noted: 'Nobody is likely to shed tears at the arrival of Traveller caravans outside the offices of Clare County Council in Ennis.' This, it suggested, was an opportunity for councillors and officials to learn about the hardships experienced by Travellers: 'They can learn, for example, what it is like to sleep, eat, cook, wash and socialise in a confined space without running water or sanitary facilities … if they're really alert, they may even learn something important about human dignity from a group of human beings so marginalised that they are effectively ostracised from mainstream society.'[63]

The occupation had some impact on the accommodation crisis insofar as plans to identify official sites were stepped up.[64] One site for eight families was designated.[65] Contrary to the requests of Traveller representatives, these places were offered to incompatible families. Those selected were threatened with fines and imprisonment if they did not comply.[66] The council's response suggested that its principal aim was to respond to community demands that Travellers be moved. Many other families remained without access to legal accommodation in the town. The movement of some families onto a housing estate precipitated the aforementioned threat of vigilante action. Other families, who moved onto the grounds of a school, were described in a *Clare Champion* editorial as intimidating children.[67] An Ennis Chamber of Commerce statement referred to the 'deep anger and hurt that the settled people in Ennis feel'.[68] The school organised a protest march against the Travellers to the council offices.[69] Traveller representatives alleged that on one occasion a 'group of vigilantes' drove past the school and fired shots into the air and that on another there was a petrol bomb attack on a Traveller caravan elsewhere in the county.[70]

The 2002 Housing (Miscellaneous Provisions) Act permitted local authorities to respond to political pressure from anti-Traveller groups insofar as evictions and other sanctions could be employed even when no official sites for Travellers were provided. Threats against law and order by settled people could be alleviated by the expulsion of Travellers. Following the first evictions in Ennis, the local Catholic bishop allowed twelve caravans to relocate onto the grounds of his official residence. He described this as a response to intimidation: 'If somebody knocks at your door as someone did the other night – she has a child of two years old and is pregnant with another child and terrified that her caravan is going to be taken – one is put in a position where one has to respond in a Christian way.'[71] The Clare Traveller Support Group has argued that Travellers become vulnerable to violence because the unwillingness by local politicians to develop authorised sites exposed them to the hostility of residents groups. It has also described an unwillingness by the local authorities to provide support for Travellers experiencing intimidation from neighbours.[72]

CONCLUSION

Intimidation and violence have historically played a central role in anti-Traveller racism in Ireland. It is argued that such racism is partly an ideological expression of an Irish nation-building project dating from the late nineteenth century that emerged, again partly, in opposition to colonialist constructions of the Irish as deviant, feckless and violent. Parallels have been identified between colonial anti-Irish racism and expressions of racism against black peoples.[73] Continuities can be seen between past anti-Irish racism and present-day anti-Traveller racist discourse. Irish nation-building to some extent internalised colonial understandings of deviance and reflected a Victorian project of racial hygiene and social control that subjected Travellers to similar forms of racism to those experienced by Irish 'underclass' immigrants in nineteenth-century

Britain. Both the Irish and Travellers were identified as dangerous uncivilised out-groups at odds with social modernisation and were subjected to forms of colonisation and assimilation. Violence against Travellers in today's Ireland and present-day versions of the 'violent Traveller' discourse are to some extent manifestations of the ideological modernisation of the dominant imagined community. This has resulted in racist politics grounded in a perceived irreconcilable social distance between both and in coercive state practices.

Present-day threats of violence against Travellers can be understood to some extent as part of a politics of exclusion aimed at expunging Traveller ways of life from Irish society. Traveller culture was depicted as increasingly at variance with dominant social norms as Irish society modernised. Since the 1960s social policies have sought to achieve the assimilation of Travellers. These policies were problematic both in terms of meeting the needs of Travellers and in terms of political acceptability. A deepening hostility to unsettled Travellers over the last four decades has been accompanied by a growing unwillingness to designate sites for Travellers. Anti-Traveller politics has been predicated upon resistance to efforts to provide legal accommodation for Travellers and simultaneous efforts to displace Travellers with no access to such sites. The imposition of legislation in 1997 requiring local authorities to develop accommodation for Travellers and a resultant unwillingness of the courts to evict those whose statutory entitlements were being ignored arguably deepened political hostility to Travellers. Similarly, anti-discriminatory legislation introduced in 2000 also prompted anti-Traveller activism. In both cases this activism has been sufficient to undermine earlier progressive measures. The criminalisation of unofficial halting sites under the 2002 Act has, if anything, reduced the impetus to adhere to legislation requiring the development of Traveller accommodation. It has increased the vulnerability of Travellers to violence and harassment and has deepened the potential for institutional racism.

Allport viewed racist speech (verbal rejection) and discrimination as preconditions for racist violence and intimidation. In the case of Travellers, racist speech about violence (violent speech) is central to the articulation of prejudice and is central also to acts of intimidation. Violent speech functions, like any threat, as a negotiating tool. In this case what is sought is the expulsion of Travellers. Violence therefore serves modernisation goals of social rationalisation where assimilation and colonisation have failed. This points to the relevance of a functionalist thesis about the relationship between racism and violence.

However, as Allport noted, prejudice fulfils both rational and irrational functions for its bearer.[74] So too do acts of violence and intimidation. Violence and intimidation need to be seen alongside discrimination and institutional racism as part of a larger repertoire of coercive mechanisms. Accusations of violence by Travellers, on the other hand, serve to legitimise goals of expulsion. The ideological stigmatisation and racialisation of out-groups is again part of the coercive repertoire. For these reasons concerns about violence, as something to be consciously overcome, must be central to efforts to address racism in social policy.[75] This suggests the need for stronger legislation against incitement to hatred. However, such legislation does not in itself address the causes of such hatred or the politics of exclusion perpetrated by it.

POSTSCRIPT

The above was written before the occurrence of two tragic incidents that suggest widespread tolerance of violence towards Travellers in twenty-first century Ireland. On 14 October 2004 John Ward, a Mayo Traveller, was killed by Pádraig Nally, a farmer, with a shotgun. Nally wounded Ward. He then proceeded to beat him repeatedly with a heavy piece of timber. As Nally described it: 'It was like hitting a stone or a badger. You could hit him but you could not kill him.' Then Nally reloaded his shotgun, followed Ward down a lane and, according to the state pathologist, killed the crouching and severely injured victim with a shot fired at close range. Nally was convicted of manslaughter but released on appeal in December 2006. Nally never claimed that Ward assaulted or threatened him. Nally's defence was that he was living in fear of Travellers and, as accepted when the case went to appeal, this, combined with Ward's trespassing on Nally's property, was sufficient provocation. Throughout the trial and appeal Nally received widespread support and was, to a considerable extent, portrayed as the victim of Travellers.

In Ennis on 23 June 2007 Michael Doherty, a fourteen-year-old Traveller, was stabbed to death by a seventeen-year-old youth. The incident occurred outside Supermac's fast-food restaurant on O'Connell Street just before 11 p.m. on a Saturday night. Michael Doherty had come to town to buy a bag of chips with a friend after a day working at the Spancil Hill horse fair. The following day the street was sealed off by the Gardaí as part of their investigation. I subsequently spoke to a number of people in Ennis about Michael Doherty's death and found sympathy in short supply. A barman who overheard one such conversation interjected: 'Oh, you're talking about the knacker who got himself killed.' A teenager I interviewed said that 'the knacker probably had it coming to him'. Another townsperson recounted a complaint by a woman inconvenienced by the street closure as overheard some days later. She concluded her grumble with an off-hand remark that it was time that people stood up to Travellers in the town.

CHAPTER FIVE

The Politics of Racism

The focus of this chapter is on the years leading up to the 2002 general election, beginning in 1997 when the hysterical response of some sections of the media to the arrival of growing numbers of asylum seekers signalled the arrival of a new political issue. The chapter offers some comparisons between political responses to asylum seekers and the political exploitation of anti-Traveller racism. It examines both the political mainstream and groups more usually associated with racism in politics.

Mainstream political parties and politicians in Ireland and elsewhere strike populist positions on social issues aimed at creating and maintaining broad support. Inevitably this involves a 'big tent' approach to accommodating diverse interests and opinions. The political mainstream inevitably reflects societal prejudices against ethnic minorities such as Travellers and anxieties about immigrants and asylum seekers which are grounded in racism and xenophobia. At the same time it embodies perspectives which might be described as forms of political correctness but are generally shared within society, that some manifestations of racism, such as 'hate-speech', are patently unacceptable. Mainstream politics, as such, can reflect a range of responses to societal racism at any given time. Extreme positions, such as those held by national front groups in various European countries, may not be sustainable within the political mainstream. Yet, mainstream parties may seek to encroach upon the positions of such groups to maintain or broaden their appeal, as has happened in recent years in the case of asylum and immigration issues. The political centre on such issues has moved to the right in a number of European countries. At the same time some forms of racism have never been more unacceptable. Clumsy or even unwitting expressions of racism and xenophobia can damage political careers. Efforts by politicians to exploit societal racism can backfire. Yet the ways in which racism in society are exploited in politics have become more sophisticated. In such a context, politicians punished for racism are penalised for being inept rather than for their views.

THE POLITICAL CURRENCY OF RACISM

Racism has a political currency because it proffers exceedingly simple explanations for complex social problems. For example, housing shortages or urban decline might be blamed on immigrants or ethnic minorities rather than upon, say, bad planning or inadequate funding. In such a context societal racism is a commodity with potential political value. Second, racism justifies various forms of inequality and exploitation which may be politically endorsed. Slavery, colonialism, apartheid, the denial of civil rights and formal and informal discrimination in areas such as education, housing and employment have all been ideologically justified or fostered by racism. The ideological power of racism is that such inequalities can be depicted as natural. They are blamed on the presumed moral, biological or cultural inferiority of excluded black and ethnic minority groups.

Racisms have always drawn on the authority of dominant paradigms of knowledge and truth. Racist stereotypes are anchored in a long history of representations of non-Western peoples as inferior. Nineteenth-century abolitionists such as Frederick Douglass sought to contest popular perceptions that slavery was sanctioned by God. Anti-Semitism, too, was sanctioned by religious doctrine. Religious justifications for racism were succeeded by racisms justified by scientific knowledge and subsequently, when biological 'scientific' racisms became discredited, by cultural racisms rooted to a degree in social science. As put by Adam Lively, old wine was poured into new bottles.[1] Racist beliefs have had the status of truth for centuries in the West. The displacement of religious justifications for racism, as in the case of anti-Semitism by the time of Vatican II, and the discrediting of racism grounded in assertions about biological inferiority after the Holocaust have not led to the demise of racism. Instead, 'race' became coded as culture. Cultural racism presumes that the qualities of social groups are fixed, and are in fact natural.[2] Difference is explained as deviance.

The political currency of contemporary racism is fixed to the gold standard of dominant cultural values and norms. In recent decades extreme and populist right-wing parties and even skinhead movements have ceased to use overtly racist arguments and instead have come to argue for the exclusion of 'others' on cultural grounds. The French National Front, the Austrian Freedom Party, the Pym Fortune List and the Irish Immigration Control Platform argue, at times, that they respect diversity but do not want their culture to be swamped or diluted by the cultures of immigrants. Such cultural fundamentalism relies to a degree upon the subconscious acceptance of a hidden text of racist claims about the threats posed by outsiders. The proponents of the 'new racism' can tap into deeply rooted codes which can be easily employed in political discourse.[3] This allows politicians opposed to the presence of black and ethnic minorities to deny racism ('of course we don't believe that black people are inferior') and at the same time pursue racist goals of exclusion by alluding to the imagined grievances of the (white) community.[4] An analogy for such forms of racist discourse can be found in advertising. Fifty years ago manufacturers claimed that smoking cigarettes soothed sore throats. One much reproduced image showed Ronald Reagan extolling the health benefits of Chesterfields. Subsequently, manufacturers were required to include warnings about the health risks of smoking on their products and restrictions were placed on advertising. They were prevented from depicting people smoking in advertisements or even from showing the product. Yet manufacturers continue to spend huge amounts on print images aimed at reinforcing their brands. The Marlboro cowboy no longer smokes himself but he still sells cigarettes.

Racism in politics is similarly sophisticated. Racist fears can be conjured up, alluded to or endorsed without resorting to crude denigrations of people on the basis of their colour or ethnicity. Racism in politics appeals to deeply rooted stereotypes and beliefs. Newspaper headlines proclaiming that Ireland is being flooded, swamped or invaded by an influx of asylum seekers tap into visceral fears. In 1904 Fr Creagh had declared from the pulpit that Jews were leeches that sucked the lifeblood of the Irish nation. Arthur Griffith used his platform in the *United Irishman* to similar effect.[5] There is a clear continuity in the imagery which fuelled the Limerick pogrom of 1904 and that which depicted the arrival of a few thousand asylum seekers as a national crisis in 1997.[6]

THE GREAT FLOOD OF '97

Nothing since has quite matched the shrill tenor of media coverage of asylum seekers during mid-1997. Headlines such as 'Crackdown on 2000 "sponger" refugees',[7] 'Floodgates open as a new army of poor swamp the country',[8] 'Why Irish eyes aren't smiling on the great Romanian invasion'[9] and 'Refugee rapists on the rampage'[10] were matched in tone by the responses of some politicians and officials to what was represented as a national crisis.[11] Asylum did not emerge as a formal election issue in 1997. Instead, it was the subject of a political consensus that traversed the rainbow coalition and its successor in government. This consensus was marked by the use of anti-asylum seeker rhetoric to justify restrictive policies. These included the non-implementation of refugee legislation, border controls that appeared in breach of obligations under international law, punitive welfare policies and the dispersal of the perceived burden of asylum seekers. The Fine Gael Minister for Justice, Equality and Law Reform, Nora Owen, and her successor in the new Fianna Fáil government, John O'Donoghue, both endorsed policies aimed at discouraging people from seeking asylum in Ireland. Both also endorsed excluding asylum seekers from participating in Irish society. As put by Nora Owen: 'I do not consider it appropriate to allow people, with temporary permission to remain in the state, to work and put down roots.'[12] In the dying days of the rainbow government, she introduced new border controls which effectively allowed immigration officers to turn away people attempting to seek asylum at ports, airports and along the Northern border.[13] By October 1997 some 800 people had been refused entry to the state. There is some evidence that the order was implemented in a racist manner. For example, a black British citizen on a visit to Ireland was deported illegally to the North and students of Chinese origin from Coleraine University en route to a seminar in Dublin were turned back by Special Branch officers stationed at Connolly Station.[14]

John O'Donoghue made the case for punitive welfare policies aimed at discouraging asylum seekers from coming to Ireland in a speech to the Irish Business and Employers Confederation on 30 September 1999 by depicting them as welfare scroungers. As he put it: 'Our current economic boom is making us a target.'[15] Subsequent welfare discriminations against asylum seekers, in the form of a system of direct provision, were introduced alongside a plan to disperse asylum seekers around the country. There was a good case for a regional settlement programme.[16] However, the case made by some Dublin politicians emphasised the dispersal of the burden of asylum seekers by either claiming that their constituencies had more than a fair share of this burden or by reinforcing stereotypes that asylum seekers were welfare scroungers and exploiters of the Irish people. The latter seemed to be the case, when the chairman of the Eastern Health Board, Ivor Callely TD, made a provocative statement about asylum seekers just prior to the introduction of the dispersal programme that shifted responsibility for the welfare of some to other health boards.[17] One problematic consequence of such rhetoric was that it seemed to sanction hostility to asylum seekers within communities designated as part of the dispersal programme. Some statements of community opposition to dispersal in the summer of 2000 reflected a broader racialised discourse which portrayed asylum seekers as AIDS- ridden and as criminals.[18] Arguably, these reflected the tone of a broader politically sponsored hostility to asylum seekers within Irish public policy. This hostility found decisive expression when in 2000 a deliberately punitive separate welfare system for asylum seekers was introduced.[19] 'Direct Provision' removed existing entitlements to universal social assistance administered by the health boards. Weekly rates of payment were set at £15 (€19.05) per adult and £7.50 (€9.53 per child). These rates were far less than those for any other categories of welfare recipient.

In reality, there was little to distinguish mainstream political responses to the asylum seeker issues from the position of 'extreme' groups such as the Immigration Control Platform which had most of its policies adopted by the last government. These included the deportation of rejected asylum seekers, amendment of the 2004 Nationality and Citizenship Act so as to limit the rights of Irish-born children of immigrants to reside in the state and opposition to a right to work for asylum seekers.[20] The Immigration Control Platform was launched in Ennis in December 1997. A few weeks earlier the *Clare Champion* ran a front-page article under the headline 'Refugee influx causes concern'.[21] This was fairly innocuous compared to some which appeared in the national press. However, the article reported at length ill-informed claims by some local councillors that the presence of asylum seekers would result in the withdrawal of funding from local health services and that local people in need of accommodation were being discriminated against by asylum seekers. As stated in large bold type at the beginning of the article: 'Concern has been expressed this week that people on local authority housing lists in Clare are being neglected and discriminated against while state agencies off-load refugees in Ennis as a cost-saving measure.' The article was balanced by an editorial that pretty much summed up the context within which contemporary racisms are manifested in discussing the temptations of blaming marginal outsiders for social problems:

Because of economic success Ireland is attracting immigrants of its own but the benefits of the commercial boom haven't filtered down to the poor and marginalised in our own society. In short we have failed to grasp the message that success brings increased responsibility to those excluded from a share in the new prosperity. In providing refugees with good quality accommodation in the Ennis area the State is rightfully fulfilling its obligations under international law. The problem is that it doesn't appear to have the same conscience when it comes to accommodating its own children. The irony is that the simmering resentment is being directed at the refugees and not towards the government.

At one level these events were a storm in a teacup. A political vacuum was temporarily exploited by a few councillors with no direct remit for asylum seekers. Anti-racist groups interrupted the inaugural meeting of the Immigration Control Platform in Ennis. Perceptions of a race crisis in Ennis contrasted somewhat with a generally positive response to asylum seekers. The town has come to be held up as an example of good practice largely due to the efforts of the voluntary sector and the Mid-Western Health Board.[22]

At another level comparisons could be made between responses to asylum seekers and Travellers. Opposition to asylum seekers in Ennis pales in comparison to a long history of anti-Traveller racism. *Clare Champion* headlines such as 'Fifteen houses for itinerants amid angry objections by residents', 'Itinerant problem heading for explosive situation', 'Outrage over plans for halting site' and 'Halting site to spark residents' revolt' demonstrate the longstanding acceptability of hostility to Travellers in local politics.[23] The language employed to express such hostility has been less guarded than that employed to discuss asylum seekers. In Clare, Travellers have been depicted as a threat to the dominant community by local politicians on an ongoing basis within a racist discourse that bears some similarities to that associated with Enoch Powell in Britain. If there was no references to 'rivers of blood' there were plenty of apocalyptic ones by councillors and officials to 'explosive situations' and 'fuses that have been lit'. Most local authority debates on Traveller issues in Clare between 1963 and 1999 were characterised by vehement anti-Traveller rhetoric.

THE 2002 ELECTION

By the time of the 2002 election the main political parties effectively had manifesto positions on the asylum issue. The parties had agreed to adhere to an anti-racism protocol devised by the National Consultative Committee on Racism and Interculturalism (NCCRI). The few instances where politicians openly courted anti-asylum seeker prejudice met with controversy, notably in the case of Noel O'Flynn, TD for Cork North Central. His statements were described as a populist effort to exploit anti-asylum racism by candidates from other political parties and indeed his candidacy was endorsed by Áine Ní Chonaill, leader of the Immigration Control Platform, who had stood unsuccessfully for election in 1997 in Cork South West.[24] They were also the subject of an investigation by the Gardaí under the 1989 Incitement to Hatred Act. Although the leadership of Fianna Fáil distanced itself from Deputy O'Flynn, no disciplinary action was taken and he topped the poll in Cork North Central.

A decade after the Incitement to Hatred Act was first introduced, just one case involving an alleged breach of the Act had been referred to the Director of Public Prosecutions. In March 1999 a Mayo county councillor, John Flannery, was acquitted of inciting hatred at Galway District Court. He had described Travellers as dogs and argued that they ought to be tagged so that the authorities could keep track of them.[25] In September 2000 the first conviction under the Act was secured against a Dublin bus driver. Earlier that month the Minister for Justice, Equality and Law Reform acknowledged that the Act was ineffective and stated that new legislation was necessary. This was because of the extensive burden of proof required to show that racist acts had been incited.[26] The Act was introduced, in part, to counter the publication of racist materials by far right groups from other countries in Ireland. In the era of the internet this goal has become more problematic but it is also the case that such groups now employ more subtle modes of racist discourse. The website of the Irish People's Party, a Dublin-based racist organisation, in the run-up to the 2002 general election made its case using a selection of newspaper stories about asylum seekers.

The asylum seeker issue was pretty much a damp squib in the run-up to this election in contrast to elections in France, Holland and Britain. Unlike 1997, the main parties had identifiable policy positions and candidates from some of the larger parties were expected to keep to the party line.[27] Fianna Fáil opposed allowing asylum seekers to work and favoured lower welfare entitlements for asylum seekers. Individual candidates did not break ranks on these issues. Fine Gael supported a right to work after six months (the position taken by the Irish Refugee Council and other NGOs) and promised to review direct provision.

The Labour Party adopted a similar position. Individual candidates from the Progressive Democrats, the Green Party, Sinn Féin, the Socialist Party and the Workers Party openly supported both the right to work and the repeal of direct provision. Áine Ní Chonaill achieved 926 first preferences in Dublin South Central out of a total poll of 44,768 (less than 2.1 per cent). She was eliminated on the fifth count. Her votes were distributed both to candidates who shared and opposed Immigration Control Platform policies. Just under 21 per cent of her transfers went to Fianna Fáil, just under 12.5 per cent to Fine Gael, almost 19 per cent to Labour, almost 24 per cent to Sinn Féin, just over 9 per cent to the Green Party and just over 7 per cent to the Progressive Democrats. The presence of just one candidate on an anti-asylum seeker ticket can be read two ways. On the one hand, single-issue candidates tend to poll well on topical issues. For example, public concerns about health services were reflected in voting for independent candidates standing on a health ticket. An optimistic reading suggests that most Irish people do not have a problem with asylum seekers. On the other hand, single-issue candidates might fare poorly on issues that have been adsorbed into the mainstream. This suggests that anti-asylum seeker feeling is adequately addressed within the political mainstream, notably within Fianna Fáil.

By contrast, the mainstream parties openly exploited anti-Traveller racism in the run-up to the 2002 election. A bill which sought to criminalise Travellers who halted on unofficial sites, put forward by a Fine Gael TD, Olivia Mitchell, was endorsed by the government. The 2002 Housing (Miscellaneous Provisions) Act was passed with unseemly haste by an overwhelming cross-party majority and without any evaluation of the adequacy of current Traveller accommodation plans, discussion of the needs of Travellers or consultation with Traveller organisations. Anti-Traveller racism has long been a staple of local politics. The 2002 election marked its emergence for the first time within national party politics. On 16 July 2002 the caravans of four Traveller families were 'forcibly removed' to Ennis Garda station following the first successful prosecution under the provisions of the Act. Ennis had been without a permanent halting site since 1997.[28]

CONCLUSION

Societal racism is a commodity with potential political value. It can be exploited within local, national and international politics. Yet it must not be forgotten that racism, discrimination and sectarianism can be and are opposed within the political system. At its best, politics can provide the basis for tolerance, pluralism, innovation, peace and prosperity. To date, political responses in Europe to the complexities of immigration have been marked by simplistic xenophobic posturing and oppressive measures. One result has been the criminalisation of immigration into a European Community which needs about 1.2 million immigrants per annum to maintain its existing population levels. The response of many mainstream parties in a number of European countries to apparent increases in racism has been to move to the right. In the Europe of today ministers charged with developing policies aimed at promoting tolerance and contesting racism play to the gallery with tough talk that serves to endorse racism. The 2002 Seville summit saw some European leaders stoop to new lows in proposing that overseas aid be withheld to pressurise emigrant countries to restrict the movement of their own populations. Yet these proposed sanctions were opposed by France and Holland, where extreme right-wing parties have performed strongly. They were put forward by Britain, where such parties perform poorly and are routinely castigated as racist by government ministers. The new Irish Minister for Justice, Equality and Law Reform, Michael McDowell, publicly endorsed the proposals of Britain and Spain at Seville, contrary to the formal position of the Irish government.

The wild imagery of 1997, the year of the great flood, has been put to one side but racism in Irish society has arguably deepened. Here, it is important to distinguish between manifestations of racism, which have increased as the black and ethnic minority population of Ireland has grown, and the creeping internalisation of racism within society and politics. Crude rhetoric has been superseded by a new administrative brutalism. It is now respectable to discriminate against asylum seekers or imprison them. The notion that the constitutional rights of some Irish-born children can be undermined by the state has become politically accepted.

CHAPTER SIX

Migrant Children and Institutional Neglect

This chapter examines responses by statutory and voluntary sector service providers in Ireland to the children of asylum seekers and to migrant unaccompanied minors with a specific emphasis on the challenges facing social workers. The focus here is on the consequences of institutional barriers resulting from racism and on how lesser rights and entitlements can contribute to the risk of institutional neglect. The Irish case examined here suggests that not only are migrant children endangered by lesser rights, they are also placed at risk by the perception that they have lesser rights than Irish children even where they do not. The direct provision system was, to labour a metaphor, like a wolf that cut asylum seekers away from the pack, away from a solidarity of shared welfare rights and entitlements with citizens. Once sundered legally and administratively from the main population, their fates became a matter of greater general indifference. For example, the paltry welfare payments they received – modelled initially on hospital rates of social assistance to allow welfare receipts to buy toiletries while away from home – were frozen year-on-year while benefit levels for citizens across the board rose routinely with each annual budget. Weekly rates have not been increased since direct provision was piloted in 1999. In 2008 these remained at €19.05 per adult and €9.53 per child. In the Irish case, responsibility for the care of asylum seekers was effectively privatised. A 2001 report by the Irish Refugee Council, eighteen months after the introduction of direct provision, described it as 'wholly inadequate', 'inhumane and discriminatory'.[1] Since then the situation has got worse. Asylum applicants who entered the state after 1 May 2004 were no longer entitled to child benefit, thus increasing the risks of migrant child poverty.[2]

The following analysis of how unaccompanied migrant children in the care of the state found themselves exempted from statutory protections set out under the 1991 Child Care Act suggests that the problem of institutional neglect is not just one of lesser rights. It was first published in 2004 and is accompanied here by a postscript aimed at bringing the analysis up to date. The introduction of separate administrative arrangements for migrant children in care created a two-tier system within which standards, deemed necessary under law for citizen children, could be flouted by the very health services charged with administrating the Children's Act. The neglect of migrant children discussed in this chapter *is* institutional insofar as it reflects a broad thrust of policies aimed at deliberately marginalising asylum seekers. No wonder then that children's rights under Irish law became easier to disregard in their case.

RACISM AND RIGHTS

Racism can be expressed through the acts of individuals or in the values, presumptions, structures and processes of social, economic, cultural and political institutions. For example, Article 2 of the UNESCO Declaration on Race and Racial Prejudice emphasises the role of structural and institutional barriers in producing racist barriers in society:

> Racism includes racist ideologies, prejudiced attitudes, discriminatory behaviour, structural arrangements and institutional practices resulting in racial inequality as well as that the fallacious notion that discriminatory relations between groups are morally and scientifically justifiable; it is reflected in discriminatory provisions in legislation or regulations and discriminatory practices as well as in anti-social beliefs and acts ...[3]

There has been considerable international debate, in the wake of the Macpherson report, about how institutional racism impacts upon black and ethnic minorities. Macpherson's inquiry into policing in London defined institutional racism in the following terms:

> The collective failure of an organisation to provide an appropriate and professional service to people because of their colour, culture or ethnic origin. It can be seen in processes, attitudes and behaviour which amount to discrimination through unwitting prejudice, ignorance, thoughtlessness and racist stereotyping which disadvantage ethnic minority people.[4]

The consequences of institutional racism include unequal access to services and unequal outcomes on the basis of ethnicity. Services configured towards the cultures, expectations and needs of majority groups which wittingly or unwittingly neglect those of minority ethnic groups are likely to produce unequal outcomes for minority ethnic groups.

The issue of structural racism warrants similar consideration. The migrants who comprise the new minority ethnic groups within Irish society, as in other European countries, often have lesser rights and entitlements than citizen ethnic minorities. These encounter structural barriers to participation in society that compound institutional barriers resulting from racism. Some non-citizens face exclusion on a number of levels within Irish social policy. First, they tend to have lesser social rights and entitlements. They may be categorised by the state as outside the remit of a range of policies and programmes aimed at tackling disadvantage. Second, they may be excluded from official equality discourse, that is, excluded from how inequalities in society are conceptualised and discussed in official research, reports and within the remit of policies. In this context, social policy considerations may become subordinate to policies of excluding such groups or of limiting their rights and entitlements. A dominant logic, which distinguishes between the citizen and the non-citizen, allows non-citizen groups to be categorised as outside of the communities within which they live. It supposes that the fate of these communities can be disconnected from the fate of non-citizen neighbours. The resulting exclusions can be understood as the institutionalisation of a narrow definition of community increasingly at odds with the real social membership of Irish society.

The Irish state stratifies groups of non-citizens on the basis of decisions about their entitlements. A distinction between citizen rights and social citizenship and what Christian Joppke refers to as 'alien rights' underlies a state process which allows non-citizen/alien groups to be treated differently from each other by the state. Migrant workers, immigrants with Irish-born children, people with refugee status and asylum seekers are each deemed by the state to have different levels of rights and entitlements.[5] In all cases, these are less than the entitlements of EU citizens living in Ireland. The result has been a hierarchy of differential rights – less than those of citizens in each case – which shape the responses of social policy and social work service providers to migrants and non-citizen ethnic minorities.

Such inequalities and welfare stratifications sit uneasily with Ireland's obligations under the UN Convention on the Rights of the Child, which was ratified by the government in 1991 and applies to all children within the jurisdiction of the state. Article 2 states that all children should be entitled to basic rights without discrimination. Article

3(1) states that the best interests of children should be a primary consideration in all actions concerning children (whether undertaken by public or private social welfare institutions, courts of law, administrative authorities or legislative bodies). Other articles specify a right to the highest attainable standard of health and to have access to health and medical services (Article 24), a right to benefit from social security (Article 26), a right to an adequate standard of living with a duty on the state to assist parents, where necessary, in fulfilling this right (Article 27) and a right to participate in leisure, recreational and cultural activities (Article 31).

CHILD PROTECTION AND INSTITUTIONAL NEGLECT

In the case of asylum seeker and migrant children, a range of potential roles for social work in Ireland can be identified. The roles of social workers as agents of social control and as service providers occur with respect to asylum seekers and migrants within a context where the services which they provide are inevitably stratified by the fact that non-citizen groups have lesser social and economic rights and welfare entitlements. It is arguably the case that the advocacy role with respect to such groups is more problematic than with respect to clients who are Irish citizens. For example, social workers may have fewer options when seeking to support clients who are not deemed entitled to social housing. Clients who experience lesser rights and entitlements are likely to present more challenges to social workers than citizen clients. Groups such as asylum seekers and migrants will have distinct advocacy needs relating to the specific barriers they experience. Examples include language barriers in accessing services, information and advocacy issues relating to asylum and immigration processes and, of course, racism.

Since the mid-1990s social workers have been increasingly drawn into more explicit 'policing' of the internal and external boundaries of the state.[6] Alistair Christie argues that the social work profession in Ireland, as elsewhere, has acquired a potential role in regulating national and super-national boundaries by working with asylum seekers as residents and as 'potential citizens'. He draws upon Zigmunt Bauman's description of the welfare state as a 'gardening state'.[7] Within this analogy social workers are depicted as maintaining borders and regulating the growth of the different parts of the 'garden' or, more specifically, by using social work practices to integrate families and individuals within society using techniques of moralisation, normalisation and tutelage. Insofar as social work may reflect the dominant culture, the social control role can be affected by cultural differences and by racism. For example, assessments relating to child protection are likely to be affected by attitudes to and understandings of clients from black and ethnic minorities among social workers. Furthermore, the advocacy and social control roles of social work will inevitably be affected by the power inequalities wrought by lesser rights and entitlements. They will be affected by the specific social control circumstances of immigration processes. The advocacy role may be undermined by the strictures of asylum application processes whereby social workers become involved in the assessment of such applications.[8]

There is some evidence that suggests that the anti-racist critique of British social work put forward by writers such as Lena Dominelli is relevant in the Irish case. This critique emphasises the importance of addressing racism within social work as well as the role of social work in addressing the racist experiences of clients from black and ethnic minorities.[9] For example, a 1999 article in *The Irish Social Worker* describes the experiences of a black social worker in Dublin of being rejected by her clients because of her colour. Furthermore, the social worker's children experienced racist harassment from other children and her home had been attacked on a number of occasions.[10] The lack of a historical focus on racism in Irish social work suggests that issues identified by Dominelli such as institutional racism, social dumping and avoidance may be problematic.

The complexities of addressing racism in social work have recently been highlighted by the report of the inquiry into the death of Victoria Climbie in London.[11] The inquiry examined how the relevant services failed to prevent her death. Victoria had come into contact with four social service departments, two specialist child protection teams and three housing departments. She had been admitted to two different hospitals. The inquiry highlighted a number of factors that may have contributed to her death but placed particular emphasis on the poor coordination of child protection services. It concluded that racism 'did play its part' in Victoria's death.[12] The inquiry report quoted the director of the London borough of Haringey's Race Equality Unit:

> There is some evidence to suggest that one of the consequences of an exclusive focus on 'culture' in work with black children and families is (that) it leaves black and ethnic minority children in potentially dangerous situations, because the assessment has failed to address a child's fundamental care and protection needs.[13]

The report of the inquiry stated that 'it may be assumptions made about Victoria and her situation diverted caring people from noting and acting on signs of neglect and abuse'.[14] It described how, on more than one occasion, medical practitioners who noted marks on Victoria's body considered the possibility that children who have grown up in Africa (Victoria was African) may be expected to have more marks on their bodies than children who have been raised in Europe. It noted that such assumptions may have prevented a full assessment on Victoria from being made. The report referred to other assumptions made in this case, including those relating to discipline in Afro-Caribbean families. Other factors, noted by the inquiry, included fear among white workers of being accused of racism and feelings that they were not as qualified as black workers to make decisions about black children. The report quoted a statement by one QC who participated in the inquiry to illustrate this point: 'Assumptions based on race can be just as corrosive as blatant racism ... racism can affect the way people conduct themselves in other ways. Fear of being accused of racism can stop people acting when otherwise they would.'[15]

The context of Victoria's death was one of inadequate access to services, advocacy and support due to lesser rights and entitlements and a lack of responsiveness from service providers. She received inadequate support from a welfare system poorly configured to meet the needs of vulnerable migrants. Arguably, the Victoria Climbie inquiry points to the risks engendered by lesser status as well as racism. Marginal non-citizen populations can be seen as particularly at risk from institutional neglect in areas such as child protection.

Some insights into the causes of institutional neglect are suggested by Michael Lipsky's 'street-level bureaucracy' thesis. This maintains that workers in public services have wide discretion over the dispensation of benefits and public sanctions.[16] Lipsky argues that street-level bureaucrats – these can be professionals or non-professionals – have enormous power over the consumers of services but also considerable autonomy from their employing agency through the exercise of discretion and demand control. A number of forms of demand control are open to officials, such as perpetuating delay, withholding information and stigmatising the process of service delivery. Street-level bureaucrats do not simply deal with occupational hazards by limiting client demand. They modify their own activities, perceptions of their jobs and perceptions of their clients to better match their ability to perform. This may lead to psychological withdrawal, resulting in workers relatively unbothered by the discrepancy between what they are supposed to do and what they actually do.[17] Lipsky argues that street-level bureaucrats who are unable to provide all clients with their best efforts develop conceptual mechanisms to divide up the client population and rationalise the division, even though the consequence of this may be at variance with the formal goals of the organisation, by 'creaming off' those clients who seem most likely to succeed in terms of bureaucratic success criteria or distinguishing between those clients deemed to be deserving and undeserving. The 'street-level bureaucracy' thesis suggests that 'hard to help' clients, such as migrants with lesser rights, may be particularly vulnerable.

The risks of institutional neglect can be illustrated in the Irish context by a 2001 study of asylum seeker mothers in Ireland by Patricia Kennedy and Jo Murphy-Lawless. The research found that some women respondents chose to remain in violent relationships with their children because of fear of risking status. It described how some women felt 'not listened to' when they came into contact with doctors and midwives.[18] The potential for institutional neglect resulting from a cocktail of bad practices, racism and lesser rights is suggested by one example included in the study. This describes the dismissive treatment by a midwife of a woman experiencing domestic abuse. The woman had become distressed about being unable to breastfeed her baby soon after its birth:

> The baby was crying and she felt helpless ... A midwife came back and rebuked her, saying that she was 'too demanding'. And her husband, when he came to see her a few minutes later, agreed with the midwife. When she came home with the baby, there was no one to help her and she felt weak and depressed. Her partner began to abuse her physically at this point.[19]

A number of studies have found that material deprivation was exacerbated by extreme accommodation deprivation resulting from chronic overcrowding in hostels. Three studies of asylum seekers in direct provision found that respondent families living in hostels and hotels generally shared a single room irrespective of the age of the children.[20] The inappropriateness of such accommodation is illustrated by the following example, again from the study by Kennedy and Murphy-Lawless:

> Three generations of a Polish family shared one bedroom, which measured about 12 by 12 feet. The grandparents slept on the floor on two single mattresses. The 17-year-old mother slept on a mattress on the floor while her baby slept nearby in her pram. There was no room for a cot. The young mother explained that she had

to stop breastfeeding, as it was too difficult during the nights in such close proximity to her father.[21]

The dangers of institutional neglect in such cases are potentially exacerbated by inadequate coordination of services for children in the Republic of Ireland. The 1998 report by the UN Committee on the Rights of the Child on Ireland's implementation of the UN Convention on the Rights of the Child identified poor coordination between and within the nine government departments involved in the area of early childhood. It also identified a history of poor communication and coordination between statutory and voluntary providers of early years care and education.[22] With respect to social work, there is a need for a focus on potential risks facing asylum seeker children, unaccompanied minors and other categories of 'hard to help' migrant children emanating from institutional neglect.

UNACCOMPANIED MINORS

These challenges are particularly acute in the case of separated children under eighteen years of age seeking asylum in Ireland. Some 861 such unaccompanied minors arrived in Ireland in 2002, of which 506 were subsequently re-united with parents or relatives. These are predominantly accommodated in the Dublin area and are the responsibility of a dedicated unit comprising social workers and link workers. Unaccompanied minors have been exempted from the dispersal programme. Accommodation centres for them are subject to regulation; every voluntary or private agency is required to register all non-statutory children's residential centres with the Registration and Inspection Service of the relevant health board.[23] The National Standards for Children's Residential Centres set out requirements for management, staffing, monitoring, children's rights, statutory care plans, child protection, education, health safety and the role of social workers.

Supervising social workers have clear statutory obligations towards all young people, including unaccompanied minors in residential care. Staff members in centres are required to be trained in the principles and practices of child protection. They have a clear obligation to report any child protection concerns. The national standards explicitly state that young people should have a room of their own and that centres must have age-appropriate play and recreational facilities. There is also a requirement that the health board be satisfied, by undertaking a proper risk assessment, that centres are safe and secure places for young people to live in. The national standards also require that centres should be subject to outside monitoring by a health board-appointed authorised person, in line with the 1995 Child Care (Placement of Children in Residential Care) Regulations on an annual basis. The authorised person must ensure that all children have an allocated social worker and that a care plan has been prepared and looks for evidence that decisions have been acted upon.[24]

It is questionable whether the care of at least some unaccompanied minors in Ireland meets the national standards. For example, one centre that has been used exclusively for unaccompanied minors since September 2002 accommodates sixty-six young people aged from twelve years of age upwards. These generally share rooms with one or more other young people and have minimal facilities and support. No qualified care workers are employed on site. As put by a social worker employed by a voluntary sector drop-in centre for asylum seekers in February 2003: 'There is no care.' She described the level of support to the children provided by health board social workers and project workers as minimal.

In 2004 there was just one dedicated long-term residential unit in Ireland for unaccompanied minors – Bellevue House in Tallaght, run by Clann Housing Association. It had eleven qualified staff members and provided care for six separated children between the ages of seven and fifteen. According to the manager of the unit, such dedicated accommodation facilities for unaccompanied minors are vital because their needs are wholly distinct from those of other children in residential care.[25]Unaccompanied minors may experience extreme psychological trauma as a result of both pre-migratory and post-migratory experiences. The former category includes bereavement, rape and torture. Post-migratory stressors can include racism, loneliness, insecurity and anxiety about the asylum process. According to Jennifer Ryland, many unaccompanied minors are in danger of being overwhelmed by anxiety and loss. By definition, they have been thrust prematurely into independent life without family and community supports. As described by one seventeen-year-old unaccompanied minor: 'I miss someone to advise me and to take care of me. I am too young to have to do this alone.'[26] A study of minors who had been living in Ireland for between two and thirteen months with a mean age of 16.29 years found indications of 'moderate problem or severe problem behaviour' in more than 50 per cent (fifteen out of twenty-eight) of respondents:

> Few had any contact with Irish people ... The longer these adolescents were in Ireland, the greater the psychological distress.

Current stressors contributed to psychological dysfunction and there was little integration into Irish culture. Social support networks consisted of other unaccompanied minors or asylum seekers. Unaccompanied minors are a highly vulnerable group and current asylum policies may add to behaviour symptoms and psychological distress.[27]

The study found that experiences of racist discrimination caused respondents to become more socially withdrawn. Most respondents (89 per cent) were found to have experienced racist discrimination. Notwithstanding the exemption of unaccompanied minors from lower direct provision benefit rates, most respondents (71.4 per cent) identified poverty as a problem. The study recommended that the number of dedicated social worker and project worker posts should be increased.

MIGRANT CHILDREN AT RISK

Asylum seeker children in direct provision and unaccompanied minors account for just some of the potentially vulnerable migrant children living in Ireland. Labour immigration from non-European Economic Area (EEA) countries has generally been subject to restrictions in relation to the immigration of dependant children. Migrant workers on non-transferable work permits are currently not allowed to apply for visas for dependants during their first year in the country. However, there are indications that some migrant worker parents have sought to reunify their families in Ireland with the result that the number of undocumented children living in Ireland has risen. The formation of immigrant ethnic minority communities and households consisting of a potential mixture of documented and undocumented persons has a number of implications. Undocumented adults or children are particularly vulnerable members of Irish society. Households consisting of undocumented persons or of both documented and undocumented persons are likely to have low household incomes as a result of low pay and a lack of entitlement to child benefits and other forms of income support. Children in such households face potentially high risks of institutional neglect insofar as they may not come into contact with many children's services. They may encounter institutional barriers as a result of having lesser rights and entitlements and because of racism.

Such marginal groups are often invisible within policy debates and programmes. In Ireland the 2002 Revised National Anti-Poverty Strategy (NAPS) identified migrants and ethnic minorities as a distinct target group. It established a goal of ensuring that migrants and members of ethnic minority groups resident in Ireland are not more likely to experience poverty than majority group members.[28] However, the current absence of data was identified within the Revised NAPS as an impediment to the establishment of specific targets with respect to poverty among migrants and ethnic minority groups and to the inclusion of minority ethnic groups within anti-poverty strategies in Ireland. The difficulties suggested by the present exclusion of migrants from anti-poverty policies are likely to be reflected in other areas. These include a lack of strategic and administrative focus upon the needs of migrants within existing programmes (institutional barriers) as well as a lack of dedicated resources. In such a context, migrant children may come into contact with social services which are ill-prepared to acknowledge and address their needs. The risks of institutional neglect potentially faced by migrant children may exceed those of asylum children and unaccompanied minors who may be more visible to social workers.

The only area where social workers in Ireland have statutory responsibility to work with asylum seekers and refugees is that of childcare.[29] The 1996 Refugee Act specifically extends the provisions of the 1991 Child Care Act to refugees and asylum seekers. Under the 1991 Act, each health board is required to 'promote the welfare of children in its area who are not receiving adequate care and protection'. This obligation has been acknowledged in responses to unaccompanied minors. However, such children are more properly *under* the care of health boards rather than *in* their care.[30] Accommodation for unaccompanied minors often resembles the sort of privatised minimalist and overcrowded provision experienced by asylum seekers living in direct provision. The potential vulnerability of migrant and asylum seeker children is partly due to lesser rights and entitlements. It is vital that social work responses to such groups address the needs of such children emanating from institutional barriers to welfare services. There is arguably a need for a broader definition of institutional racism than that set out in the Macpherson report. Such a definition must take into account barriers relating to lesser rights and entitlements. In Ireland, as elsewhere, these disproportionately affect black and ethnic minorities. It also needs to take into account barriers that affect 'hard to help' persons with lesser rights, emanating from avoidance and social dumping, in areas not affected by lesser rights.

POSTSCRIPT

The preceding analysis dates from 2004. It emphasised the potential risks to vulnerable asylum seekers and migrant children from institutional neglect. It saw a potential danger that vulnerable children would fall through the cracks in the absence of a clear and sufficient collective focus on their needs by service providers. In the Irish case, asylum seeker and migrant children have not been adequately defined as a target group by statutory services in the area of social work. Furthermore, there are indications that asylum seeker and migrant children are disproportionately dependent upon the voluntary sector yet marginalised within this sector. A number of studies and assessments of policy inadequacies in addressing the needs of 'at risk' migrant children in Ireland suggest that these are poorly protected from the dangers fatally encountered by Victoria Climbie in London.

Unaccompanied minors in Ireland remain a particularly vulnerable group. A study by the International Organisation on Migration (IOM) concluded that these were not being afforded the same child protection rights as Irish children.[31] The 2003 report revealed that some 250 separated children had disappeared from the 'care' of the health boards in the Dublin area from 2001, accounting for close to 10 per cent of the total number (2,717) of separated children who had arrived into the country between 1999 and 2003. Some forty-eight such children disappeared in 2004. In January 2005 its author described how minors, some as young as twelve, were living in hostels run by caretakers with little training in dealing with troubled children. Visits by social workers were not regular. Many, she emphasised, were at risk of ending up in the sex trade or in forced labour. Others, it was implied, vanished, fearing what would happen to them on becoming 'timed-out' at eighteen years of age. Former unaccompanied minors faced the risk of deportation. There had been a number of identifiable instances where children were being lured out of hostels and into questionable relationships with people from outside.[32] The IOM study noted that some unaccompanied minors placed unsupervised in hostels had been victims or suspected victims of sex trafficking. In 2001 just four out of a then total of 422 minors 'in care' were accommodated in designated children's centres. As for the rest, the National Standards for Children's Residential Centres did not apply to them because they were living in adult or homeless hostels under Part 11, Section 5 of the 1991 Child Care Act. Such hostels were deemed to fall outside the remit of the Social Services Inspectorate.

In the absence of adequate day-to-day supervision or inspections of overall standards, child welfare depended on access to social workers. However, here the IOM report identified that the ratio of social workers to children was 1:50 when the acknowledged desirable ratio was 1:12.[33] In January 2005 the Irish Refugee Council stated that there appeared to be 'no concern' and a 'lack of investigation' of cases of children who had gone missing. A substantial article in *Village* magazine reported evidence of inadequate investigation by the Gardaí when children in hostels went missing and a lack of follow-up on behalf of the heath services with statutory responsibility for ensuring the welfare of these children.[34] Following coverage in early 2005 of the under-protection of migrant children in the care of the Health Services Executive (HSE), Mary Harney, the Minister for Health, indicated that hostels for unaccompanied minors would come under the remit of the Social Services Inspectorate but, according to the Irish Refugee Council, it was 'unclear how high a priority this is'.[35]

By 2008 when the issue again received media attention, little had changed. By then about one fifth (328) of all migrant children in HSE care had vanished. Most of these were at least sixteen years old but some were as young as eleven.[36] Back in November 2000 the Irish government launched a National Children's Strategy. This endorsed two of the guiding principles of the 1989 Convention on the Rights of the Child – that all children should be entitled to basic rights without discrimination and that the best interests of the child should be a primary consideration in all actions concerning children.[37] Such a remit is particularly important given the profound gap which exists between commitments to children's rights adopted by the Irish state and existing policies and responses to asylum seeker children, unaccompanied minors and migrant children in Ireland.

However, the case against extending safety nets to vulnerable immigrants has influential advocates. Since 2004 a Social Welfare liaison officer has been working with the Department of Justice, Equality and Law Reform to close off access to social services by persons subject to deportation orders.[38] This offers a concrete example of the subversion of the caring and advocacy roles of social work depicted by Alistair Christie. The Department of Justice, Equality and Law Reform (the reference to equality seems farcical) produced a report making the case for prohibiting access to public services to 'non-nationals' who are not legally resident in the state, the exception being access to emergency medical treatment. Such proposals, as the analysis of the 2003 IOM report makes clear, would include vulnerable former unaccompanied minors who were 'timed-out' at eighteen years of age if their applications for refugee status were turned down.[39] The institutional neglect of vulnerable migrant children is, to some extent at least, deliberately manufactured. It is, to a considerable extent, the consequence of an ethos that fosters discrimination and condones official indifference to their welfare.

CHAPTER SEVEN

Hospitality, Solidarity and Memory

This chapter assembles three polemical essays that first appeared in 2003 and 2004.[1] As reproduced here they communicate a sense of anxiety about the future from what is now the past. Each sought to make sense of the ratchet of administrative, legal and constitutional measures directed against immigrants in the first few years of the twenty-first century. Their common focus was on the mechanics of exclusion whereby cognitive, administrative and legal barriers reinforced one another within the systems of the Irish nation-state. These were the years when cognitive distinctions between 'nationals' and 'non-nationals' were encouraged, when Irish people got used to living in a society where different groups of non-citizens could have lesser rights and entitlements from each other as well as from citizens, when the rules of belonging for the new guests of the nation were being firmed up.

In 2000 asylum seekers were cut out of a welfare system that hitherto made few distinctions between citizens and non-citizens. With the introduction of 'direct provision' social policy became an instrument of internal border policy. Lesser welfare entitlements for asylum seekers were defended as necessary to tackle an asylum 'crisis'. Subsequently the right of all Irish-born children to citizenship was undermined. Back in 1987 the High Court had determined, in *Fajujonu v. Minister for Justice*, that Irish-born children of non-citizens had a right to live in Ireland with the protection of their families. The upshot of this was that these were routinely advised that they could safely withdraw their applications for asylum. However, the government began to refuse leave to remain to such families, knowing that that this would trigger a test case in the courts. In April 2002 the Fajujonu ruling was overturned in the High Court (*Lobe v. Minister for Justice*). On 23 January 2003 the Supreme Court upheld *Lobe v. Minister for Justice*. An Irish citizen child of non-citizens could now be deported unless their parents agreed to be deported without them. This ruling was effectively superseded by the June 2004 Referendum on Citizenship that removed the citizenship birthright from the Irish-born children of non-citizens. 2004 also saw the passing of an Act that removed many welfare entitlements from new immigrants.[2] In such terms the hatches were battened down. When it came to rights and entitlements the importance of being Irish was emphasised as never before. The future was to be faced by anchoring rules of belonging more firmly to the past.

Such measures seemed to make it harder for Irish nationals to find a common cause with many new guests of the nation. The problem of promoting empathy and solidarity with those outside the dominant imagined community finds no easy answer. Philosophers such as Immanuel Kant and John Rawls have influentially (among some academics, intellectuals and jurists, that is) made a rational case for hospitality towards and solidarity with strangers, one that has many colloquial equivalents. Local examples include the (questionable) notion of an Ireland of the welcomes, a specific sense of cosmopolitan solidarity rooted in the Irish Diaspora – the much-voiced nostrum that Ireland should treat immigrants well because the Irish needed a welcome elsewhere – as well as a tradition of Christian humanism reflected in Irish social justice ideals and commitments to international aid. Such perspectives might count for little before a juggernaut of anxious ethnocentrism. However, as these essays argue, they offer valuable tools for challenging the viability of a narrow chauvinism.

(I) HOLOCAUST MEMORIAL DAY

In February 2003 Michael McDowell, the Minister for Justice, Equality and Law Reform, was interviewed on the radio programme 'Morning Ireland' about his statement to mark Ireland's first Holocaust memorial day apologising on behalf of the Irish government for discrimination against Jewish refugees before, during and after the Holocaust. He was asked whether it was possible that some future minister would have to apologise in a similar manner about the present-day treatment of asylum seekers in Ireland. He retorted that the comparison was facile. The question put to the minister echoed a comment I had made two days earlier in another radio discussion when asked about my views on commemorating the Holocaust in Ireland. I answered that the best form of commemoration would be to ensure that our current responses to asylum seekers did not warrant apology at some future date. At face value, current Irish responses to asylum seekers have little in common with the anti-Semitic policies that openly remained on the books until the late 1950s. The principle difference was made by Ireland's ratification of the UN Convention Related to the Status of Refugees (1951) in 1956. Before then, ministers and their officials effectively decided who could be admitted, without reference to any fixed criteria. The upshot of these differences was that Jewish refugees could be and were legally discriminated against. In the words of a typical memorandum of the pre-1956 period: 'It is the policy of the Department of Justice to restrict the immigration of Jews.' The department continued to routinely portray Jews as enemies of the nation until the 1950s.[3]

In my book *Racism and Social Change in the Republic of Ireland* I maintained that anti-Semitism in Ireland had much in common with anti-Semitism in Nazi Germany. Both countries espoused policies of attaining and maintaining societies that were *judenfrei* or 'without Jews'.[4] Our starting place was a dominant sense that Ireland was a homogenous Catholic country. This discounted the existence of a small Jewish minority. The 'problem' was presented in terms of preventing Jews from entering the country. The Nazi 'Jewish problem' initially consisted of some 600,000 German citizens. This rose to more than ten times that number following Nazi conquests to the east and west. The historian Raul Hillburg maintains that the Holocaust was made possible by the construction, under the Nuremberg Laws, of a legal definition of Jewishness.[5] Once the Nuremberg Law categories were in place it became natural and rational to treat Jews differently from other human beings. The Irish state, to some extent, internalised a logic analogous to that of the Nuremberg Laws when it allowed the Irish Co-ordinating Committee for the Relief of Christian Refugees, a voluntary body set up in response to the annexation of Austria, to vet refugee applications. The committee excluded most 'legally defined' Jews from its remit but accepted the Nuremberg category of *Mischlinge*, Jews who had converted to Christianity.[6] One theory of the Holocaust was that it was a specifically modern event whereby people became dehumanised within what Max Weber termed an 'iron cage of rationality'. By this he meant the expansion of formal rationality, embodied in laws and regulations, at the expense of other forms of reason, reasonableness and empathy. The terrible atrocities of the Holocaust were furthered, to some extent, by the rule of law. So too has the human cost of 'Fortress Europe', where restrictions on asylum seekers are administered by polite airline employees enforcing carrier liability laws rather than by brutal border guards. The frozen bodies that fall from the undercarriages of aircraft bound for Fortress Europe, the drowned ones washed up on the beaches of its south shores or the asphyxiated corpses found in long-distance lorry containers are but some of the casualties.

Thirty years ago, in a book called *The Irony of Irish Democracy*, David Schmitt argued that one of the consequences of authoritarianism in Irish society was a kind of perverse ambivalence towards laws and regulations. Deference to those in power, be they politicians or clergy, went hand in hand with an general unwillingness to accept or impose regimentation.[7] For instance, Schmitt argued that the Gardaí were flexible and humane in their treatment of people compared to many other police forces. He speculated that while Ireland might conceivably become an authoritarian dictatorship it was unlikely to develop into a highly regimented one like Nazi Germany. Schmitt's view of the Gardaí seems to have been borne out by the way in which a Limerick superintendent coolly debunked a series of histrionic accusations made against Hungarian refugees accommodated in a former army barracks outside the city at Knocknalisheen in 1956. The Irish Red Cross had pressed the government to remove, among others, Lazlo Pesthy, the elected leader of the refugees, for reasons of personal immorality. The Garda report explained that 'the woman of the night' Mr Pesthy was accused of consorting with in the camp was, in fact, just seeking musicians to play in a band in the city.[8]

The crude forms of social control attempted at Knocknalisheen, which prompted all adult refugees in the camp to go on hunger strike in May 1957, can be read as a conflict between the well-meaning but essentially authoritarian Irish officials and refugees described in government reports of the day as 'vociferous' in demanding their rights. Many of the refugees had previous experiences of contesting state oppression. For example, Lazlo Pesthy had been a political prisoner in Siberia for twenty-nine months and was subsequently imprisoned in Hungary. He was reported to have taken part in the original demonstrations against the Hungarian communist regime with students of the polytechnic university in Budapest and in the fighting that followed. He was used to standing up for his rights. The Hungarians were better able to do so than the indigenous Irish victims of authoritarianism in orphanages, Magdalene laundries and other institutions. The best remedy for such authoritarianism is an emphasis on rights.

However, the rights of refugees, under the 1951 UN Convention on the Status of Refugees, are being increasingly undermined in Ireland and other European countries and the asylum issue has become a lightning rod for racism and xenophobia. The term 'asylum seeker' refers to a legal or administrative category used to refer to refugees who have yet to be accepted as such by the state. It has become increasingly accept-able to treat those people categorised as asylum seekers differently from other people living in Irish society. Only in the last few years, since the announcement of direct provision in 1999, has the legal category of asylum seeker been used to drive discriminatory social policies. In Ireland, as in Britain, social policy has become a tool of exclusionary 'Fortress Europe' border policy. Politicians and officials spoke of the need to discourage asylum seekers and the process of seeking asylum became stigmatised. People categorised as asylum seekers came to be depicted as an undeserving group and as the legitimate target of resent-ment. Harsh social policies and exclusionary border policies were justi-fied by the presumed existence of 'bogus asylum seekers'. The term incorrectly implied that the persons so labelled did not have a right to apply for asylum. It was part and parcel of an officially sanctioned hos-tility to asylum seekers. In the last few years of the twentieth century when the number of refugees rose the category of asylum seeker became a vehicle for racism in Irish society.

A few years ago asylum seekers were central to Irish debates on racism and multiculturalism. It seemed as if there was an understanding that government responses to asylum seekers could not be separated out from anti-racism policies. Government policies denying asylum seekers a right to work were opposed by churches, NGOs, trades unions and employers' organisations. Subsequently, direct provision was opposed by many of the same groups. Arguments that direct pro-vision was both discriminatory and bad social policy were made, to no avail, in the consultation process for the Revised National Anti-Poverty Strategy (2002). The new strategy set a crucial goal for Irish social pol-icy of ensuring that migrants and ethnic minorities do not encounter disproportionate risks of poverty alongside other goals such as address-ing child poverty. However, the extreme relative poverty encountered by asylum seeker children remains, to a considerable extent, due to other government policies. This doublethink, to use a word coined by George Orwell, is sustained by the exclusion of asylum seekers from debates about racism and social exclusion. Government-funded anti-racism campaigns are backed by laws such as the Equal Status Act that makes it illegal to discriminate in the provision of goods and services. Yet, discrimination against asylum seekers in the provision of welfare goods and services also has a legal basis.

Asylum seekers are currently the poor relations within Ireland's immi-grant communities. Overall, they are just a small minority within a larg-er minority. In February 2003 the backlog of unprocessed applications for asylum stood at almost 7,000. By contrast, over 40,000 work permits – some 16,000 of which were renewals – were issued to non-EU nationals during 2002. New immigrant communities, churches and civil society are going from strength to strength. It has become increasingly politically necessary for official Ireland to acknowledge and celebrate multicultural or 'intercultural' Ireland. The attraction of a cosy interculturalism that excludes proscribed asylum seekers is all too evident. If we have borrowed some disastrous asylum policies from the United Kingdom, there is also a risk that Irish racism will increasingly resemble the British case where hostility to asylum seekers among the white majority is accompanied by antipathy from anti-racist bodies and established black and ethnic minority communities.

On 8 May 2003 the High Court ruled that the detention of a Nigerian asylum seeker, Ms Bola Ojo, was illegal and the refusal of her application for residency was unfair. She was arrested on 27 January with her six-week-old Irish-born son when she went to a police station to register a new address. Her application for asylum had been turned down but, following the Supreme Court ruling in February 2003 that undermined the right of Irish children of non-citizens, she became part of a backlog of some 10,000 cases now living in fear of deportation. The detention of the Ojos was overturned on a technicality. Further imprisonments and deportations can be anticipated as a logical outcome of semantic legal distinctions between 'Irish' and 'non-Irish' Irish children.

The ideal of citizenship has become the bedrock of Western thought about equality. Yet, while citizenship rights have deepened, for example to take account of gender inequalities and the rights of children, they also justify many forms of discrimination and inequality experienced by those not part of the club. Modern day inequality resulting from citizenship and immigration laws can be as insidious as the Nuremberg Laws that led to Catholic and Protestant churches alike excluding *Mischlinge* from their congregations prior to the Holocaust. Then, as now, laws and regulations insist that some of our neighbours are really not part of society. One of the purposes of separate welfare systems such as direct provision and the growing use of dedicated facilities to accommodate asylum seekers is to drive a wedge between asylum seekers and other members of our communities. The creation of a legal category governing some Irish-born children of immigrants, specifically aimed at dislodging them from Irish society, has a similar administrative role to the legal categories imposed on some German citizens under the Nuremberg Laws. It serves to justify differential treatment and potentially provides a focus for further discrimination.

One retort to the injustices inherent in existing systems of justice that favour some groups at the expense of others has been advanced by John Rawls.[9] His theory of justice starts from the simple premise of imagining what fair rules and social arrangements might be drawn up under a 'veil of ignorance'. The asylum or citizenship arrangements that would be considered just by people hypothetically not aware of where they were to be born nor knowing their gender, sexuality, class position, social status, skills, abilities or religion would differ somewhat from those currently in force. The development of various non-citizen castes, each with different levels of rights and entitlements, has intensified as a response to immigration. There is nothing inherently good, reasonable or necessary about such efforts to categorise human beings. Rights enjoyed by citizens can be extended to people from other jurisdictions, as has occurred in the European Union. The Czech asylum seekers deported last year can be welcomed as prospective EU citizen immigrants this year. Direct provision could be reformed. It is only an administrative system. Asylum seekers could be allowed to apply for work permits, for people can be workers as well as asylum seekers. The rights of Ms Ojo's child could be protected rather than flouted, for that child is no less Irish than anybody categorised as such.

(II) DISPOSABLE PEOPLE AND THEIR CHILDREN

Irish society has changed profoundly in recent years. It has become a demonstrably multicultural society and this is taking some getting used to. An initial period of openly histrionic and, at times, naïve racism during the late 1990s has abated or at least gone underground. A number of positive initiatives have emerged notwithstanding the absence of coherent thinking about integration. The existence of bodies such as the Equality Authority, the National Consultative Committee on Racism and Interculturalism and the government's 'Know Racism' campaign suggest a degree of acknowledgement that racism and discrimination are not acceptable in twenty-first century Irish society. Yet, in 2004 a very different message emanated from the ruthless efforts of the government to undermine the rights and entitlements of immigrant workers and their children. Alongside the undermining of welfare rights from non-citizens announced in March 2004 the government promoted a referendum proposal to strip entitlements to citizenship from Irish-born children not descended from Irish parents. It was marketed under the slogan 'common-sense citizenship' and was passed by an overwhelming majority of the Irish electorate on 11 June 2004.

The present drive to reduce welfare entitlements to non-citizens and citizenship entitlements to non-nationals cannot be separated from a longstanding hostility towards 'unwanted' immigrants such as asylum seekers or, indeed, Jewish refugees before, during and after the Holocaust. Citizenship is a legal concept. It serves to institutionalise ideological understandings of community. Dublin's Portmarnock golf club excluded women from membership by means of rules set by its exclusively male membership. So also can the citizens of nation-states set the rules that determine the treatment of non-nationals. Rights to welfare, whether or not they are tied to citizenship, define who is to be considered as a deserving member of the community. If 'Irishness' becomes legally defined in terms of being descended from those who are already accepted as part of the Irish nation, we are left with little more than a nineteenth-century conception of the Irish 'race' as a definition of twenty-first century Irish society.

Irish politicians and journalists increasingly distinguished between 'nationals' and 'non-nationals' in the months before the referendum. This dualism functions as a simplistic 'us' and 'them' that is poorly equipped to make wise decisions about complex changes to Irish society. Efforts to deny citizenship rights to Irish-born children who are not 'Irish' or deprive immigrants of a welfare safety net previously available to everyone are not mere exercises in pragmatism. Yes, other countries in the European Union do not allow all people born in their jurisdictions to become citizens. However, many have a long track record of immigration and naturalisation. Some, like Germany, have sought to address the legacy of excluding generations of foreign workers from citizenship. Others, such as Belgium, Italy and Spain, have periodically naturalised cohorts of legal and irregular immigrants. Yes, Britain has decided to exclude some new immigrants from its welfare state. However, the reasons for this were political. New Labour caved in under the pressures of right-wing populism. The case put to the Irish people was not that such restrictions on rights and entitlements were regrettable but these were, in the words of Mary Coughlan, Minister for Social and Family Affairs, 'prudent and sensible'.[10] The Irish government consciously sought to maximise welfare restrictions on immigrants in the current political climate. In particular, the decision to remove children's allowances from immigrant children, including those who are Irish born, whose parents may be nurses or teachers, seems difficult to square with the argument that entitlements were removed to prevent welfare tourism from the countries that joined the European Union in 2004.

The experience of other countries tells us that equal citizenship rights do not by themselves secure the integration of immigrants. However, the absence of rights does much to socially exclude minorities. In the United States, past discriminatory access to welfare and the denial of civil rights has contributed to present-day black inequality.[11] In the late 1960s many Irish commentators drew parallels between such inequalities and those in Northern Ireland. Yet in both the North and in America the problem was one of discrimination against some citizens rather than the denial of citizenship rights *per se*. The starting place for most debates about multiculturalism and integration has been, until recently, a concern that some groups were likely to experience their rights as citizens differently because of prejudice and discrimination. In this present era of globalisation the question becomes a more difficult one of securing the integration of immigrants in the face of pressures to deny them rights and entitlements.

There are perhaps two main elements in the ideological gridlock that is misshaping current legal and policy responses to immigration. Both are intertwined. The first is a nativist conception of Irishness that takes the form of ideological begrudgery towards 'non-nationals'. The second is a willingness to treat immigrants as disposable beasts of burden. Many non-EU immigrant workers are on non-transferable work permits. If they complain, they may lose their jobs. If they lose their jobs, they lose their right of residency. People from other European Union countries can change jobs, but without access to the welfare safety net they fund as taxpayers they also might easily be dislodged if surplus to requirements. There seems to be a presumption that immigrants will self-deport if and when they are no longer wanted. Indeed, it has been suggested that they are to be helped on their way with travel grants if that is what it takes to get shot of them.

The big, big problem of immigration in the era of globalisation is that rights and recognition have become wedded to citizenship but that more and more people are outside citizenship in the place where they live. The category within which a human being finds herself has come to supersede any consensus about human equality within democratic societies. The notion of the human being has become something of a category error. Somebody categorised as an asylum seeker or a 'non-national' on a non-transferable work permit is deemed to be a sort of non-person. Against this rationalisation of human existence stand various secular and religious conceptions of social justice, human rights, community and solidarity that would define Irish society in broader terms than those presently institutionalised in the state. Non-governmental organisations, refugee support groups, faith communities, trades unions and organisations representing immigrant communities – in short a significant portion of Irish civil society – have at times contested dominant narrow conceptions of Irish society. For example, on 12 March 2004 the Irish Bishops' Conference called for residency rights to be granted to the backlog of some 11,000 immigrant families with Irish-born children who at the time feared deportation.

Looking to the future, the worst-case scenario is that present-day nativism calcifies into something worse – an Ireland where a dominant powerful community becomes captured by a siege mentality, where the present indifference to the welfare of immigrants mutates into fear and hate. The reappraisal of what it means to be a member of Irish society is not something to be left to chance. It is a crucial project for the present generation of citizens and immigrants alike. Like it or not, many immigrants are here to stay. Their deliberate marginalisation serves to sabotage an inevitable common future. The children of immigrants are needed as much as the children of citizens to provide for the retirement-age welfare of the current generation. It ill behoves us to wilfully impoverish the present or next generation of immigrants.

Yet, crucially, so much of the current politics of immigrant exclusion focuses on attacking the rights of children. Michael McDowell, Minister for Justice, Equality and Law Reform at the time, claimed that the impetus for the government's policy of removing citizen rights from immigrant Irish-born children came from the pleas of the masters of Dublin's maternity hospitals to do something about the growing numbers of non-national expectant mothers.[12] The government's Supreme Court challenge in 2003 to an earlier legal precedent that gave humanitarian leave to remain in Ireland to the Irish-born children of nonnationals, the removal of the birth right to citizenship and the removal of rights to welfare including children's allowances each constitute specific attacks on children and therefore upon the future of Irish society. The principle that humans should not be treated as the ends of others remains central to numerous distinct and sometimes contradictory conceptions of justice and freedom. The notion that human beings are oppressed when their own ends are violated remains central to moral philosophy. It is the starting place of Western theories of human rights. It is as central to Karl Marx's critique of exploitation under capitalism as it is to Frederick Hayek's free market understanding of the state as something that subordinates individuals to tyrannical collective ends. A common proposal within the moral schemes of the likes of Aristotle, Jesus of Nazareth, Immanuel Kant and John Stuart Mill is, in essence, that you should do unto others as you would have them do unto you.[13] Within such terms immigrants can find themselves misused and abused. The philosopher John Rawls maintained that the basis of the human motivation towards justice is intergenerational. He argued that: 'For anyone in the next generation, there is someone who cares about him in the present generation.'[14] He concluded from this that everyone, whatever his temporal position, is forced to choose everyone. It comes down to what 'we' want the future to be. We (all of us) need some conception of a good society that speaks to a common future rather than one that rationalises the exploitation of immigrants and sanctions the abuse of children in the name of common sense.

(III) NEW GUESTS OF THE NATION

By necessity, any exploration of the present relationship between the rules of citizenship and dominant ideals of 'Irishness' requires some historical focus. To paraphrase Neal Ascherson, with every pun intended, present-day understandings of Irish nationality have been forged from the past. Much has been written about nations as imagined communities ideologically sustained by invented traditions. Bastille Day was created in 1880 some ninety-one years after the storming of the Bastille. Gaelic football was invented as a 'traditional' Irish game in the late nineteenth century to displace soccer. As the curiously Irish-named character O'Brien put it in Orwell's *1984*, he who controls the present controls the past. Streets, parks and tower blocks can be named after icons of the national past. National sports can be invented. Ethnic groups can be written into or written out of official history. David McCrone in *The Sociology of Nationalism* concludes that, all in all, 'the past' is a powerful source of legitimacy for those seeking to change the present for a new future.[15]

The title of this article alludes to a 1931 short story by Frank O'Connor. *Guests of the Nation* is about the reprisal execution of two English hostages during the war of independence. It has had an ongoing resonance within debates on belonging and exclusion since it was first published in 1931. The title is heavy with irony for it is a story of remorseless and inexorable exclusion on behalf of the nascent state. It is a slap in the face to the clichés of the 'Ireland of the welcomes'. It is a story of friendship and fellowship between four young men and one old woman caught up on different sides of a war. The two prisoners are on their way to becoming, as put in another cliché of the story of the Irish peoples, 'more Irish than the Irish themselves'. This phrase referred to the assimilation of Norman incomers who adopted the Gaelic language and local customs. If it suggests possibilities of inclusion, the title of Frank O'Connor's story has come to evoke the opposite. As the narrator, Bonaparte, says of his orders on behalf of the fledgling state:

> I could not at the time see the point of myself and Noble guarding Belcher and Hawkins at all, for it was my belief that you could have planted that pair down anywhere from this to Claregalway and they'd have taken root there like a native weed. I never in my short experience saw two men take to the country as they did.

The final tragedy and irony of *Guests of the Nation* is that the two Englishmen are 'planted' in a bog grave. In the end, friendship and fellowship do not carry the day. Orders must are carried out. The rules of the new state have to be obeyed. George Orwell published a similarly themed essay, *A Hanging*, also in 1931. The young Eric Blair – George Orwell was a pen name – presided over executions as an assistant police commissioner in British-controlled Burma. Both O'Connor's story and Orwell's essay address the mechanics of exclusion by the state and feelings of complicity and powerlessness among people who were just following orders. Max Weber offers the following sociological explanation of such acts:

> The honour of the civil servant is vested in his ability to execute conscientiously the order of superior authorities, exactly as if the order agreed with his own conviction. This holds even if the order seems wrong to him and if, despite the civil servant's remonstrances, the authority insists on the order.[16]

Max Weber argued that bureaucratic processes remove the imperative for moral decisions in how organisational roles become defined. The human objects of bureaucratic tasks cease to be subjects of moral demands. Such bureaucratic rationality is evident within the administrative and decision-making processes of Western societies where they affect groups such as immigrant workers, refugees, citizen welfare recipients as well as persecuted minorities. For example, the way in which refugees or immigrants are administratively classified determines whether or not they are to be regarded as members of the society within which they live. Gradations of rights between citizens and non-citizens, immigrant 'guest' workers, undocumented workers, refugees and asylum seekers have emerged in a number of Western countries that as recently as a century ago operated few restrictions on immigration. In effect these are the result of placing people in different administrative categories. Under the logic of citizenship it becomes 'natural' that the non-citizen should not have social and economic rights. Citizenship, according to Michel Peillon:

> ... becomes the wall, the barrier which protects an abstract national community. Citizenship grants privileges to those who belong at the very same time as it denies them to the non-citizen. Most expressions of prejudice and intolerance, most strategies of rejection, are based on the boundaries which have been traced around citizenship.[17]

A further layer of state-sanctioned exclusion occurs when the rules of citizenship are bent to build higher walls to keep out or marginalise immigrants. The conscious actions of the Irish government to seek to remove the residency entitlements of the families of Irish-born immigrant children suggests a perception of immigrants as an 'out-group' from whom the 'real Irish' citizens must be protected. Before the Supreme Court decision in January 2003 to deny the family of Irish-born Kevin Lobe the right to remain in Ireland, a previous court ruling on *Fajujonu v. Minister for Justice* (1987) held sway. The Fajujonus were a Moroccan and Nigerian married couple with two Irish-born children. They successfully contested a deportation order on the basis that their children were Irish citizens. They argued that their children, as Irish citizens, had a right to family life, in accordance with the rights of the child under the Irish Constitution.[18] This was interpreted by the High Court as a right for the child to live in Ireland with his or her family. The practice, which emerged following the Fajujonu judgement, of granting leave to remain to asylum seeker families with Irish-born children, served to promote the social inclusion of some immigrants. The benefit entitlements of such families increased. They gained access to rent allowances and parents became entitled to work. For example, 4,071 people were granted leave to remain in the state in 2002. Some 75 per cent of these were currently or had formally been asylum seekers. However, almost 25 per cent had never been asylum seekers. In effect, the Fajujonu judgement allowed for the regularisation of a significant number of immigrants. That is, until the rules were changed.

Media accounts of the issue sometimes referred to loopholes in the citizenship laws as if to say people had become Irish citizens who were not supposed to become so because they were not 'Irish'. As such, efforts by the government to limit the rights of the 'non-Irish' Irish-born are aimed at protecting an alleged 'national interest'. These have followed efforts to diminish the welfare rights and entitlements of non-citizen migrants. In 2000 a punitive system of direct provision was introduced to discourage asylum seekers from seeking asylum in Ireland. In February 2003, the cabinet debated a proposal to remove a right to child benefits from non-Irish and non-EU country citizens.

Administrative distinctions between 'Irish' citizens and 'non-Irish' Irish citizens may be implemented dispassionately but these are predicated upon exclusionary ideological constructions of 'Irishness'. The formulations of social membership that become institutionalised within the rules of citizenship are grounded in biological and spatial conceptions of community. Distinctions can be made between biological *jus sanguine* conceptions of citizenship that define it in terms of blood relationships and *jus soli* definitions of citizenship in terms of birthplace. Under the former, the immigrant can never become Irish because he or she does not have Irish blood and is not part of the Irish 'race'. There is no melting pot. Instead immigrants can be likened to donor organs rejected by antibodies of the biological host. Immigrants do not get to be Irish, let alone 'more Irish than the Irish themselves'. The imagined Irish race becomes a biological reality. It is presumed that immigrant minority communities can never become part of the abstract national community and as such should be prevented from becoming citizens on grounds of their different ethnicity. Under a *jus soli* definition of Irish everybody born in Ireland is recognised as Irish. *Jus soli* citizenship was reiterated in the Good Friday Agreement. Anybody born on the island of Ireland, as distinct from within the Irish nation-state, was entitled to Irish citizenship. However, these rights have been partially undermined. The first Irish-born child was deported in February 2003. At the same time, the Europeanisation of citizenship rights has undermined the viability of *jus sanguine* conceptions of Irishness. A *cordon sanitaire* around the existing imagined community is unsustainable.

Karl Marx emphasised how social stratification occurred on the basis of social class. Max Weber considered that society was stratified on the basis of economic factors, status (which, of course, included citizenship) and power. Conflict theories of social stratification derived from the work of Marx and Weber by Randall Collins emphasise a need to take account of the material arrangements that affect social interaction. On the other hand, structural functionalist theories, derived from the sociology of Talcott Parsons, considered that social inequality was necessary for the proper functioning of society. The problem here was not how to promote equity but how to get the right people into the right positions so as to best meet the needs of society. Social order was understood as the product of consensual social norms that, again, served a functional purpose. This suggested that people accepted inequality but it also implied that as society changed the functional necessities for social order changed too.[19] As such, sociological theories of stratification suggest that a range of inequalities are perpetrated by the rules governing full social membership. These theories also suggest that there will be an institutional impetus to accommodate changes in the real membership of society but not necessarily by addressing social inequalities. At the same time Parsons accepted a clear relationship between citizenship rights and social equality.[20] The converse of this, of course, is some presumed causal relationship between a lack of rights and inequality.

Many Western societies have dual labour markets as a consequence of stratifications between the social, economic and political rights between citizen and non-citizen groups. One consequence of dual labour markets is that immigrant workers tend to enjoy lesser pay and conditions to indigenous workers. They are vulnerable to discrimination and exploitation. They experience greater risks of poverty. Research has shown that immigrants with lesser rights throughout the European Union are disproportionately represented in forms of poorly paid and insecure work and that they are disproportionately unemployed. Furthermore, second and third generations of migrant-descended communities who have been born, raised and educated in European member states continue to encounter disproportionate levels of social exclusion. Discrimination caused by racism in areas such as employment or housing can be compounded by lesser rights and protections. Where immigrants and asylum seekers have lesser welfare entitlements or rights to education they may experience greater levels of poverty. Labour market stratifications combined with welfare stratifications in Ireland have the potential to create an Irish society where some minority ethnic groups face disproportionate levels of inequality. It goes without saying that lesser rights and entitlements impede the integration of immigrants. Such stratifications are, from a structural functionalist perspective, ultimately dysfunctional.

The new guests of the nation are guest workers, asylum seekers, migrants and non-citizen ethnic minorities. Irish society has changed hugely in the last decade. Just under one quarter million immigrants came to Ireland between 1995 and 2000. Of these about half were returned Irish immigrants. Some 18 per cent were from the UK, 13 per cent from other EU countries, 7 per cent from the United States and 12 per cent from the rest of the world. Large-scale immigration has become a component of the National Development Plan even if it has yet to be so acknowledged within the ideological processes of nation-building. The 2003 Employment Permits Bill proposed that immigrants from the EU accession states would have full access to the Irish labour market from May 2004. This meant that immigration restrictions would be lifted from citizens of the Czech Republic, Estonia, Latvia, Lithuania, Hungary, Poland, Slovenia and Slovakia. In 2003 these accounted for some 35 per cent of all immigrants with work permits. However, Mary Harney, the then Minister for Enterprise and Employment, stated that the new legislation will allow for these rights to be temporally revoked in the event of an economic downturn.

In Ireland, both citizen and non-citizen black and ethnic minorities live outside the dominant imagined community. Yet dominant constructions of 'Irishness' have shifted since these became institutionalised in the state following independence in 1922. The legacy of the nineteenth-century nation-building that led to the establishment of the new state was a narrowly constructed monocultural religious (Catholic) ethnic conception of nation. The Irish-Ireland hegemony of the first half of the twentieth century froze these ideological constructions of citizenship in aspic. Nation-building before and after independence coincided with the displacement of Protestant, Jewish and Traveller minorities from the dominant imagined community. Irish-Ireland had eroded by the 1960s.[21] Ireland became more secular but remained ideologically monocultural. During the 1990s, President Mary Robinson employed the metaphor of the 'fifth province' to refer to an enlarged 'Diaspora' definition of Irishness that included citizen emigrants and their non-citizen descendants.

This symbolic fifth province was effectively monocultural. However, it was a crucial reckoning with a history of mass exclusion of 'surplus' population within Irish nation-building. In 1841, Ireland was one of the most densely populated countries in Europe. By 1954, it was among the most sparsely populated. During the nineteenth and twentieth centuries mass emigration was ideologically represented as necessary and inevitable. Post-Famine economic and social pressures produced stratifications within households and communities. For example, Tom Inglis has described the emergence of a post-Famine sexual morality that consigned family members without the prospect of inherited land or dowries to celibacy within the community or emigration.[22] Within the new state, ambivalence to emigration constituted an implicit social policy. Emigration was constructed as unavoidable and even as a good thing; as a social and economic safety valve. The moral argument that Ireland should welcome immigrants because Irish emigrants have been welcomed in other countries has often been made on calls to radio programmes and in letters to newspapers. However, a sociological analysis of Irish modernisation reveals that Irish society became proficient at excluding displaced and unwanted Irish people and that this can be done to invited guest workers and unwanted migrants alike just as easily.

Irish ethnic-national chauvinism has, in the past, coincided with a self-image (and tourism marketing image) of the Ireland of the welcomes. Welcomes for tourists coexisted in the past with the exclusion of emigrants. Now they are to be found alongside the marginalisation of immigrants. A well-known (American) song, sung to generations of tourists in Jury's Cabaret and elsewhere, goes:

> If you're Irish come into the parlour
> There's a welcome there for you.
> If you're name is Timothy or Pat,
> so long as you come from Ireland
> there's a welcome on the mat.
>
> If you come from the mountains of Mourne
> or Killarney's lakes so blue,
> we'll sing you a song
> and we'll make a fuss,
> whoever you are you're one of us.
> If you're Irish this is the place for you.

State, society and nation can each be viewed as potential sites of inclusion and exclusion. Social and political rights are formulated by the state subject to the will of 'the people'; that is, those who are already citizens. In this first sphere, 'Irishness' is enshrined in the state and legally defined by the granting of citizenship. In the past citizens have extended the franchise, given rights to women and broadened their own social and economic rights. Citizens have the run of the parlour. The second sphere is demographic. It includes everybody living in Ireland and not just those legally defined as Irish by the state. There may well be people from Nigeria, China or Iraq living in Killarney or in the mountains of Mourne. State definitions and rules of Irishness have yet to catch up with this multicultural reality. The extent to which these can ever do so will depend, in part, upon the extent to which dominant constructions of social membership become and remain inclusive. Nation-building is an ongoing process of ideological and material change. As the first line of the song suggests, much depends on how 'Irishness' is defined. Once again (with feeling): '... whoever you are you're one of us. If you're Irish this is the place for you.'

CHAPTER EIGHT

The Citizenship Referendum
(with Fidele Mutwarasibo)

The political responses to immigration that are the focus of this chapter cannot be understood without some reference to past nation-building or national preoccupations about economic development in an era of globalisation. Two legacies of Irish modernisation must be emphasised in making sense of the politics of the 2004 Citizenship Referendum. The first is a process of exclusionary nation-building which contributed to the development of the Irish Republic as an ethnic nation-state rather than as a civic nation-state.[1] The second relates to recurring distributional anxieties shaped by past economic fatalism – evident in past political acceptance of emigration – that have persisted into an era of prosperity defined in neo-liberal terms. The 2004 referendum emerged from economic as well as cultural formulations of Irishness.

Cultural reformulations of Irishness emerged in the decades prior to the 2004 referendum but there remained for the most part monocultural ones. For example, during the 1990s the Robinson presidency sought to institutionalise a Diasporic conception of Irishness.[2] This spatial reckoning with the 'race' memory of exclusions resulting from emigration among emigrant communities extended Irishness to, as Yeats put it, 'wherever green is worn'. The formulation of identity subsequently central to the 2004 referendum was again effectively monoethnic. It distinguished existing citizens of the nation-state from Irish-born children of immigrants hitherto entitled to citizenship. This was expressed in popular parlance as a distinction between 'nationals' and 'non-nationals'.

Second, the referendum as a political response to immigration was bound up with the politics of economic growth and past distributional conflict. Economic isolationism in the wake of independence failed. From the 1950s a project of economic development centring on national development plans and foreign investment emerged with limited initial success. It coexisted with the depiction of emigration as a useful economic safety valve.[3] A copious indigenous literature – including critiques of underdevelopment during the 1980s and analyses of post-Famine distributional conflict – emphasised an ongoing sense of Malthusian fatalism. This depicted emigration as a manifestation of overpopulation. An increase in population was not to be condoned because under zero-sum 'rules' it would mean a decline in living standards for the rest. Joseph Lee identified the emergence of a 'zero sum' mindset whereby people saw the advancement of others as only possible at their own expense: 'The size of the cake was more or less fixed in more or less stagnating communities and in small institutions. In a stunted society, one man's gain did tend to be another man's loss. Winners could only flourish at the expense of losers. Status depended not only on rising oneself but on preventing others from rising. For many, keeping the other fellow down offered the surest defence of their own position.' In Lee's account an essentially liberal project of modernisation found itself in contestation with deterministic thinking about social problems. The fact of emigration itself became the criterion of population excess. Emigration dispensed with the need to do anything about its causes.[4] All this evokes a sense of a people thinking with their bellies rather than, as Bismarck exhorted the Germans to do, with their blood.[5] The Irish nation-state, no less than others, could be ambivalent even towards its own ethnic membership.

Nineteenth-century liberalism, no less than Catholicism, contributed to the social and sexual regulation of Irish society. Both held that the state should only act when the male breadwinner was proven to have failed to provide for his dependants. Post-independent Ireland was in many respects a privatised nation of breadwinners and dependants. The link between welfare and work within early twentieth-century legislation remained consistent with the exclusion of 'surplus' population from the remit of Irish social policy. Neo-liberalism has arguably displaced Catholicism as a dominant ideology in the wake of secularisation and urbanisation. The fatalism Lee identified has been superseded by a valorising of individual agency in prevalent neo-liberal accounts of the Celtic Tiger.[6] Irish free-market neo-liberal responses to globalisation find expression in what has been variously described by Roche and Craddon as a 'lean corporatism' that prioritises national competitiveness over social considerations or by George Taylor as a fundamental political shift whereby free-market policy solutions to social problems have increasingly moved to the fore.[7] Peadar Kirby argues that such 'consensual' responses to globalisation cannot be understood in isolation from earlier anxieties about underdevelopment. These, he argues, are 'hidden behind a discourse with a strong emphasis on national community'.[8] It is suggested that such political responses to globalisation cannot but impact on political responses to immigration.

Both modernisation legacies were evident in the politics of the referendum. The campaign of Fianna Fáil, the largest party in government, employed the slogan of 'commonsense citizenship' that tapped into existing distinctions between the still-predominantly monoethnic 'nationals' and 'non-nationals'. That of the Progressive Democrats (a party that emphasised the economic benefits of immigration) centred on racialised claims about asylum seekers and 'baby tourists' exploiting health services. It portrayed 'non-nationals' as disposable economic actors with no claim on the nation-state.

ASYLUM SEEKERS, IMMIGRANTS AND IRISH POLITICAL PARTIES

The nativist politics of the referendum played out within overwhelmingly monocultural political parties. In the Irish case, immigration, predominantly depicted in terms of an asylum seeker crisis, had become politicised in the years prior to the 2002 general election. Just one single-issue anti-immigrant candidate emerged to contest the 2002 general election. By contrast, a number of single-issue independent candidates emerged to contest health issues. Two of these were elected. As noted in Chapter 5, under Ireland's proportional representation system such candidates tend to poll well on topical issues inadequately addressed by the mainstream political parties. One reading of the relative absence of single-issue politics on asylum and immigration was that populist concerns had been successfully absorbed into the political mainstream. Specifically, it could be suggested that the 'punitive' policies on asylum put forward by the successfully returned government parties, Fianna Fáil and the Progressive Democrats, contained anti-asylum populism within the political mainstream. Government policies of actively promoting large-scale market-led labour immigration, or the consequences of these, did not become a political issue in the 2002 general election. Immigration continued to be politicised in terms of asylum seekers even though these were a fast-declining proportion of overall immigration. Subsequently, in the run-up to the 2004 Referendum on Citizenship, racialised hostility towards asylum seekers was mobilised in advocating the removal of the rights of the children of immigrants (including asylum seekers) to Irish citizenship.

In the run-up to the 2002 election each of the six main political parties endorsed an anti-racism protocol. This outlined commitments to send 'consistent and clear' messages that signatories rejected racism, and to condemn campaign materials susceptible to inciting hatred on the grounds of 'race', colour, nationality, ethnic origin or religious belief.[9] The protocol was much cited in criticism that one Fianna Fáil candidate, Noel O'Flynn, politically exploited hostility towards asylum seekers in Cork during the run-up to the election. O'Flynn topped the poll and was not subject to formal censure subsequently by his party. The protocol advanced norms of conduct which were generally adhered to. However, it included no commitments to promoting the participation of immigrants or ethnic minorities within Irish politics.

In 2003, before the referendum was announced, the Africa Solidarity Centre (ASC) undertook research aimed at fostering responsiveness by Irish political parties to immigrants as prospective voters, party members and candidates.[10] The study was influenced by campaigns in the United Kingdom aimed at addressing under-representation of black and minority ethnic communities in British political parties.[11] The impetus for the ASC research in 2003 was twofold. There was a perceived need to challenge potential exploitation of racism in the 2004 local government election. There was also a longer-term concern to promote inclusionary politics.[12] The ASC argued that the 2004 election offered an important and positive opportunity to promote the participation of immigrants and ethnic minorities in Irish politics. Rights to vote in the 2004 local elections depended upon residency criteria rather than citizenship. Under Irish law, non-citizens – including asylum seekers – were entitled to register to vote in local government elections subject to a six-month residency rule.[13] Furthermore, in local government elections it was not necessary to be an Irish citizen to be elected as a public representative.[14] The ASC survey complemented an immigrant voter registration campaign conducted by some NGOs and the Catholic Church directed at local authority officials responsible for maintaining electoral registers. This anticipated, correctly, that asylum seekers and other non-citizen immigrants entitled to vote in the local elections would experience difficulties in registering their vote.[15]

In their responses to the first (2003) ASC survey none of the six major political parties, including Fianna Fáil and the Progressive Democrats in government, identified specific policies or good practices adopted to encourage members of immigrant communities and ethnic minority groups to become party members. The response of Fianna Fáil, the main government party, was the most extensive but made no specific reference to immigrants and ethnic minorities. Instead, it outlined a general ethos of inclusion grounded in the democratic republican ideals of the party. This promised to 'guarantee religious and civil liberty, and equal rights, equal treatment and equal opportunities for all'.[16]

Media coverage of the ASC research emphasised the finding that the constitution of the Progressive Democrats contained a provision preventing non-Irish or non-EU member state citizens from becoming party members.[17] Media criticism was specifically directed at Michael McDowell, party president of the Progressive Democrats who, as Minister for Justice, Equality and Law Reform, was responsible for Irish immigration policy. The ASC argued that parties which prevented non-citizens from joining could potentially be open to legal challenge on human rights grounds. It emphasised that the British Labour Party had overturned a ban on members from Northern Ireland at its 2003 conference following legal advice that it had a weak case on such grounds.[18] The Progressive Democrats promptly agreed to amend their constitution.[19]

During the 2004 local government elections no party retained formal barriers to membership from immigrant communities yet institutional barriers were strongly evident. Political activism by immigrants and ethnic minorities emerged outside the party system. Several immigrant and ethnic minority candidates contested the elections as independents. Two of these were elected: Dr Taiwo Matthew to Ennis Urban District Council and Rotimi Adebari became a councillor in Portlaoise. Concerns raised by NGOs months in advance of the election that non-citizen immigrants entitled to vote in the local government elections would encounter difficulties in registering to vote proved justified. As late as 22 April, asylum seekers entitled to vote were prevented from registering to vote in the June 2004 local government elections.[20] The identity cards issued by the Department of Justice, Equality and Law Reform to asylum seekers stated that these were not to be accepted for the purposes of legal identification. The result was that many people entitled to vote were prevented from including their names on the register of electors. It took several requests to the Department of Justice, Equality and Law Reform and the Department of Environment and Local Government before clarification regarding how such people could register was forthcoming. A statement by the Irish Refugee Council, issued prior to the amendment, summed up the problem in the following terms:

The strength of any democracy is in the extent to which all who are entitled to vote are encouraged and enabled to do so. In this regard the Irish Government has, to date, singularly failed Ireland's immigrant communities. A failure to rectify this situation will be a missed opportunity for significantly enhancing the integration of Ireland's new communities into Irish society.[21]

On 22 April 2004 the Minister for the Environment, Heritage and Local Government amended the electoral regulations to allow recognition of temporary Resident Certificate and National Immigration Bureau cards.[22]

THE CONTEXT OF THE REFERENDUM

Immigration emerged as the dominant issue during the 2004 polls because of a government decision, announced in March 2004, to hold a referendum on the removal of the constitutional right to citizenship from the Irish-born children of immigrants on the same date as the local government and European elections. The 1998 Belfast Agreement had copper-fastened a *jus soli* constitutional right to citizenship for all children born on the island of Ireland just as asylum and immigrant numbers began to rise. Asylum seekers and other immigrants with Irish-born children were entitled to leave to remain for the benefit of their children as a result of an earlier High Court ruling in 1987 (*Fajujonu v. Minister for Justice*) (see Chapter 7).

This position, according to Donnacha O'Connell and Ciara Smith, put the government in a bind. It was politically impractical to change the Belfast Agreement but it was too much to allow a carefully constructed asylum system to be undermined by a 'procedural bypass'.[23] Therefore a policy decision was made to begin to refuse leave to remain to asylum seeker families in the knowledge that this would trigger a further test case in the Supreme Court. In Ireland, persons granted leave to remain by the Minister for Justice, Equality and Law Reform may acquire citizenship after a period of five years resident in the state in Ireland. In April 2002 the Fajujonu ruling was successfully overturned in the High Court (*Lobe v. Minister for Justice*). On 23 January 2003 the Supreme Court upheld this ruling. In essence the court ruled that the Irish citizen child of non-citizens could be deported with its parents unless the non-citizen parent agreed to be deported without their child. The government subsequently sought to remove the constitutional *jus soli* birthright to citizenship by hitting on a *jus sanguinis* formula that would ensure that both those from Northern Ireland and from the Republic whose parents were already 'Irish' could still become citizens. Patrick Weil has influentially emphasised the need for a state-oriented approach to theorising what he sees as an international convergence in the regulation of immigration. He identifies a number of forms of convergence. These include the adaptation of state immigration polices to meet obligations under the 1951 UN Convention and under subsequent conventions. Second, similar restrictive responses to migrations emanating from colonial relationships emerged in a number of countries. Third, in the European case, a degree of policy harmonisation became inevitable in the wake of the 1991 Maastricht Treaty. That said, a general convergence in terms of immigration law and policy does not, for Weil, explain immigration outcomes within specific countries. The rationale for specific immigration practices continues to be influenced by state priorities.[24]

To some extent, the 2004 referendum might be represented as a form of convergence with other European states. Ireland's birthright citizenship, it was argued by supporters of the referendum, contravened some European state citizenship norms of qualified rights to citizenship at birth.[25] At the same time, state priorities such as the 1998 Good Friday Agreement influenced the specific proposals put forward. Articles 2 and 3 of the Irish Constitution had been amended as part of the symbolic politics of the 1998 Agreement, followed by the 2001 Citizenship Act.[26] It replaced an all-island claim of sovereignty with a *jus soli* citizenship birthright to all children born on the island of Ireland. The benefit to immigrants was unintentional. In effect the 2004 referendum sought to safeguard the birthright of persons with Irish ancestry while denying, as Germany did, nationality to the children of immigrants. Within this new settlement there were some similarities to German *jus sanguinis* citizenship in the post-Second World War era insofar as it privileged a community-of-descent criterion over one of residence. The Citizenship Referendum proposed an automatic right to citizenship only for Irish-born children of citizens. It removed pre-1998 rights to citizenship of the children of 'non-nationals' born in the Republic of Ireland.

THE POLITICS OF IMMIGRATION

The referendum was held on the same date as the local government elections. It became the main focus of the election campaigns of the two parties in government. Fianna Fáil's campaign was structured around the slogan of 'common sense citizenship'. The campaign of the Progressive Democrats centred on Minister Michael McDowell's claims about the exploitation of Irish maternity health services by immigrant mothers seeking Irish citizenship for their children. In essence, the minister claimed that a crisis in maternity hospitals had been precipitated by the exploitation by 'non-national' mothers of 'loopholes' in the Constitution that allowed them to claim citizenship for their Irish-born children. Minister McDowell argued that in the thirteen months or so since the Supreme Court ruling there had been 'no diminution in the numbers of non-nationals arriving heavily pregnant'.[27] As he put it when the referendum was first mooted in March 2004:

> Our maternity services come under pressure because they have to deal at short notice with women who may have communications difficulties, about whom no previous history of the pregnancy or the mother's health is known, and who in about half the cases of first arrival (according to the Master of the Rotunda, Dr Micheal Geary, as interviewed on RTE during the week) are already at or near labour.[28]

The essence of what the media referred to as the 'baby-tourism' argument was that immigrants stereotyped as asylum seekers were exploiting the Irish health system to gain access to Irish citizenship.[29] The masters of the Rotunda and the Coombe, two maternity hospitals in Dublin, sought to distance themselves from claims repeated on a number of occasions by McDowell 'that they had pleaded with him to deal with the problem', arguing that a lack of funding for maternity services should not be used to introduce a referendum.[30] In contrast, two studies undertaken in 2001 identified cases of extreme material deprivation among asylum seeker mothers and their babies. Both found cases of post-natal malnutrition that necessitated mothers abandoning breast-feeding.[31] It was subsequently confirmed by a civil servant memorandum (prepared for the government in August 2003) that many of those women presenting late and depicted as 'baby tourists' were actually dispersed asylum seekers coming up from rural areas to Dublin maternity hospitals.[32]

Claims by the minister that 'non-nationals' were exploiting maternity services emerged in a context where health service problems had already become highly politicised. As put by a prominent Irish political commentator: 'It is clear that the deliberate unsubstantiated stereotyping of immigrant mothers as exploiting the health services was stage managed to build political support for the idea of the referendum.'[33] Yet cabinet members repeatedly distanced the government from potential accusations of racist intent.[34] As put by Minister McDowell:

> I can reiterate now that the Government campaign in support of the proposal will not be racist because the proposal itself will not be in any way racist. I simply won't allow the proposal to be hijacked by those who wish to further a racist agenda; but equally I will be harsh in my criticism of those on the other end of the political spectrum who claim to detect racism in any action, however rational, fair-minded or soundly based, that affects immigration or citizenship or immigration policy.[35]

The Labour Party argued that holding the referendum on 11 June would encourage racist tendencies during the local and European elections.[36] Fine Gael indicated their support for a 'yes' vote in the referendum but did not campaign on the issue. As expressed by a party spokesperson: 'It's such a complex and sensitive area, there is a danger that by having this referendum on the same day as the local and European elections, it will become a black and white issue, if you forgive the terminology.'[37] As put by one Fianna Fáil councillor who opposed the referendum: 'The proposed referendum is designed to remove what has always been a fundamental right in this State, namely a person's right to citizenship by virtue of birth. The corollary of the proposed change is the underlining and increased supremacy of citizenship by virtue of blood.'[38]

A dissident Progressive Democrat senator, using parliamentary privilege, equated the politics of the 2004 referendum to the exploitation of the asylum issue in North Cork during the 2002 election. This he described as 'a chilling reminder of what happens when individuals turn the sensitive issue of race and citizenship into a political football'.[39] Senator Minihan claimed that Deputy Noel O'Flynn had engaged a politically successful high-profile campaign against asylum seekers and that this resulted in 'a heightening of racial tensions in the city'. The senator described the human cost of such politics:

> A university student visited me in a distressed state. Her father was from Hong Kong, her mother was born and educated in Cork, and resided there. She was as much a Corkonian as I am. However, because of her different ethnic looks, she was now a victim of racial taunts. A mother of two foreign adopted children contacted me. Her children had settled into school and had been in Ireland since they were a few months old. They were now being taunted

in the school yard. Cork people who had married non-nationals who had become integrated into the community, and who had worked and lived in Cork for a number of years, contributing to our society, were now being racially abused. Elderly ladies living alone were in fear of being assaulted or raped by non-nationals who according to myth were rampant on the streets of Cork. This was a result of stirring it up, of playing with people's emotions. Fuelled by some local journalists, the myths and tensions grew.[40]

The referendum proved overwhelmingly popular with the electorate. It was passed with a three to one majority. The extent to which this result was influenced by the 'baby tourism' claims is difficult to ascertain. Despite considerable trenchant criticism of these claims the government, including Minister McDowell, were not politically damaged by allegations of racism. Indeed, the argument put forward by the minister that groups who levelled accusations of racism were irresponsible was generally accepted in media debates.[41]

THE RACIALISATION OF IRISH NATIONALITY?

The 'national/non-national' dualism became prevalent during the early years of this decade when general perceptions of immigrants as asylum seekers had yet to be displaced by perceptions that most asylum seekers were labour migrants. A number of non-pejorative terms emerged within academic and policy discourse during this period, including migrants and ethnic minorities (the category used in the National Anti-Poverty Strategy) and 'new-communities' (used in a number of NGO reports and by some social researchers). However, 'non-national' became institutionalised in official discourse when in 2001 it replaced the term 'alien' in legislation.[42] The term was used by the Department of Justice, Equality and Law Reform in security debates, in reports about crime, human trafficking and illegal immigration, and by the Department of Enterprise and Employment to describe immigrant workers. By 2004 the national/non-national dualism had become the prevalent commonsense conceptual framework for debates about immigration.

This dualism codified debates about belonging within Irish society with primary reference to ideological accounts of an Irish monocultural past. From the late nineteenth century a prevalent 'Irish-Ireland' cultural nationalism at times equated nation with the Irish 'race', emphasising at times the superiority of the Irish and the inferiority of the non-Irish. The linking of race and nation continues to have a degree of resonance in popular Irish discourse. During the twentieth century Jewish, Protestant and Traveller minorities were excluded from the dominant imagined community. Such exclusions were addressed in James Joyce's *Ulysses*, where the character of 'the citizen' calls into question the 'Irishness' of the Jew Leopold Bloom.[43] Present-day racialisations of 'Irishness' have their historical antecedents. The prevalent categorisation of immigrants as 'non-nationals' suggests a cognitive continuity with past nationalist ethnocentrisms.

A second characteristic of the term 'non-national' was the presumed absence of identity it conferred upon those so categorised. Descriptions of immigrants as 'non-nationals' allude to their invisibility within the dominant imagined community, except when they become visible through the evocation of pejorative stereotypes which are then projected onto the immigrant population as a whole. Existing hostility towards asylum seekers and their babies, towards 'baby tourism', can be projected onto the Irish-born children of all immigrants. 'Non-national' also implies that those so categorised are stateless rather than immigrants, with their own distinct histories of belonging and recognition. Statelessness, as Hannah Arendt noted, all too easily becomes equated with a perceived absence of 'a right to rights'.[44] In such terms the presentation of 'non-nationals' as stateless within the jurisdiction of the Irish state exempted them from the republican ideals of 'equal rights, equal treatment and equal opportunities for all' espoused by Fianna Fáil in its reply to the Africa Solidarity Centre survey.

THE RACIALISATION OF POLITICS AND CITIZENSHIP

Minister McDowell's role in precipitating the Citizenship Referendum suggests some parallels with that of Enoch Powell in politicising immigration at a national level in the United Kingdom. Powell's 'Rivers of Blood' speech in 1968 was widely criticised as being racist and inflammatory. Differences between the roles of both can be considered with reference to the literature on the emergence of 'new racism' discourses aimed at circumventing accusations of racist intent.[45] Writings on 'new racism' emphasise how contemporary expressions of racism are coded in language about 'culture'.[46] The avoidance of explicit race narratives becomes a political imperative, as do a degree of public commitment to anti-racism, yet prejudices about racialised groups continues to be exploited for political gain. These may be expressed through the administrative categories that regulate migration. The last decade has witnessed the growing racialisaton of human beings defined exclusively by their inclusion in the administrative category of 'asylum seeker' – in essence a person exercising a right under the 1956 United Nations Convention Relating To The Status of Refugees. What is striking is that this mobilisation of racism, xenophobia and ethnocentrism in politics and law has occurred at a time when social and legal norms opposed to racism and some other forms of discrimination have never seemed so strong.

The racialisation of Irish politics was to some extent expressed as a populist response by the political centre-right mainstream to rapid social change. More than half of the respondents to an Irish attitudinal survey conducted in 2002 believed that minorities increase unemployment, that education suffers due to the presence of minorities and that minorities were given preference in obtaining local authority housing. Almost 70 per cent considered that minorities abuse social welfare. In each case the percentages endorsing these negative statements had risen from 1997 when a Eurobarometer survey posed the same questions. Such findings have considerable implications for Irish politics. So too do indications that the referendum precipitated a significant increase in racist incidents.[47]

McDowell's populism, unlike Powell's, frequently emphasised the economic benefits of immigration. It sought to undermine potential immigrant dependency. The Irish 'Celtic Tiger' case for immigration to some extent emphasised the disposability of immigrant workers. This was evident in government unwillingness to reform a non-transferable work permit system which had been much criticised for fostering the exploitation of immigrants. In Ireland, as in Britain, the accession of the new EU member states (one month prior to the referendum) was accompanied by a time-limited prohibition on welfare entitlements designed to prevent 'welfare tourism'. The narrowing of citizenship due to the 2004 constitutional resettlement occurred in parallel with the explicit linking, for the first time, of some welfare entitlements to citizenship.

It must be noted that a number of key social rights, such as rights to welfare, were not restricted to citizens under the 1937 Constitution.[48] In other words the *jus soli* formulation of citizenship outlined by the 1937 Constitution was reflected in welfare practices which linked entitlements to residency. Domicile, rather than citizenship, underpinned a longstanding welfare settlement. For example, the 1993 Social Welfare (Consolidation) Act set out a statutory right to supplementary welfare allowance (SWA) which extends beyond citizenship. Section 171 of the

Act states that: 'Subject to this Act, every person in the State whose means are insufficient to meet his needs and the needs of every child dependant of his shall be entitled to SWA.'[49] Under Section 180(1) of the Act, health boards were charged with assessing entitlement to SWA on the basis of the needs of the person.

Christian Joppke argues that in society with well-developed social rights citizenship becomes a precondition of inclusion. Yet he suggests that the gap between social citizenship (rights to welfare goods and services) and social membership is most problematic where social citizenship is most developed.[50] Gradations of rights between citizens and non-citizens, immigrant 'guest' workers, 'illegal' workers, refugees and asylum seekers have emerged in a number of Western countries that as recently as a century ago operated few restrictions on immigration. In such a context citizenship becomes not just a set of rights but also a mechanism of exclusion. It becomes a mechanism of civic stratification, a form of inequality in which groups of people are differentiated by the legitimate claims they can make on the state. In the Irish case, the introduction of 'direct provision' in 2000 shifted the basis of SWA entitlement from domicile to citizenship. The 2004 Social Welfare (Miscellaneous Provisions) Act removed entitlements to children's allowances and other non-contributory benefits previously available on a universal domiciliary basis. However, in February 2006 the government acknowledged that EU law (EU 1408 of 1971) imposed reciprocal obligations on EU state to recognise the entitlements of citizens from other EU countries resident in their own countries. This meant that the removal of entitlements set out under the 2004 Act could not apply to immigrants from EU countries. However, the two-year residency eligibility criteria introduced by the Act continues to apply to immigrants from non-EU countries.

CONCLUSION

The overwhelming endorsement of the 2004 Citizenship Referendum by the Irish electorate (by more than 80 per cent of voters in the 11 June election) occurred for a number of reasons. First, that a racialised conception of citizenship was articulated within populist political responses to immigration. This was anchored in past exclusionary monocultural nation-building ideologies of Irishness. Here the new 'commonsense citizenship' proposed by the government ideologically reflected the established nation-state. Central to this was a recurring distinction between the legitimacy of claims by nationals and non-nationals

upon the nation-state. The break with *jus soli* citizenship followed a
series of measures that undermined established domiciliary entitlements
to which non-citizen immigrants were entitled. Here, social citizenship
has become coterminous with political citizenship and shaped by reciprocal rights enjoyed by citizens of EU member states but not by other
immigrants such as Africans.

Second, the referendum result reflected an ethnic nepotism of Irish
politics. To some limited extent activism, including action-research by
the Africa Solidarity Centre, promoted new norms of responsiveness to
immigrants and ethnic minorities. It also promoted some awareness of
the political necessity of acknowledging racism and institutional barriers
within political parties. The most striking outcome of the research was
the prompt removal of the prohibition on people who were not Irish or
EU member state citizens (reported in the media as a ban on 'non-
nationals') becoming members of the Progressive Democrats at the
instigation of Michael McDowell. The ASC research also indicated a
disjuncture between a degree of willingness to promote political inclu-
sively and the perceived populist political imperative of undermining
political and social citizenship rights. Here, the entitlement of some
immigrant non-citizens to vote in local government elections and stand
for election allowed for a crucial challenge to the dualism of 'national'
and 'non-national' at a time when the proportion of immigrants who
are entitled to apply for citizenship was low. Following the referendum,
new legislation allowed for immigrants to apply for citizenship after
three years' residency.[51] Future Irish elections are likely to include
greater numbers of immigrant citizen voters and candidates and as such
contest the ethnic distinction between 'national' and 'non-national' that
shaped the politics of the 2004 referendum.

Third, the exclusionary politics of the referendum reflected a culture
of anxiety arising from past distributional conflicts where outsiders
were defined by economic rather than ethnic status. This history of economic 'othering' – and its cultural and ideological centrality to nation-
building – suggests that support for 'commonsense' restrictions on citizenship cannot be explained solely in terms of racism and nationalist
ethnic chauvinism.

To some extent the 2004 politics of immigration were structured by
tensions between domiciliary rights – including the right to vote in local
government elections – and citizenship rights. The ASC research sought
to foster domiciliary political responsiveness to recently established
immigrant communities so as to contest the 'national/non-national'
dualism which partially moulded political responses to immigration

and, as such, challenge the absence of identity presumed by the 'non-national' archetype. The successes of this immigrant politics of recognition occurred outside the political mainstream where two candidates were elected as independents and a small cohort of seasoned immigrant candidates had emerged. At a pre-referendum seminar organised by the ASC one subsequently unsuccessful candidate described her ambition to become the first Nigerian woman elected to the Dáil. She also recounted how her election agent had defected from Fine Gael to manage her campaign because as the Irish grandmother of 'a mixed race child' she could not support the party's support of the referendum. Such solidarities, no less than the anticipated growth in the numbers of citizen immigrants, suggest an inevitable degree of future mutability in distinctions between 'nationals' and 'non-nationals' if not between citizens and non-citizens.

CHAPTER NINE

The Rules of Belonging

It is a cliché to describe the past as a foreign country. To some extent everyone can be a foreigner in their country of origin, citizenship or domicile. The nation-states that emerged in the modern West were somewhat like the big brand names, the multiples that homogenised the high streets and squeezed out many idiosyncratic small shops. Like other nation-states the Republic of Ireland was preceded by the emergence of mass ideas of identity and belonging. These were sustained by mass literacy and education. It became possible to conceive of an identity that was shared with someone living at the other end of the country. People who would never meet came to define their Irishness in the same way. At the same time, they could label 'others' they actually lived alongside as not really Irish. Human beings in all their diversity can become subordinated to dominant ideal formulations of national citizenship, of religious denomination, of ethnocentric tribe or of rule-bound social movement. They may be judged and found wanting by the Platonic ideals of 'real' nationalism, 'real' religion and 'real' cultural authenticity. Ideals of belonging encroach like the shadows in Plato's cave on the flesh and blood world of day-to-day existence. Such ideals may well shelter some within the cave but also insist that others are not really British, not really Irish, not really feminist or not true believers in a particular religion. Identity imposes orthodoxies slaved to ideals of belonging.

What Phillip Larkin said about families – 'They fuck you up, your mum and dad' – sometimes holds for motherlands and fatherlands. The Irish nation-state was forged out of violence. 'We may,' Patrick Pearse wrote in *The Coming Revolution*, 'make mistakes and shoot the wrong people; but bloodshed is a cleansing and a sanctifying thing, and a nation which regards it as the final horror has lost its manhood.'[1] During the late 1970s intellectual nationalists of different shades of green interrogated what Richard Kearney influentially described as the

Irish Mind, an atavistic collective unconscious depicted in Jungian terms as somehow intrinsically authentic and distinctive.[2] Identity so understood is strong stuff, a family quarrel with no place for outsiders, intellectual or otherwise, and no room for disloyalty or dissent. Thirty years later, in the belligerent post-11 September 2001 world of homeland security, wars of terror and wars on terror, the relationships between identity and intolerance have become everyone's urgent business. As recently put by Amartya Sen in *Identity and Violence: The Illusion of Destiny*, the so-called clash of civilisations serves to classify and incarcerate people within rigid conceptual boxes.[3]

To come to terms with ethnocentrism, racism or sectarianism is to confront the shortcomings of one's own tribe. The writers who would engage with the foibles of their own nation or ethnic group – be it Orhan Pamuk today or Seán Ó Faoláin during the 1940s – might find themselves censored or censured at home then maybe readmitted posthumously like James Joyce on foot of outside recognition, as iconic proof of the greatness of the people from which they had sprung. A willingness to engage with the capacity of one's own tribe (however defined) to exclude or discriminate is crucial to addressing problems such as racism and discrimination. All peoples, all nations and all societies – whatever their own histories of being oppressed – are capable of oppressing those they define as others. It is not possible to paper over the cracks by saying that your own people's history of being oppressed means you cannot oppress others. Post-colonial claims of mutual solidarity between different societies with a history of oppression play well as ideological politics but when tested – say by the presence of migrants from other colonised countries – may perform poorly as a basis for facing up to the racism and discrimination one's own society is capable of. In the Republic of Ireland, as elsewhere, dominant ideas of social membership emerged at a cost to minorities. Those perceived as deviant from the norms of the dominant 'imagined community' – and of the Constitution and laws that institutionalised these – were required to choose between assimilation (the surrender of visible difference as the price of social membership) or rejection. To look at the social history of the Republic of Ireland from this perspective is to challenge comfortable orthodoxies. A focus on the Republic of Ireland's specific history of excluding minorities might well be denigrated as 'revisionist'. Accounts, for instance, of the murders of Protestant and Traveller civilians in west Cork by IRA fighters during the War of Independence and Civil War pose considerable challenges to national myths about emancipation.[4] Studies of the experiences of Jewish refugees before, during and after the Holocaust, as distinct from the invented experiences of Joyce's imaginary Irish Jew, demonstrate that Ireland was by no means exempt from the anti-Semitism common in other European nations. These suggest that ethnic nationalism, anti-colonialist or otherwise, can be at odds with anti-racist aspirations or, at the very least, will have a hard time reconciling a real Irish society in all its diversity with an imagined Ireland rooted in the past and the legacy of real sectarianisms. Joyce's *Ulysses* contains a definition of a nation as 'the same people living in the same place'. The reality is that nation-states have tended to subordinate difference to national ideals of homogeneity. Small minorities might find themselves written out of history, swallowed up like corner-shops in the face of the big brand names.

This has been part of modernity, part of nation-building. It is important to understand the mechanics of such exclusions in coming to terms with the challenges of integrating new immigrants. In 1904 Fr Creagh urged a boycott against the Limerick Jewish community. Creagh combined the then prevalent secular European anti-Semitisms that depicted Jews as enemies of nation-states with religious anti-Semitism. He portrayed the Jews as oppressors of the Irish people. Under Creagh's Catholic nationalist formula anti-Semitism was represented as contributing to the emancipation of the 'Irish'. He cast the Jews as oppressors of the Irish 'worse than Cromwell'. In post-independence Ireland Jews became officially defined as a threat to the state before, during and after the Holocaust. For instance, a Department of Justice memorandum, dated 28 February 1953, noted a policy of official anti-Semitism: 'In the administration of the alien laws it has always been recognised in the Departments of Justice, Industry and Commerce and External Affairs that the question of the admission of aliens of Jewish blood presents a special problem and the alien laws have been administered less liberally in their case.'[5]

A key plank of racist politics is the proposition that vulnerable minorities somehow oppress the dominant group. Anti-Semitism within Irish nationalism drew on the language of anti-colonialism. Irish anti-colonialism no less than 'imperialism' can play host to nativism, ethnocentrism and racism. Overt racism is often piously despised within the political mainstream yet the old sour wine has been poured into the new bottles of the West versus the rest, Fortress Europe and Irish distinctions between 'nationals' and 'non-nationals' rooted in stereotypes of despised asylum seeker mothers and their 'non-Irish' Irish-born children. The concern remains that anxieties about social change become exploited by populist politics that mobilise racism and ethnocentrism to offer simple answers to complex questions.

Ethnocentrism has acquired a new credibility in the wake of 11 September 2001. Multiculturalism has been attacked from the left and right. Public intellectuals such as David Goodhart, the editor of *Prospect*, tell us that 'ethnic nepotism' is natural and that welfare solidarities do not work in diverse societies. Multiculturalism has to some extent been supplanted by a new muscular liberalism that proposes that the big Western tribe must (again) become intolerant of the rest. An American advocate of this muscular liberalism, the philosopher Richard Rorty, writing in 1994 described his position as one of anti-anti-ethnocentrism.[6] It scorned efforts by liberals to extend pluralism to include those who do not share their beliefs. Rorty argued that Western liberals should 'accept the fact that we have to start from where we are, and this means that there are lots of views which we cannot take seriously'.[7] He argued that Western liberals get themselves into a bind because their beliefs pull them in two incompatible directions. On one hand they possess no doubts about human equality. On the other they become aware that most of the world does not share their values. They cannot, as he puts it, stick up for their beliefs without getting in a muddle or without choosing to be ethnocentric.[8] An early definition of ethnocentrism offered by Theodor Adorno was to regard one's own group as normal and others, by comparison, as strange and inferior.[9] It is often suggested that ethnocentrism is natural because human societies tend to be suspicious of outsiders.[10] However, the stereotypes that sustain ethnocentrism are often implausible, whether they are applied by nationalists to the presumed enemies of nations or by liberals to presumed enemies of freedom.

Isaiah Berlin has offered a liberal understanding of pluralism that contrasts with Rorty's case for ethnocentric solidarity. Berlin insisted that it is important to recognise the existence of a plurality of differing human ideals and values. He advocated a pluralist liberalism that permitted the pursuit of plural ideals and values. Berlin argued that it is important to acknowledge the existence of a plurality of differing human ideals and values. He considered that their character and their pursuit are part of what it means to be a human being. He depicted multiple yet finite values as part of the essence of humanity rather than arbitrary creations of mankind's subjective fancies. Berlin was no relativist. He argued that we may well find a particular way of life intolerable but we must never forget to recognise it as a human pursuit:

> If I am a man or a woman with sufficient imagination (and this I do need), I can enter into a value-system which is not my own, but

which is nevertheless something I can conceive of men pursuing while remaining human, while remaining creatures with whom I can communicate, with whom I have common values – for all human beings have common values or they cease to be human, and also some different values else they cease to differ, as in fact they do.[11]

The essence of Berlin's pluralism was not a willingness to surrender one's own values but an unwillingness to ever forget that other values are, for those who hold them, objective expressions of their humanity.[12] Solidarity is inconceivable without empathy. Empathy sometimes amounts to understanding some connection between one's own fate and that of others or, at least, perceiving others from some recognisable vantage point. Here art can have a powerful role. This article was prompted by a film installation by Jackie Doyle that was commissioned by the Belfast Film Festival in 2005. *Connections* consisted of a bank of television screens typical of an airport departure lounge. Information on flight destinations gave way to short overlapping films where forced migrants told stories of torture, persecution and consequent trauma. The central device of Doyle's installation was simple. Actors with Northern Irish accents narrated the testimonies of forced migrants from other countries and vice versa. Foreknowledge of the punch line – human stories of oppression and exclusion can be interchangeable – in no way lessened the visceral impact of the piece. At the time of writing (May 2006) forty-one 'asylum seekers' from Afghanistan had just ended a hunger strike in St Patrick's cathedral in Dublin. Their protest was timed to coincide with the twenty-fifth anniversary of the IRA hunger strikes in the North. It too could be seen as a conscious effort to create an Irish connection; to penetrate the Irish Mind, so to speak. However, making such connections is never easy for racialised groups.

This, for me, is Jackie Doyle's point and what is missed by Isaiah Berlin's liberal humanist bonhomie. Their problem, one shared with the real forced migrants whose stories were presented by Doyle, is that recognition of their humanity is mediated by nation-state politics of belonging. For Hannah Arendt the big practical problem with human rights was the absence of a 'right to rights'.[13] Arendt understood that, empirically (what is, rather than what ought to be), rights spring from membership of a nation-state rather than from the human condition. She argued that those exempted in one way or another from citizenship found no protection in the abstract nakedness of being human. As she put it in her book, *The Origins of Totalitarianism*, drawing on the Irish political theorist Edmund Burke: 'The survivors of the extermination camps, the inmates of concentration and interment camps, and even the comparatively happy stateless people could see without Edmund Burke's arguments that the abstract nakedness of being nothing but human was their greatest danger.'[14] Human rights depend, as such, upon what states (and their citizens) will or will not do about them.

The Republic of Ireland must begin the business of integrating or otherwise coming to terms with the one in ten living in Irish society who were not born there. It must do so in the knowledge that an unwillingness or inability to integrate immigrants sets up big problems for the future. It must do so in the knowledge that the efforts of other countries have often been flawed. It must do so knowing that integration cannot be bought off the shelf but must be grounded in local effort. Engagement with the local rules of belonging is required. Existing national ideas of belonging are a necessary starting place but so too is recognition of how past and present rules of Irishness have failed indigenous minorities.

To date, the integration of immigrants has been for the most part restricted to the economy. The grocer's republic, to borrow loosely from Yeats, now exists within a globalised economy that brings large numbers of workers with scant thought about where they will fit within Irish society. Everything we know about human migration leads us to expect that many will be here for good. Everything we know about the experiences of other immigrant societies tells us that we have a vested interest in their success. To paraphrase John Rawls, our fates are intertwined; the fates of their children and our children even more so. For this reason alone ethnic nepotism – excluding emigrants from social rights and entitlements – makes little practical sense. However, the experiences of other countries tell us that even when rights are extended to immigrants all sorts of dangerous institutional barriers can persist. These have everything to do with culture and identity. Difference is all too often portrayed as deviance from dominant cultural norms and this in turn gives licence to discrimination.

In Ireland, as elsewhere, a reckoning with dominant ideas of belonging cannot be avoided. Engagement with these seems to be crucial if projects for securing the integration of immigrants are to have any political legitimacy. Yet in the Republic of Ireland, no less than the United Kingdom (where there has been a Commission on the Future of Multi-Ethnic Britain), the precise national identity that immigrants are required to engage with is somewhat unclear. In France, a republican ideal of equal citizenship represents the state as culturally neutral. It has become all too clear that this republicanism is ethnocentric and that its hidden purpose has been the assimilation rather than the integration of immigrants. In the Irish case the big question is whether republican conceptions of equal citizenship can transcend its ethnic nationalist past. Martin McGuinness has spoken of the need to persuade, as he puts it, 'our people' of the unionist tradition 'that they are a cherished part of the Irish nation' who 'will not have to give up anything they cherish in what will be a multicultural, multiracial, multilingual secular society'.[15]

The problem here is that one person's inclusionary republicanism is another person's ethnocentric monoculturalism. There is more to the business of integrating immigrants than convincing them to get in touch with their inner Irishman or Irishwoman – saying that you can have your multiculturalism any colour you like as long as it is green.

CHAPTER TEN

The Fighting Irish

There is a need when coming to terms with questions about integration – especially the big one: integration into what? – to face up to the extent to which the whole business of Irishness has been such a bitterly contested one within the intellectual politics of the last generation. A flavour of how and to what extent Irish intellectuals bicker among themselves about who they are is suggested by the following, originally published as a review of a 2005 collection of essays on Edmund Burke by Seamus Deane. The dilemmas it identifies for Irish academic and intellectual engagement with questions of belonging thrown up by immigration are signalled in a postscript.

Deane's first published essay on Burke appeared, auspiciously enough, in 1968, that year of campus revolution and new social movements. *Foreign Affections: Essays on Burke* assembles thirteen previous essays and lectures into nine chapters. Burke then is very much a sustained preoccupation within Deane's 'Irish Studies' oeuvre.[1] The new essays are chronologically divided into meditations about thinkers who preceded Burke, most notably Montesquieu but also Swift and Diderot and thinkers who came after him, notably Lord Acton and Cardinal Newman; that is, possible influences on Burke followed by some considerations of his legacy.

The question that most often comes to the fore in *Foreign Affections* is whether liberty is compatible with colonial rule? *Yes*, answered Burke, unless such rule escaped the rule of law and was replaced by arbitrary power. This answer, for Burke, endorsed revolution in America but not elsewhere, Deane argues, where colonial atrocity was condoned while revolutionary violence condemned. Deane casts Burke as a reluctant critic of colonial atrocity. His focus though is not on teasing out the ambiguity of Burke's positions on political legitimacy, empire and the Irish question. Rather his position is one of general antipathy to both Burke and what Deane thinks is Burke's political legacy, a liberal anti-revolutionary position on violence and progress. Something gets conflated at times between what can be fairly attributed to Burke and to what might be construed as part of Burke's broader legacy. Deane's engagement with both occurs through the 'Irish Studies' lens of the present-day Catholic nationalist post-colonialist thought. Orwell's dictum that whoever controls the past controls the present and whoever controls the present controls the future comes to mind. Insofar as this applies to Irish historiography it also applies to readings of literature and political philosophy. The account of Burke presented here is never less than partisan and is sometimes sectarian.

Foreign Affections makes no reference whatsoever to the main competing text that has placed Burke's preoccupations about the Irish question at its centre. Conor Cruise O'Brien's *The Great Melody: A Thematic Biography of Edmund Burke* gains entry to Deane's bibliography but is not mentioned in *Foreign Affections*.[2] There is no reference to O'Brien in the index despite the prominence of his efforts to rehabilitate Burke. This is a glaring omission and obviously a deliberate one, the petulance of which undermines the creditability of Deane's scholarship. Deane and O'Brien have for decades prowled the battlefields of the culture wars that have shaped the school of 'Irish Studies' built by the former. Both represent implacably opposed intellectual positions on the Irish question. Deane's approach to the matter suggests the pretended indifference of a family feud (Do not mention his name. I will not hear his name spoken in this house). Almost thirty years ago in *The Crane Bag*, an Irish journal that aspired to the sort of intellectual conversation avoided here, Deane dismissed O'Brien's 'liberal humanism' and introduced some of the criticisms of Burke found in *Foreign Affections*. This dismissal occurred in a debate between Deane and Seamus Heaney published in 1977.

'Do you not think,' Deane asked Heaney, 'that the kind of humanism which Conor Cruise O'Brien sponsors is precisely that kind of humanism, totally detached from its atavisms, which, though welcome from a rational point of view, renders much of what he says either irrelevant or wrong; particularly in relation to the North where bigotry is so much part of the psyche?' The obstinate voice of rationalist humanism, Heaney retorted, was important for if that was lost everything was lost. He argued that O'Brien did an utterly necessary job in rebuking all easy thought about the Protestant community in the North: 'It is to be seen in this way: seven or eight years ago there was tremendous sentiment for Catholics in the North among intellectuals, politicians and ordinary people in the South. Because of his statements O'Brien is still reviled by people who held these sentiments; yet now these people harbour sentiments which mirror O'Brien's thinking, and still they do not cede to the clarity or the validity of his position.'[3] But surely, Deane objected, did not O'Brien's 'bourgeois form of humanism' impose a rational clarity upon the Northern position that was untrue to the reality? Heaney replied that O'Brien's real force was in the South rather than the North: 'It is not enough for people to simply say "ah, they're all Irishmen" when some Northerners actually spit at the word Irishman.' O'Brien's contribution was an obstinate insistence on facing up to this kind of reality.[4]

Deane wrote explicitly about Burke for an issue of *The Crane Bag* that he edited in 1978. Curiously, the piece, entitled *An Example of Tradition*, is not listed among those reworked for *Foreign Affections*. It emphasised the revival of Edmund Burke's writings on Ireland by Matthew Arnold and the centrality of Burke to nineteenth-century liberal-thinking Ireland; for instance the thinking that led to the repeal of the Penal Laws and efforts to kill home rule with kindness between 1891 and 1914. In 1881 Arnold produced an anthology, *Edmund Burke on Irish Affairs*, and argued in its preface for a degree of Celtic cultural independence.[5] Deane cast Arnold (and Burke by association) as parent to the subsequently prevalent archetype of the vitalic 'Celt as dreamer, imaginative, unblessed by the Greek sense of form, at home in wild landscapes' and so as the antithesis of Europe's anxious anaemic political and social modernity. Arnold's idealisation of the Celtic race, according to Deane, informed a sectarian and even racial conception of Irishness. This, he maintained, was distinct from the Anglo-Irish tradition that W.B. Yeats created out of Swift, Berkeley, Goldsmith and Burke. It was distinct from the heroic revolutionary tradition that Pearse created out of Wolfe Tone and Robert Emmet. Through Arnold, Deane argued, a notion of Celtic Ireland had 'removed itself to Britain, encased in Burke's capricious reputation', to later return as an unlikely (and presumably inauthentic) influence on the Irish literary revival.[6]

In *Foreign Affections* Deane outlines Burke's positions on political legitimacy, colonialism and the plight of the Catholic Irish under the Penal Laws. He quotes a contemporary account by Tom Paine – one accepted by Burke – which maintains that Burke would defend the British Constitution in its entirety, 'loaded with all its incumbrances, clogged with its peers, and its beef; its parsons and its pudding, its commons, its beer, its dull slavish liberty of going about just as one pleases'. Deane explains this as an argument that the Constitution of England, the old Constitution of France, European civilisation in all its faults, disorders and incoherence accorded with the unpredictable and complex nature of history and the human person. These amounted to a social complex order that could be discerned but never properly understood. Its complexity could be fatally disrupted if it were to be replaced by an artificial man-made order. Burke feared that the result would be despotic and dehumanising. Revolution, the surrender of experience to abstract principle, amounted to the surrender of civilisation (however flawed) to barbarism.

For Deane, the British liberty defended by Burke, as exported to Ireland, was 'the exclusive preserve of colonists'. Burke opposed the Penal Laws yet legitimised the system that imposed them. This disjuncture is at the heart of Deane's difficulty with Burke. As he put it: 'The late attacks of 1792 on the Penal Laws in Ireland are of a piece with his earlier writings, they remain almost entirely free of the new version of political obedience that he forged for his anti-revolutionary philosophy.' The question, then, answered differently by Burke and Deane, is whether one can oppose tyranny without having a revolution. For those who answer in the affirmative (and no doubt it is easier to do if one has not experienced tyranny) Burke will always be an attractive figure. Not so for those for whom the answer is no.

The chapter on Newman exemplifies Deane's approach at its most nuanced. His thesis is evident in the title: 'Newman: Converting the Empire'. It links Newman's championing of Catholic institutions in Ireland with a mission of Catholic colonial expansion. The connection with Burke concerns first his views about the ambiguity of both vis-à-vis British imperialism. Deane also views Newman as an inheritor of Burke's views about universalism and counter-revolution. For Burke legitimacy depended much upon tradition. Deane draws parallels with Newman's theology on the legitimacy of the pre-Reformation universal church. For both, Deane suggests, counter-revolutions could never reinstate worlds that had earlier been lost. They could only pretend to do so while inaugurating new ones. Deane likens Newman's pursuit of the liberty of Catholics in Ireland to Burke's efforts. However, he views both as imperial crusaders. Neither opposed the legitimacy of empire, be it in Ireland or elsewhere.

Deane acknowledges the scope of Burke's concern about colonial oppression. However, he contentiously states that this concern is incoherent and can be intellectually dismissed. His case is that Burke's claims about 'an external conspiracy of illuminati, philosophers and Freemasons to overthrow the altar and throne in Europe' discredit the main planks of his thought. Deane's dismissal is pretty much an absolute one. To put it colloquially, if Burke subscribed to the flaky conspiracy theories of his day, then:

> Burke is not to be taken seriously as a political thinker, especially on Irish affairs. As an intellectual, or a rhetoritician, or as a hired gun for the Whigs, or as an apologist for the Irish Catholics, the French émigrés or the Begum of Outh, he is too partisan to be reliable.

This is much the same as arguing that Newton's theory of gravitation must be false because Newton believed in alchemy. The damning reference to Burke's allegedly crackpot beliefs reads like a textbook example of an *ad hominom* argument. The reader is offered no footnote, no context, not even a secondary reference. Deane uses the term 'conspiracy' here but there is no entry in the index for the term (nor ones for illuminati or Freemasons) to help the perplexed reader. As for the judgement about Burke's partisanship, the problem with this line of attack is that it always cuts both ways. To illustrate this, just change the reference to eighteenth-century Whigs into one about twentieth-century Northern Irish nationalists and replace Burke's foreign affections with present-day post-colonial colonial preoccupations. Similar dismissive tactics are employed elsewhere in the book. For instance, the first page of Deane's opening chapter refers to 'routine' assessments of Burke's thought. He provides just the one example, this from Luke Gibbons, the author of another volume in the same Critical Conditions: Field Day 'Irish Studies' series that includes *Foreign Affairs*. The supposed 'routine' verdict is that Burke did not clarify the philosophical foundations of his thought; 'either because he was a practising politician, and not that way inclined, or because his thought was so confused, his betrayal of principle so stark that these foundations could not but have been murky'.

In his introduction to a subsequent chapter – one entitled 'Freedom Betrayed' – Deane notes that Burke, like Adam Smith, became incorporated by the likes of F.A. Hayek into 'the Manichean view of history that prevailed during the Cold War'. This observation is an interesting starting point but is not developed any further than throwaway attacks mentioned above. The parallel between present-day appropriations of Smith and Burke, not discussed by Deane, warrant consideration. John Kenneth Galbraith has argued that Smith, as a moral philosopher, would not have approved of the present-day neo-liberal idealisation of market forces that have become linked to his name.[7] Smith's moral philosophy emphasised the interdependence of people in society. His opposition to eighteenth-century trade barriers emerged in a specific context. Galbraith argues that his position on laissez faire might well have been different had he lived a century later.

Similar arguments might be made in the case of Burke. Neither can be blamed for whatever Manichean world-view held by those who would appropriate them posthumously. Deane tellingly quotes an assessment of Burke quoted from Thomas Moore's 1825 biography of Richard Brinsley Sheridan:

> Burke was mighty in either camp; and it would have taken *two* great men to effect what he, by this division of himself, achieved. His mind, indeed, lies parted asunder in his works, like some vast continent severed by a convulsion of nature, each portion peopled by its own giant race of opinions, differing altogether in features and language, and committed to eternal hostility to each other.

Deane identifies two Burkes – one who is the defender of liberty, another the betrayer of liberal causes – but likes neither. More sympathetic readings of Burke, especially the Burke of Irish affairs, are ignored. *Foreign Affairs*, in addressing just one side of the story, fails both.

POSTSCRIPT

The fighting Irish, Deane and O'Brien, have both sought to arbitrate who could legitimately define themselves as Irish and under what terms. Deane's post-colonial studies project was to 'remind the Southern state of what it has forgotten or betrayed in Northern Ireland'.[8] O'Brien sought to challenge nationalist aspirations for a United Ireland that would ignore those of Unionists. However, the nationalists he criticised hardly recognised themselves in his depiction of them. O'Brien's assault on their shibboleths was experienced as cultural intolerance. Yet, as Ernest Gellner has observed, O'Brien was no less trapped in the same hall of mirrors as those nationalists he criticised. He could not stand back from the presumption that nationality was *the* basis of identity and solidarity rather than a relatively recent historical invention.[9] It was as a heretic rather than as a heathen that he set himself against some of its dogmas.

Post-colonial Irish studies grew out of the Field Day Company that did much to reinvigorate Irish theatre; notably through plays of Brian Friel, from *Translations* (1980) onwards. Field Day published a number of influential pamphlets, including ones from Edward Said, Fredric Jameson and Terry Eagleton, that in Jon Cleary's summary situated modern Irish culture 'within the context of colonialism, imperialism and anti-colonial nationalism'.[10] This movement grew in influence during the 1990s, notably through the work of Declan Kiberd and Luke Gibbons.[11] Cleary depicts the post-colonial movement as a challenge to the modernisation perspectives that accompanied revisionism in the Republic of Ireland. These, he argues, bundled reactionary nationalism and Catholic conservatism together as dysfunctional enemies of economic and social modernisation. But the main intellectual achievement of post-colonial Irish Studies, Cleary suggests, was to challenge the denigration of nationalism as reactionary and sectarian, and instead represent it as the basis of social and political emancipation in common cause with anti-colonialist and anti-imperialist liberation movements, therefore in solidarity with oppressed peoples elsewhere.[12]

For its critics, notably Stephen Howe, the insertion of Ireland into wider arguments about imperialism and decolonisation using what has come to be known as colonial discourse analysis has often been superficial. Howe argues this presents the coloniser and the colonised in terms of Manichean stereotypes and polar antithesis.[13] This way of thinking about culture and society all too easily denigrates those like O'Brien whose purpose was to play rogue devil's advocate to his own tribe. That said, the tribe was by no means homogenous. O'Brien was born into a Catholic elite that expected their moment to come within a home rule parliament. The 1916 revolution scuppered that.[14] Perhaps it was this sense of displacement that opened him up subsequently to unionist anxieties. Deane's experiences of growing up in Derry's Bogside (evoked in his fine novel, *Reading in the Dark*) provided a very different vantage point.[15] In some respects their experiences of being Irish were very different indeed. These were perhaps no less profound that those between some Westerners and some Muslims now stereotyped as a clash of civilisations. O'Brien's liberalism, for all that criticised intolerance, was vehemently intolerant. For instance, in a 1978 memorial lecture for Christopher Ewart-Biggs, the British ambassador killed by the IRA, he referred to the 17.1 per cent of Irish identified in a survey as having anti-British attitudes as 'either intellectually retarded or emotionally disturbed'.[16] Deane's much-cited 1977 criticism of O'Brien as seeking to impose a rational clarity upon the Northern conflict is telling here. O'Brien, a cosmopolitan Irishman, 'a voice of sanity in the Irish mess', gained kudos for explaining to the wider Western world just how irrational Irish nationalists were for 'raking dead fires'.[17] The differences on both sides were ontological as well as political. Post-colonial critics shared the perspective of an earlier generation of

Romantic nationalist intellectuals, notably Daniel Corkery, which presented the Enlightenment as a colonial imposition upon native Irish culture.[18] The post-colonial analysis drew attention to the past racialisation of the Irish as feckless and irrational. Not unreasonably, it experienced criticism from O'Brien as cultural disparagement. This very sensitivity may well prove an asset that counsels against being blindsided by present-day ethnocentric liberal revulsion toward Islam, the Roma, Travellers and other groups 'irrationally' out of step with Western modernity. Such experiences of being disparaged constitute a potential basis of post-colonial nationalist solidarity with some new guests of the nation. However, a proprietary claim to victimhood all too easily condones xenophobia. The Catholic Irish were beleaguered in Northern Ireland. In the Republic they ruled the roost. The next chapter explores how fealty to post-colonial orthodoxies can obscure ethnic nepotism in this latter context.

CHAPTER ELEVEN

Against the 'Racial State'

Efforts to understand racism in the Republic of Ireland have inevitably appropriated ideas and concepts originating elsewhere. Sometimes events in other countries have affected Irish sensibilities. For example, during the 1980s some Dunnes Stores workers endured a long strike aimed at promoting a boycott against imports from apartheid South Africa. More than a decade earlier the civil rights movement in Northern Ireland was inspired by the American civil rights movement opposed to racial segregation in the United States. For decades Irish readers have had some access to the conceptual toolkits for addressing racism developed elsewhere. For example, in a 1951 review for *Studies*, Daniel Lyons S.J. sought to explain the workings of racism in the United States and the scale of political, economic and social injustices faced by what are now called African Americans. He explained the prejudice they encountered ('a whole framework of theories against the Negro' that allowed them to be treated as inferior) as efforts to rationalise the consequence of these injustices. They were stereotyped as criminal but 'their paltry thievery reflects mainly on the white society that subjects them to severe economic discrimination'.[1] Gradually such understandings of how inequalities were justified and perpetuated by prejudice began to impact on Irish social justice debates.

By the 1970s the international debate about racism had broadened out to include ethnic minorities like the Irish in Britain. These, like victims of anti-Semitism, were understood to encounter *racialised* processes of prejudice and discrimination. Here justifications for prejudice were seen to shift from claims about intrinsic biological inferiority to stereotypes that claimed intrinsic cultural inferiority. The growth of immigration has prompted academic efforts to understanding racism and *racialised* discrimination in the Irish case. In a nutshell these have sought to understand how the Irish experience is similar to and distinctive from what has transpired elsewhere. Of course, much depends on which understandings of the Irish experience prevail. The focus of this chapter is on the shortcomings of current academic efforts to conceptualise racism in the Irish context. Two interrelated tendencies warrant concern. The first uncritically imports theories of state racism without treating these as propositions to be tested empirically in the Irish case. The second, at its simplest, portrays racism as an import and remains in denial about indigenous forms of exclusion emanating from local identity politics.

COLONIALISM AND THE 'RACIAL STATE'

Ireland did not have an empire but the Irish helped administer one and, in doing so, inevitably imbibed beliefs about racial inferiority than justified Western imperialism. Noel Ignatiev, in *How the Irish Became White*, examines accounts of complaints by nineteenth-century Irish immigrants, fresh off the boat in Boston, that 'coloured people did not know their place'.[2] The Republic of Ireland, all this suggests, came into being with the software of Western racism preloaded. This might, for instance, account for the experiences of recent African immigrants, noted in survey after survey, of very high levels of racist incidents. The software kicked in when they arrived.

A recent effort to conceptualise Irish racism, *After Optimism? Ireland, Racism and Globalisation* by Ronit Lentin and Robbie McVeigh, falls within this school. Their core argument, using a concept developed by David Goldberg, depicts the Republic of Ireland as a *racial state* in the process of becoming a racist state.[3] Goldberg argues that race is integral to the emergence, development and transformation (conceptually, philosophically, materially) of the modern nation-state.[4] Nation-states, he continues, were initially conceptualised as racially homogenous and, in the case of colonial powers (the original racist states), developed conceptually and materially through processes of racial exploitation and differentiation.[5] Goldberg here seems to imply that all nation-states fit his *racial state* archetype. Elsewhere he limits the typology to states that govern populations in explicitly racial terms, that is, where racial groups are identified legally or administratively 'as inherently inferior or historically immature'. By historically immature Goldberg means those judged and found wanting within Western narratives of discovery ('they' did not exist until they were found) and progress (bringing civilisation and salvation to uncivilised, backward peoples). For Goldberg the racial state emerged and was ideologically sustained by 'historicism' so defined.[6]

Goldberg quotes the nineteenth-century Irish historian Lord Acton by way of example. 'Inferior races,' Acton proposed in a spirit of benevolent despotism, 'are raised by living in political union with races intellectually superior' and 'exhausted and decaying nations are revived by the contact with the younger vitality'.[7] It has lived on, he suggests, within Western liberalism, where commitments to pluralism and even anti-racism bear new claims of higher civilisation.[8] The recent shrill expressions of triumphal liberalism that have emerged alongside the war on terror seem to bear this out. Here the duty of the civilised liberal is to be intolerant of intolerance. A new instance upon Western cultural superiority seems to underpin opposition to multiculturalism within a number of Western states.

No firewall protects Ireland from the software of Western or, as Goldberg would have it, historicist racism. Whether it makes sense to insist that the Republic of Ireland is a 'racial state' (and Northern Ireland a 'racial statelet') is less clear. The key events that, for them, define Irish state racism – treatment of Travellers and asylum seekers, the emergence of a Fortress Ireland within Fortress Europe and the outcome of the Citizenship Referendum – cannot solely be explained in terms of the state. The question as to whether the Irish state fits the racial state ideal-type developed by Goldberg requires some empirical resolution. It also depends on how the state is defined. Lentin and McVeigh seem to define the state in Marxist terms, as an all-encompassing denial of society, so that empirical distinctions between racism institutionalised within the state and racism within society are seen to be unnecessary.

Their account of racism in what they term the Northern Irish 'racist statelet' is a case in point ('we insist that the key responsibility for racism lies with the state'). Here racism is attributed to colonial institutions even though much emphasis is placed on the 'affinity between Loyalism and racism'.[9] The inference here is that the Northern Catholic nationalist community cannot be racist. The same presumption migrates across the border where racism is simply attributed to the racial state.

This approach seems unhelpful when it comes to explaining why 80 per cent of voters supported the 2004 constitutional amendment that stripped the birthright of citizenship from Irish-born children of immigrants. It was introduced at short notice and strongly supported by both the parties in government. Fianna Fáil's poster campaign emphasised 'commonsense citizenship' in reassuring pastel colours. The Minister for Justice, Michael McDowell, played the race card by dishonestly raising the spectre of African women exploiting the health system. Many of those detrimentally affected by the outcome of the referendum were black Africans. That racism played some part in the outcome of the referendum cannot be doubted but the extent to which it was a factor remains unknown.

The first problem with simply presuming that the Irish state is a racial state is that distinctions between the cultural software and institutional hardware of racism become lost. The second problem is that other causes of prejudice and discrimination are ignored. In other words, more than one form of software is likely to prevail. For example, the crucial distinction institutionalised in 2004 was one between 'nationals' and 'non-nationals'. The 'national/non-national' dualism codified immigration in terms of longstanding debates about belonging within Irish society. Here it arguably drew on a history of exclusionary nationalism that equated Irishness with ethnic homogeneity.

FROM ETHNIC NATIONALISM TO ETHNIC NEPOTISM

Lord Acton, in the language of his time, used the words 'race' and 'nation' interchangeably. In 1913 Stephen Brown S.J. published two articles that launched an ongoing debate in *Studies* about nationality and national identity: 'What is a Nation' and 'The Question of Irish Nationality'.[10] The former opened with a series of quotations, one from Tom Kettle's *The Open Secret of Ireland*: 'The open secret is that Ireland is a nation.'[11] Brown then outlined and discussed the extent to which the Irish case fitted criteria for nationhood identified by 'anthropologists and sociologists' in the 'truly vast body of literature dealing with the connection between national character and race'.[12] The specific criteria outlined – physical environment, race, language, custom, religion, common interests, history – were broadly equivalent to those evoked in the late twentieth century in definitions of ethnicity. Ethnicity is a term that only gained currency from the 1970s.[13] *Race* as used by Brown with some degree of equivalence referred to presumed national characteristics rather than those presumed to relate to phenotype.[14] Brown identified custom, the unwritten and traditional codes which rule the habits of people and 'by long iteration, furrows deep traits in its character' as a 'nation-building force'.[15] Linguistic distinctiveness too could have a nation-building role.

However, Brown emphasised that the boundaries of language and national belonging were by no means the same even if a common language – here he was thinking of the United States – had the power 'to weld into some sort of oneness' the 'jumble of races as is to be found within its borders'.[16] Religion, he argued, was 'the strongest and most important of the elements which go to constitute nationality'. He instanced the power of Mohammedanism 'to bind its votaries into a kind of national exclusiveness'. Before the Reformation, he argued, the idea of a common Christianity was stronger that that of loyalty to separate nationalities: 'The enemies of Christianity were, so to speak, the national enemies of all.'[17] Since the Reformation, religious differences had prevented devotion to a common country but the experience of modern nations had shown 'the absurdity of the notion that there can be no national unity without religious unity'. Brown emphasised the role of historical consciousness – of Fatherland as 'the patrimony of memories that unite us to our fathers and in terms of an understanding of common origin' – as the crucial block of nation-building. Nations were held together by common memories:

> A nation looks back on its past as a lesson for its national life in the present, and as a justification of its continued national life in the future. Common memories are the nourishment of patriotism, the foundation of national consciousness and by the common hopes and aspirations that sprung from these.[18]

Taking these elements together – 'race', language, custom, religion and common understandings of history – Brown drew a few conclusions about what constituted a nation. A nation consisted of a relatively large group living together in common territory in organised social relations held together by a peculiar kind of spiritual oneness. There was, he insisted, nothing mystic about this sense of oneness. It, national consciousness, consisted 'of common memories of historic things wrought in common and suffered in common in the past, and secondly the actual consent to carry on that common life, as a distinct people, master of its destinies, shaper of its future'.[19]

In 1920 Brown's 'Recent Studies in Nationality' addressed the problem of using the terms 'race' and 'nationality' interchangeably.[20] Here, in the absence of the concept of ethnicity, he sought to explain how the term 'race', as used by anthropologists, acknowledged no racial distinctions between Europeans.[21] Race understood as nation admitted 'absurd and often unjust explanations' of the inherent qualities of different types; 'the Latin decadent, the Slav politically incapable, the Irish lazy and mendacious' and so on. Brown's literature review examined the use of abstractions such as the Teutonic, Anglo-Saxon or Celtic races. It cited refutations of the German idea of nationality understood to be 'based on the ethnographic or race theory'. Brown's account, to use a later terminology, was sceptical of accounts that presumed intrinsic characteristics of any race as nationality. Yet Brown presumed a psychology of national character.[22] Different peoples (Brown persisted in using the term 'race' for want of an alternative) cultivated distinctiveness.

Brown's pioneering articles for *Studies* were hardly the last word in what has now become a huge literature about ethnic-nationalism. This needs to be taken account of in efforts to understand the specific societal contexts where racism finds expression. What ultimately held nation-states together, according to the political theorist Ernest Gellner, was the social glue of culture and shared idea of belonging.[23] In this context distinctions between 'nationals' and 'non-nationals' express a solidarity within defined limits – an ethnocentric unwillingness to exclude others – that does not require racism even if for some, like Michael McDowell, ethnic nepotism is to be justified politically by the mobilisation of racist stereotypes.

OLD AND NEW GUESTS OF THE NATION

To some extent Irish twenty-first-century responses to immigration and social diversity will be prisoners of present and past conflicts within historiography. Nationalist post-colonialist perspectives, at their most reductionist, advance the twin theses suggested by the cover illustration and title of *Encounters: How Racism Came to Ireland* by Bill Rolston and Michael Shannon. Here is a book that begs to be judged by its cover. This depicts a group of Orangemen holding a banner bearing the slogan 'The Secret of England's Greatness' under an image of a turbaned Asian prince being handed a Bible by Queen Victoria.[24] The presumed equation is that unionism = colonialism = racism. A further inference implied by the title and the wording on the banner is that racism was imported to Ireland by colonisers. This directs the reader to the questionable presumption that anti-colonialist nationalism is by definition anti-racist. The book itself is much better than its unfortunate cover and title. It documents succinctly but effectively nineteenth-century encounters between nationalists and American abolitionists. For instance, it *does* dwell on a republican, John Mitchel's, advocacy of slavery 'as the best state of existence for the Negro'.[25] It emphasises that many such encounters were ones where Irish people, often of unimpeachedly 'green' provenance, were part of colonising forces that subjugated people of colour.[26] The dominant theme of the book concerns the possibility of present-day anti-racist solidarities rooted in the presumption of equivalence between Irish (nationalist) struggles and those of enslaved peoples. Yet by skipping adroitly from nineteenth-century encounters between the oppressed Irish and enslaved Africans it preserves an analysis that would have a difficulty in explaining the exclusions resulting from Irish nation-building experienced by Jewish, Protestant and Traveller minorities in the Republic of Ireland in the decades since independence.

For example, the people in Limerick who expelled the city's Jewish community in 1904 seemed to be as exposed to anti-Semitic stereotypes as those in many European cities. Yet Fr Creagh, who led the campaign to expel the Jews, described them as exploiters of the Irish people 'worse than Cromwell'. In Limerick anti-Semitism was expressed within a nationalist discourse. Here Creagh was not alone. Newspapers such as the *United Irishman*, edited by Arthur Griffith, reflected continental anti-Semitism which cast the Jews as national enemies.[27] By the end of the nineteenth century Protestants had become marginal within the mass politics of nationalism. With independence, the new nation-state reflected a Catholic ethnic conception of belonging. Many institutions within the new state, for example education and health, were designed so as to protect the dominant religious group from the influence of this increasingly marginalised Protestant minority. Here, an ethnic nationalism rooted in Catholicism proved capable of sectarianism. From the second half of the twentieth century onwards a growth of anti-Traveller prejudice coincided with their displacement from the rural economy. A longstanding local politics of spatial exclusion ensued whereby discrimination against Travellers was justified by a rhetoric that emphasised their cultural inferiority. Here, anti-Traveller prejudice seems to have echoed nineteenth-century colonialist stereotypes of the Irish as feckless and indolent. The *Punch* cartoons of uncouth fighting Paddy and lurid *Sunday World* accounts of Traveller deviance blur easily into each other. If the former justified colonisation for the purposes of civilisation, the latter now serves an internal colonisation whereby the modernisation of Irish society occurs through the displacement of a minority ethnic group.

In *The IRA and its Enemies* Peter Hart documents disproportionate killings of Protestants and tramps and 'tinkers' as 'informers' in County Cork during the War of Independence:

> Not all executed 'spies' and 'informers' were strangers or deviants and almost none of those who were, were in fact guilty of helping the authorities. Nevertheless, these were exceptions. The great

majority of suspects – and, it seems, most informers – were respectable Catholics but the majority of victims were not. They were killed not for what they did but for who they were: Protestants, ex-soldiers, tramps and so on down the communal blacklist. Their deaths were not just the consequence of political heresy but of a persecution that went way beyond the immediate hunt for informers. Guerrilla war transformed them from the unwanted to the enemy within.[28]

Hart concludes that violence was not merely directed at Protestants but at all out-groups: It is striking how often condemned 'spies' and 'informers' were described in terms of outraged respectability. They were not just traitors, they were 'low', 'cheap and low living', 'degenerate', 'a bad character', 'a low type, 'the tinker type', etc.[29] This part of the country, incidentally, was the location of Frank O'Connor's fictional *Guests of the Nation*.

The hostile reception to Hart's research by non-historians such as the literary critic Luke Gibbons suggests that ethnic-nationalism, anti-colonialist or otherwise, might have a hard time reconciling a real Irish society in all its diversity with an imagined Ireland rooted in the past and the legacy of real sectarianisms. His 2005 *Village* article, 'Memory without walls: From Kevin Barry to Osama bin Laden', exemplified the politics of memory (as distinct from actual history) at work here. Gibbons claimed that historians like Hart 'have sought to recast the guerrilla warfare of Tom Barry, Liam Lynch and others as "terrorism", "serial-killing" or "ethnic-cleansing"'.[30] Yet 'ethnic-cleansing', a term popularised after the break-up of former Yugoslavia, might not be inappropriate. A good deal of sectarian burning-out and forced land sales occurred between 1919 and 1923 in both parts of Ireland, particularly when the local IRA or their Northern loyalist equivalents got out of control.[31]

Gibbon's article ends with a discussion of an iconic photograph of two African women walking past the shutters of 16 Moore Street (first published in the *Sunday Tribune*), the now uncelebrated building where the rebel leaders of 1916 surrendered. Real immigrants, the new guests of the nation, can only be bit players in such post-colonialist pageants. The exclusions they experience may have much to do with racism but they also have something to do with longstanding local identity politics. In this context, to blithely insist that the Republic of Ireland is a racial state serves to mask a broader potential mechanics of exclusion.

CHAPTER TWELVE

The Wages of Fear
(with Roland Erne)

Early 2006 witnessed two apparent efforts by opposition politicians to test the waters of anti-immigrant populism. The first was widely received as a cynical effort to amplify fears of Irish workers being displaced by immigrants. After a period when immigrant worker exploitation had come under scrutiny – notably those employed by Gama in the construction sector and by Irish Ferries – the tone of the political debate seemed to shift abruptly. The issue of protecting overall employment standards became central to the 2006 social partnership bargaining between the government, the Irish Congress of Trade Unions (ICTU) and the Irish Business and Employers Confederation (IBEC).[1] The broader context was the fraught negotiations between trade unions and the government on the EU Services Directorate. The trigger was a proposal by Pat Rabbitte, then leader of the Labour Party, to consider reinstating a work permit system for migrants from the new EU countries. The second, an effort to advocate welfare ethnic nepotism, one that backfired, took the form of Fine Gael's criticism of giving childcare allowance payments to the dependants of EU migrants living in the Republic of Ireland.

In a sense both debates were the fallout of the 2004 decision to open up the Irish labour market to the ten EU accession countries. The Republic of Ireland belongs – together with the UK and Sweden – to the group of initially only three EU member states that did not impose any restrictions on the free movement of workers from the eight new central and east European EU member states.[2] But only 25,000 workers migrated to Sweden. The UK counted 290,000 arrivals between May 2004 and September 2005. Ireland, with less than one tenth of its population, issued about 160,000 new social security numbers between May 2004 and November 2005; some 86,900 to Polish migrants, 29,500 to Lithuanians, 14,600 to Latvians and 29,900 to those from other new EU member states.[3] In less than two years some of Ireland's largest immigrant communities had established themselves from scratch.

THE EXPLOITATION OF IMMIGRANT WORKERS

In April 2005, Joe Higgins, a socialist member of parliament, exposed how the Turkish corporation Gama, which had won several tenders for large public construction projects, paid wages to its Turkish employees of €2.20 per hour, far below both the national minimum wage and the then Registered Employment Agreement for the construction industry hourly rate of €12.95. The Gama workers had to stage a seven-week strike before they were awarded a settlement of €8,000 each in back money.[4] On Friday 9 December 2005 more than 100,000 trade unionists demonstrated against Irish Ferries' plan to dismiss their 550 Irish employees and replace them with employees from eastern Europe who would be paid an hourly rate of €3.60. At the same time, SIPTU seafarers and dockers blocked all Irish Ferries vessels on the Irish Sea and ICTU postponed talks on the new Irish social pact until the government had published the blueprint for legislative changes that would lead to improved implementation of agreed conditions of employment.[5] This dispute was resolved when the company agreed to protect the jobs and conditions of employment of those seafarers who wished to continue working for Irish Ferries. The company agreed to pay no less than the Irish minimum wage to all its new eastern European employees, even though it had reflagged its vessels to Cyprus. However, the issue of employment standards remained on the agenda as one of the most contentious topics in the 'Towards 2016' negotiations.[6]

Irish trade unions invoked the Irish Ferries incident in debates about the draft EU Services Directive, described by SIPTU as a monstrous 'Frankenstein directive'.[7] SIPTU characterised the first draft of the proposed EU Services Directive as a potential 'exploiters' charter' and an attempt to set in train a race to the bottom in terms of pay and conditions of employment:

> The magnificent trade union demonstrations of recent weeks were not only protesting against the race to the bottom currently being pursued by Irish Ferries management against its workers, but also against the same agenda being pursued through the EU's proposed Services Directive. If the former is the most glaring example of

how exploitation is being facilitated by the 'law of the sea', the latter is an attempt to advance the same aims by introducing the 'law of the jungle' on land.[8]

The government argued, somewhat disingenuously, that such responses to the EU Services Directive were irresponsible and alarmist. Nevertheless, the union campaign, which included the participation of an Irish delegation at a European Trades Union Congress demonstration in Strasbourg, proved to be effective. In February 2006, most Irish members of the European Parliament backed several Social Democrat and Christian Democrat amendments aimed at securing the primacy of employment standards and collective agreements of the host country in which a company is providing its services.[9]

THE BLAME GAME

On 3 January 2006 Pat Rabbitte called for a debate on the re-introduction of a work permit regime for migrant workers from the new EU states. His intervention was widely portrayed as 'political opportunism', 'appealing to the basest instincts' and as shifting the debate from one on exploitation of immigrant workers to one about protectionism. As put by one Sinn Féin councillor: 'Whether by design or accident – and it is hard to tell the difference – he has managed in one fell swoop to shift the blame for the Irish Ferries debacle and the continuing problems of worker displacement away from the policies of the Government and the employers and onto the heads of migrant workers from both within and outside the EU.'[10]

An *Irish Times* opinion poll (cited by Rabbitte) suggested that almost 80 per cent of voters wanted a system of work permits to be reintroduced for citizens from the ten new European Union member states coming to Ireland.[11] The findings were that immigration restrictions on workers from the accession states appealed to some members of all the main political parties except the Progressive Democrats. Insofar as all the parties were pro-immigration, the poll suggested a gap between party elites and some grass roots members, one ripe for political exploitation. While the poll did not identify racist or ethnocentric attitudes, it did suggest potential support for anti-immigrant political populism that would play to the kinds of views expressed by two trade union supporters of Rabbitte's comments in a blog debate:

> People whose jobs are under threat and whose wages and conditions are being undermined do not want to hear diaper Marxist

fantasies about uniting to overthrow capitalism ... What they are interested in is practical measures, and these must include immigration controls and strict regulation of the use of migrant workers.[12]

It's about time the Labour Party in this country woke up and remembered that they are the Labour Party in this country and not a pan-European labour party. Their concern should be with Irish workers, not foreign workers (who seem to have no end of advocacy groups to defend them). This is the first glimmer of hope for the future of the party that I've seen for a while. The fact is that workers doing other workers out of jobs by undercutting their wages are no different from scabs.[13]

Rabbitte argued that the findings of the *Irish Times* poll of strong cross-party support for reinstating work permits made it feasible for the social partners to extract concessions on employment standards within the 2006 revised social partnership negotiations.[14] A Labour Party report entitled *A Fair Place to Work and Live* claimed that his remarks were 'made in the context of the revival by Commissioner McCreevy of the EU's draft Services Directive'.[15] The report advocated a series of measures aimed at improving protections for Irish and migrant workers alike. These included improved legal protection, employer sanctions, emphasising the right of all immigrant workers to join trades unions and ratification by Ireland of the International Convention on the Rights of Migrant Workers. There was no reference to reinstating work permits.

THE LIMITS OF ETHNIC NEPOTISM

In early 2006 an attempt by Fine Gael to politicise the receipt of a new once-off childcare payment of €1,000 by dependants of EU migrants still living in their countries of origin backfired. Fine Gael claimed that child benefit plus the childcare payment for non-resident children could cost €150 million, of which €50 million would be for the childcare payment; the Taoiseach, Bertie Ahern, claimed that the total annual expenditure on the childcare allowance might be as little as €1 million.[16] In a 'robust Dáil debate' Ahern said to deny such payments to the children of migrant workers from the new EU member states amounted to 'a Scrooge mentality'. Another member of the government, Brian Lenihan, criticised what he described as 'an ugly outbreak of Fine Gael racism'.[17]

During the debate Ahern 'clarified' for the first time that citizens from all EU countries (but not other migrants) would be exempt from the two-year residency eligibility criteria introduced under the 2004 Social Welfare (Miscellaneous Provisions) Act introduced to coincide with EU enlargement. The Act removed rights from new immigrants to Unemployment Assistance, Old Age (Non-Contributory) and Blind Pension, Widow(er)'s and Orphan's (Non-Contributory) Pensions, One Parent Family Payment, Carer's Allowance, Disability Allowance, Supplementary Welfare Allowance (other than once-off exceptional and urgent needs payments) and Children's Allowances.

Arguably the 2004 Act was a political feint aimed at countering potential anxiety about the decision to allow migrants from the new EU-ten to work in Ireland. The main group who lost out under it were new migrants from outside the EU. In February 2006 the government acknowledged that EU law (EEC 1408 of 1971) imposed reciprocal obligations on EU states to recognise the entitlements of citizens from other EU countries resident in their own countries. This meant that the removal of entitlements set out under the 2004 Act could never have applied to immigrants arriving from the new EU member states. Throughout 2004 and 2005 it was generally presumed by government departments and NGOs that the 2004 Act applied to all immigrants. In one fell swoop Ahern demolished the opposition for being so mean-spirited as to back the presumed aim of an Act his government had passed.

It seems ironic that the Irish government hosted a conference entitled 'Reconciling Mobility and Social Inclusion' as part of its EU presidency in April 2004, just one month before legislation limiting welfare entitlements was introduced. However, the report from the conference, while couched in the rhetoric of social inclusion, placed little emphasis on welfare rights and entitlements.[18] Rather, the focus was on labour mobility and equitable access to labour markets:

> Mobile workers, and especially those who migrate from other regions and countries, are particularly vulnerable to social exclusion. Mobility can involve leaving behind the supports of family, friends, local community and one's own culture, and experiencing much difficulty in finding comparable supports in the host country. This demands that, in solidarity, we work to provide them with the supports they need to achieve social inclusion and integration. It is clearly also in our interests to do so. The social exclusion of migrants can result in their working well below their potential as well as high rates of unemployment. This has negative consequences both economically and in relation to social cohesion. Two key goals of the Lisbon agenda, greater economic competitiveness

and social cohesion, are well served, therefore, by reconciling mobility and social exclusion.[19]

Within 'Reconciling Mobility and Social Inclusion' immigrants tended to be portrayed as economic actors with little claim upon Irish welfare goods and services. The case of the 2004 Social Welfare Act suggests that Irish politicians can benefit from giving lip service to welfare ethnic nepotism and that such welfare chauvinism can limit the scope of debates about integration through social policy.[20] Ethnic nepotism is a term used in social policy debates to refer to the case for excluding immigrants from welfare solidarities developed around citizenship. The perspective is a socio-biological one which offers a deterministic account of the workings of ethnic bonds in the United States.[21] The portrayal of ethnic nepotism as 'natural' – rather than as a hypothesis about how groups might behave – is part and parcel of a larger culture of anxiety that now impedes the integration of immigrants. In the United Kingdom David Goodhart has influentially argued that there is an inevitable conflict or trade-off between social solidarity and diversity.[22] Diversity, Goodhart and some socio-biologists argue, serves to undermine the moral consensus on which a large welfare state rests.[23] However, in practice, the restriction of welfare rights to 'nationals' seems unfeasible, at least in the case of European migrants, because of EU law and *realpolitik*. Diplomatic considerations aside, the value of EU-wide welfare reciprocity is exemplified by the remittance in 2005 alone of more than €420 million from the United Kingdom for people now in Ireland, many of whom were returned emigrants who had built up entitlements in the UK.[24]

For similar *realpolitik* reasons the reintroduction of work permits advocated by Rabbitte was improbable from the onset. The main opposition parties, no less than those in government, were pro-Europe and had never opposed opening the Irish labour market to the new EU states. Irish 'competitive corporatism' has bound the state, business and the trade unions to one another in the pursuit of economic growth.[25] The unions, no less than the other social partners, have repeatedly signed up for a 'competitive corporatist' national project, rooted in a half century of developmental ideology and policy formation.[26] Trade unions are deeply embedded in such decisions.

THE BENEFITS OF SOLIDARITY

By the summer of 2006 the controversies about worker displacement had died down. David Begg, general secretary of ICTU, ebulliently portrayed the outcome of the various negotiations on worker protection as very positive, 'the single biggest leap forward in social policy initiated in this country'. These included new standards of compliance with labour laws which made the exploitation and abuse of any worker a de facto criminal offence, changes in the work permit to include the right of non-EU nationals to apply and reapply for their own work permits, legislative changes to prevent Irish Ferries-type collective redundancies, new public procurement arrangements aimed at preventing the exploitation of immigrant workers (in other words the taxpayer would no longer subsidise exploitation or sharp employment practices) and a Labour Relations Commission (LRC) Code of Practice to protect people working as domestic servants. Together, he argued, these amounted to the single biggest leap forward in Irish social policy.[27] Collectively these addressed many of the causes of immigrant worker exploitation and risks of Irish workers being displaced by immigrants on lesser working conditions. *Towards 2016* included a range of other measures, including the collaboration of the Revenue Commissioners, Social Welfare and the new Office of Employment Rights through Criminal Asset Bureau-style investigation units to target serious abuses of employment standards.[28]

The negotiations that bought this about were described by Begg as 'the most difficult project Congress has ever undertaken both in terms of its complexity and in overcoming opposition to it'.[29] As these unfolded, the Irish labour movement was faced with the apparent task of quelling internal 'dissident' xenophobic voices opposed to solidarity with immigrant workers. But the clear rationale for such solidarity prevailed. Continued exploitation of migrant workers and a corresponding ethnic layering of the labour market would erode not only overall labour standards, but, crucially, also undermine the strength of organised labour, especially in sectors such as construction, parts of manufacturing and private services. Irish workers could not but lose from the exploitation, through lesser pay and conditions, of immigrants. Rabbitte's intervention rankled because it seemed to provide a platform for xenophobic anxieties that risked undermining what Congress were trying to achieve in the 2006 negotiations.

The perspectives that prevailed potentially signal a new 'inclusive corporatism' that differs from the old economic nationalist 'competitive corporatism' of Ireland Inc. Ethno-nationalistic trade union strategies, which aim to protect domestic workers though the exclusion of migrant workers, frequently produce the opposite of the desired 'protectionist' effect. Labour standards are hardly enforceable if migrant workers do not enjoy a secure status. Undocumented immigrants will hardly make themselves visible, make claims or even co-operate with a trade union if they fear being deported. Within the Irish open economy unions have everything to gain from enlisting immigrant workers. Immigrants in turn benefit from trade union protection.[30] The number of unionised non-citizen employees rose from 24,800 to 37,100 between 2005 and 2007, an increase of over 50 per cent. Yet during this time the proportion of immigrants who were union members fell (from 13.9 per cent to 12.6 per cent) because recruitment did not match the rate of increase of the labour force.[31] Clearly unions could be more proactive in reaching out to immigrant workers.

So did it all turn out well in the end? Trans-EU welfare solidarity seemed to trump the politics of welfare ethnic nepotism. A proposal to debate the imposition of restrictions on migrants from the new EU countries was smacked down. There was, it seemed, little to gain from whipping up Irish nativist anxieties about European migrants taking Irish welfare or jobs. Europeans, it became clear, could not be stripped of benefits to which Irish citizens were entitled. Nevertheless, non-EU migrants continued to be subject to the 2004 Act. The unspoken reality was that any restrictions on immigration, any work permits revoked, could only be applied to them. They most likely will take the brunt of any future Irish antipathy towards immigrants and of any political attempts to exploit such feelings.

CHAPTER THIRTEEN

The 'New Irish'

In June 2007 Rotimi Adebari was elected mayor of Portlaoise. Ireland's first black mayor was one of two Nigerian former asylum seekers elected as independent councillors in the 2004 local government elections. In his inaugural address he mused that while he was now the first citizen of Portlaoise he was not yet an Irish citizen. In the presence of a large crowd of well-wishers, including other immigrants, the Nigerian *chargé d'affaires* and representatives from the United States, Indian and South African embassies he gave an upbeat acceptance speech which recalled something of the positive rhetoric of Barack Obama; one directed at the citizen majority at least as much as new immigrant communities: 'I say to my fellow immigrants, the sky's the limit. Ireland is not just the country of a thousand welcomes, but a country of equal opportunity. Ireland has changed and will never be the same again, but I say this is a good thing.'[1] The following week the ceann comhairle (speaker of the House) John O'Donoghue hosted a reception at Leinster House welcoming Adebari to 'the heart of Irish democracy'. O'Donoghue hailed 'a significant moment in Ireland's development' and voiced his hope that the 2009 local government elections would bring a greater cultural diversity at council level and that, further down the line, immigrants would be elected to parliament: 'I am sure that it is only a matter of time before we see some "New Irish" elected to the Houses of the Oireachtas.'[2]

Adebari's election speech and O'Donoghue's rhetoric inaugurated a new phase of symbolic politics where at least the idea of immigrant political integration is on the table. As is ever the case, timing was everything. The reception came weeks after a general election where the main political parties had neglected immigrants for the pragmatic reason that most of the 'new Irish' lacked the franchise. However, because non-citizen residents can vote in local elections, Irish political parties were somewhat more responsive in 2004 when Adebari was elected.[3] With the general election out of the way new overtures to those entitled to vote in the 2009 local government elections made sense. O'Donoghue stated his hope, perhaps referring to Adebari, that 'the future new Irish TDs and senators' might be attracted to his Fianna Fáil: 'They don't call Fianna Fáil the catch-all party for nothing.' However, the behind the scenes view of political party analysts was that such political inclusion would be gradual and slow; as put by one, a few election cycles from now which would put the matter on the back burner until at least 2017.[4]

THE LIMITS OF CITIZENSHIP

The term 'new Irish' warrants scrutiny at a time of emerging debates about integration. Not all Irish-born children get to be Irish anymore.[5] The dualism promoted by the 2004 referendum was one between 'nationals' and 'non-nationals', suggesting an empirical definition of the 'new Irish' restricted to those who become naturalised. One based on naturalisation would exclude the bulk of the immigrant 10 per cent or so of the population. The 'new Irish' so defined are likely to remain a small fraction of the immigrant population even in the longer term. The experience of other EU countries suggests that most immigrants from these countries are unlikely to seek Irish citizenship. They do not need to do so to obtain the employment and social entitlements. They are likely to be prevented from obtaining dual citizenship under their own domestic legislation. It is likely that many migrants who remain here expect to go home; the likelihood of a 'new-Irish' emerging from Ireland's large Polish community in the short term may be small. The medium-term prognosis is a large non-citizen population enjoying many reciprocal social entitlements but lesser political rights than citizens. Within this population, immigrants from non-EU countries will have a greater impetus to naturalise. What is certain is that any national project of immigrant integration will have to come to terms with the inadequacies of citizenship as a badge of social membership and as a vehicle for social cohesion.

This is a shared problem across a number of western EU countries. New waves of labour migration have come from countries without past colonial ties and hence no tradition, for better or worse, of integration or assimilation. Within this context claims have been made about cosmopolitanism as an inclusive political ideal. A cosmopolitan citizenship ideal is essentially a post-national one that allows for inclusion within the nation-state in the absence of naturalisation. Advocates of cosmopolitanism endeavour to shift the focus of debate away from the sort of adversarial 'zero sum' game of playing 'nationals' against 'non-nationals'. They emphasise an obligation to be hospitable towards immigrants rooted in a Kantian conception of reason. Kant's *Perpetual Peace* (1795) emphasised the concept of hospitality as a right that belongs to all human beings by virtue of their potential as a world citizen. Hospitality was defined as the right of a stranger not to be treated with hostility in a foreign land. The stranger may be refused entry unless refusal endangered them.[6] Cosmopolitanism, so presented, was an Enlightenment ideal that found itself sidelined by the development of the nation-state as the vehicle for rights.

The main theorists of the new cosmopolitanism are Kant's modern successors, Jurgen Habermas, John Rawls and Ulrick Beck. Habermas and Beck offer theories of modernity that emphasise a capacity for communicative action and reflexivity which translate into cosmopolitan demands on human reason to see the necessity of reciprocal justice.[7] Rawls' veil of ignorance is the successor of Kant's categorical imperative 'to act only in accordance with that maxim through which you can at the same time will that it should become a universal law'.[8] Rawls' theory of justice started from the simple premise of imagining what fair rules and social arrangements might be drawn up under a 'veil of ignorance', that is, under conditions where everybody did not know where they were to be born nor know their gender, sexuality, class position, social status, skills, abilities or religion or indeed nationality.[9] The veil of ignorance then was a technique for making rational choices about conceptions of justice. It is a formula that endeavoured to address Kant's maxim to act in a way that one's conduct might be adopted as a law by all rational beings.[10]

Reason so presented is always hard work and hardly inevitable; an expression of what ought to be rather than what is. Yet, advocates of the new cosmopolitanism emphasise how ideals have indeed become transferred into norms of international reciprocity. As summarised by Robert Fine and Vivienne Boon:

> The empirical claim of cosmopolitanism claims is to be found in the observation that the centrality of the nation-state is being challenged by such factors as increased movement of people, the formation of trans-national political and legal structures, and the onset of global risks, including environmental risks, that no state can address alone. Behind these empirical claims also lies that the

> historical awareness that the 20th century has been characterized not only by the rise of human rights to all manner of people and peoples deemed not to belong – to those 'others' who for one reason or another have been excluded from the nation, the race, the class or even the human species. [11]

Contemporary cosmopolitanism is characterised here as a new expression of humanism. However, its development is rooted in the empirical reality of genocide, racism and other 'isms' dedicated to 'the exclusion of and destruction of some from the very category of humanity'.[12] Cosmopolitanism therefore is not just a declaration of some Kantian 'ought' but is an expression of unease with the current state of affairs translated politically to the notion of binding trans-national human rights. For example, the UN Convention on the Rights of Refugees is depicted by advocates of cosmopolitanism as a practical achievement of a Kantian ideal, one realised through shifts in norms and values (in the aftermath of the Holocaust) and translated into reciprocal obligations incorporated into legislation by states. Simply put, ideals become translated into legal norms that can be seen from both top down and bottom up perspectives to impact on the nation-state.

Ulrick Beck and Edgar Grande have recently depicted the European Union as the potential vehicle for a new political cosmopolitanism.[13] Indeed, the apparent lack of anxiety about the presence in Ireland of hundreds of thousands of migrants from other EU countries suggests that some form of regional cosmopolitanism pertains; a safe European home with the Euro, free movement, Ryanair flights and reciprocal welfare rights. But rules of hospitality tend to be extended furthest to near neighbours.[14] Fortress Europe is no exaggerated metaphor when considering the refugees who drown crossing the Mediterranean or suffocate when trafficked in containers because of carrier liability legislation crafted to undermine the UN Convention on the Rights of Refugees. Post-1990 political responses to asylum seekers – the group deemed entitled under international law to Kantian hospitality – exemplify how the nation-state as a vehicle for rights can become derailed. Yet if all politics are ultimately local so potentially too are cosmopolitan politics. The NGOs at the forefront of solidarity with immigrants have both Irish and trans-national dimensions. The 'Irish' Refugee Council or the 'Irish' Council for Civil Liberties seek to influence the Irish state. Irish NGOs represented by the European Council on Refugees and Exiles (ECRE) have sought to influence policy at EU level.[15] A state agency, The 'National' Consultative Committee on

Racism and Interculturalism (NCCRI), seeks to shift local norms by promoting international protocols against racism.[16] The promise of cosmopolitanism can be seen from trans-national normative shifts and ideas whose time reflected a trans-national climate of opinion as well as local activism, for example the establishment of the Irish Commission for the Status of Women in 1970. The 1989 UN Convention on the Rights of the Child provided the impetus for the 1991 Children's Act and for debates about constitutional change.

In all this, the nation-state remains centre stage. Rights, as Hannah Arendt insisted, depend on what states will or will not do about them.[17] Cosmopolitan hospitality will be practised by nation-states or not at all. States integrate immigrants or otherwise manage them as part of an ongoing process of economic, social, political and organisational nation-building. Benedict Anderson depicted nations as imagined communities 'because the members of even the smallest nation will never know most of their fellow-members, meet them, or even hear of them, yet in the minds of each lives the image of their communion'.[18] In this context citizenship is the stuff of imagination as well as the bearer of entitlements. From the nineteenth century, the promise of citizenship was extended over time as rights were invoked to address differential experiences of citizenship by the likes of women, people with disabilities and ethnic minorities. But citizenship has remained a double-edged sword. Exclusionary forms of nation-building can be fostered through citizenship ideals of belonging. Protestant, Traveller and Jewish citizens were ideologically placed outside the Irish nation. A myth of Irish homogeneity long prevailed, particularly affecting Travellers, who have been cast as deviants from the dominant imaginary norm. Efforts to contest the 'sub-Irish' status of Travellers within citizenship have failed to a considerable extent. A state-funded Citizen Traveller project was shut down in 2002 when it criticised legislation aimed at regulating the behaviour of Travellers by the Minister for Justice, 'Equality' and Law Reform.[19] Citizenship has been as much about social regulation as about rights. Citizenship ideals of belonging bear definitions of normalcy and deviance and are concerned with social hygiene – producing certain kinds of people to fit some national purpose – as much as the promotion of ethnic nationality.

In this context the gaps between Irish and some putative 'new Irish' may be less than those between Irish and sub-Irish. So too will some immigrants find hospitality more easily than others. One can talk up the Poles as exemplary potential 'new Irish' (highly educated, hardworking, Catholic and fond of a pint) while dismissing the Roma with the very same vehemence they face in Romania.[20] In July 2007 the Irish government deported a community of Roma living on a roundabout on the M50 motorway. The main expression of cosmopolitan solidarity towards them came from Pavee Point, a Traveller NGO affiliated with Roma communities in international networks.[21] Following this, the Minister for Justice, Equality and Law Reform threatened a review of state funding received by the Traveller organisation.[22]

Travellers hardly need to consciously invoke Rawls' 'veil of ignorance' to identify solidarity with the Roma, though the rest of us might need to. Even where cosmopolitan ideals seem to prevail, solidarity and hospitality is by no means equally distributed. Kant proved personally unable to extend the categorical imperative to Negroes.[23] The experiences of the now-EU citizen Roma suggest that European solidarity among neighbours plays favourites. In the Irish case some categories of non-citizen immigrant may prove to be more welcome as 'new Irish' than others and easier to integrate within the dominant imagined community than citizen Travellers. The potential of cosmopolitan hospitality to circumvent the nation-state as the basis for inclusion and exclusion is inevitably a limited one.

THE NEW POLITICS OF ADAPTATION

The term 'adaptive nation-building' is coined here to refer to future potential resettlements which might seek to address the new disjuncture between citizenship and the composition of Irish society. It draws on Katy Hayward's account of Irish adaptive politics. This portrays the core democratic instruments of Irish statehood as being constantly recycled; with old elements being reshaped for new purposes. Within this account, the state embodies continual processes of 'recycling' in which 'history, present and future, merge in both ideational and pragmatic terms'.[24] The model presumes something of a closed loop system within which 'new Irelands' and nation-building reconstructions emerge through citizenship. However, Irish nation-building can be understood as a process that preceded and led to the establishment of the Irish nation-state. The nineteenth century witnessed processes of social modernisation that fostered cultural and political nationalism; specific ideals of belonging that subsequently became institutionalised within the Irish nation-state. Prior to independence, mass literacy and mass movement politics created a sense of common identity between Irish people who might never meet. Ernest Gellner suggests that post-independence dominant ideals of social cohesion presented a mass politics of identity in the guise of cosy community as a form of ideological glue.[25] Even as technocratic modernisation and individualism became more pronounced, the rhetoric of 'traditional' communal solidarity has prevailed. But the Irish society that now experiences immigration is arguably one that is atomised to some extent, within which some 'Irish' as well as immigrants search for inclusion and a sense of belonging. In this context a broader set of potential dislocations than those attributable to immigration can be potentially blamed on migrants. Here populist distinctions between 'nationals' and 'non-nationals' may prove an easier sell than more complex models of social solidarity. As such, integration policies should not just be directed at immigrants. The cognitive category of 'new Irish' must prove attractive to the existing Irish as well as immigrants if it is to succeed.

Recent large-scale immigration will inevitably test the capacity of the institutional model described by Hayward to accommodate social change. The twenty-first century, like the nineteenth century after Catholic Emancipation, may witness profound bottom-up challenges to the current status quo. The extent to which cosmopolitanism or a reinvented nationality proves to be the driving idea remains to be seen. If nation-building and integration ultimately come down to questions about rules and ideals of belonging, the quest for the 'new Irish' is one for solidarity and social cohesion under changing circumstances. Here a mixture of responses can be envisaged.

Firstly and inevitably, solidarity between a citizen Irish and any 'new Irish' is constituted in terms of formal belonging to the nation-state. Over time some immigrants get to be nationals but most remain 'non-nationals'. The 'commonsense citizenship' logic of the 2004 referendum is likely to persist.[26] The 80 per cent who voted in favour prove difficult to convince that expansive integration measures are in their interest. In essence they, and the opinion-formers who appeal to them, get to define the legitimacy of putative integration measures. The danger here is that zero-sum conceptions of the dominant interest will impede pragmatic responses to social change.[27] Insofar as the 'new Irish' remain a minority within the majority, ethnic nepotism and xenophobia towards non-nationals can be represented as still being in the national interest. Politically it becomes difficult to argue that measures aimed at integrating non-citizen immigrants are to the overall benefit of 'Irish' society. An example here is the 2000 government report, *Integration: A Two-Way Process*. Here refugees were to be the focus of integration efforts but not asylum seekers. Integration was to begin when someone achieved refugee status. In effect, asylum seekers were to be deliberately socially excluded. Cognitive and administrative barriers to integrating non-citizens are likely to persist. Impermeable conceptions of nationhood may prevail even when borders become porous.

Secondly and necessarily, pragmatic solidarities between citizens and denizens will find expression. Already more than 12 per cent of trade union members are immigrants. This, in the context of social partnership, opens up scope for immigrant participation in governance if not government. Participation of a mostly high-skilled and well-educated immigrant population in the workplace potentially translates into social inclusion just as it does for citizens in employment. Concrete measures of integration can be identified whereby immigrants purchase homes, raise families and acquire social capital. Immigrants may become embedded in Irish society without necessarily proclaiming themselves as 'new Irish' but in doing so challenge institutional definitions of Irishness. In this context James Joyce's dictum (spoken by Leopold Bloom in *Ulysses*) that a nation consists of the same people living in the same place cannot hold. Here, nation-building is envisaged in terms of the social, economic and cultural processes that shape social solidarity within a diverse society. The self-integration of immigrants no less than any 'top-down' process has the potential to redefine the dominant imagined community.

Thirdly, formal processes of cosmopolitan adaptation may find expression in the nation-state. The EU has a track record of promoting social solidarity. For example, it overturned Irish legislation introduced in 2004 to curtail the welfare entitlements of migrants from member states.[28] EU membership places Ireland within a range of trans-national debates about social inclusion and social cohesion. An example here is the 'Reconciling Mobility and Social Inclusion' conference hosted by the Irish government as part of its 2004 EU presidency. EU-sponsored political integration, by comparison, has been less successful. Currently, all EU citizens are entitled to vote in the European Parliament elections in the constituency in which they reside. The sole parliamentary electoral reciprocity is one between Ireland and the United Kingdom but there are no constitutional barriers to extending such reciprocity to other EU states.[29] The trigger event in each case would have to be some bilateral reciprocity. Even advocates of EU-based cosmopolitanism accept that this would be difficult to achieve.[30] Ultimately it is difficult to detach questions about citizenship from ones about sovereignty. The suggestion is that cosmopolitan ideals and norms potentially circumvent tendencies towards xenophobia and zero-sum perceptions of ths stakes within the nation-state politics of adaptation. The need for a post-national model of citizenship is envisaged.[31]

THE NEW BLACK IRISH

Here is a hypothesis. The citizen 'new Irish' will be disproportionately black or non-white European even if most immigrants continue to originate from EU member states.[32] Irish immigration policy opens Irish borders to some 400 million Europeans while imposing restrictive visa rules to non-EU labour migrants, Fortress Europe barriers to asylum seekers and time-limited student visas on Chinese migrants. The implicit expectation is that any permanent immigration population would be white Europeans, mirroring to some extent past immigration policies of Australia. In the Australian case this translated into a racialised citizenship. In the Irish case EU-based solidarity with near neighbours exempts most non-white immigrants. Non-white immigrants will experience greater initial barriers to integration than white European immigrants because of lesser rights and entitlements and because of particular vulnerabilities to racism and discrimination. Lacking access to EU-based solidarities, they are particularly dependent on ones grounded in Irish nationality. In the absence of a cosmopolitan sense of Irishness, non-white immigrants could expect marginalisation even as citizens. In a context where the 'new Irish' are more likely to be Filipino, Chinese or African than white Europeans, a number of integration dilemmas will have to be faced. These can be illustrated by efforts of African immigrants to negotiate symbolic debates about Irish hospitality and material barriers to integration.

Within the new symbolic politics the expectation is that black immigrant politicians look, as an *Irish Times* headline on Adebari put it, 'beyond race'. The bottom line is that no immigrant politician is likely to succeed without reaching out to the 'old Irish' and without representing Ireland as hospitable. That there remains a gap between rhetoric and reality is unsurprising. Adebari, not yet a citizen, cannot vote or stand in general elections. As an asylum seeker he had to traverse the punitively harsh 'direct provision' system introduced by O'Donoghue in 2000.[33] Africans have borne the brunt of Irish hostility towards asylum seekers. They, Adebari included, found themselves the specific target of the racialised politics of the 2004 Citizenship Referendum.[34]

After *Lobe v. Minister for Justice* (2003) Irish-born children entitled to citizenship and their families could be deported. At the time some 11,500 applications for residence from parents with Irish citizen children were pending. Most were from Africans and former asylum seekers.[35] Deportations made possible by the 2003 ruling proved controversial; media accounts emphasised the plight of 'Irish children' and their families. Some expressions of Irish solidarity with Africans achieved high profile, particularly in the case of Olukunle Elukanlo, a 20-year-old student living in Palmerstown, who was deported to Nigeria in his school uniform.[36] A campaign by fellow students secured his return. However, the referendum outcome de-legitimised much such solidarity; those deported were no longer portrayed as Irish. The post-referendum experience of many Africans in Ireland has been one of considerable insecurity and stress (over 10,000 were at risk of deportation) exacerbated by experiences of racism and adversity.[37]

Such experiences make the positive engagement with politics and civic participation promoted by African NGOs all the more striking. African immigrants seem 'hungry to participate' because of, rather than in spite of, their experiences of insecurity.[38] They have been at the forefront of bottom-up efforts to promote immigrant self-integration. The establishment of a successful newspaper, *Metro Éireann*, by two Nigerian journalists, Abel Ugba and Chinedu Oneyejelem, in 2000 proved an important early development. *Metro Éireann* established annual Media and Multicultural (MAMA) Awards, a showcase for 'new Irish' projects and ideals. It also serialised Roddy Doyle's stories of fictional encounters between Irish and immigrants, republished as *The Deportees*.[39]

A number of African academics and researchers have focused on the potential for African participation in Irish society. Research topics include a study of religious social capital, African elite formation in Ireland, responsiveness of political parties to immigrants and immigrant civic participation.[40] Of the six immigrant candidates who stood in the 2004 local government elections, both of those elected were African. A number of African NGOs emerged, including Akina Dada wa Africa (AkiDwa) and the African Solidarity Centre. The Africa Centre (renamed because it was felt that the term 'solidarity' elicited negative connotations among potential Irish supporters) strategic plan for 2005–2008 emphasised the promotion of active civic participation.[41] Specifically it sought to strengthen the capacity of African communities to participate in Irish society, to promote 'genuine representation of minority communities' and to promote civic integration among African communities.[42] In the absence of support from the Irish state, work by the Africa Centre on immigrant civic participation was funded by the UK-based Joseph Rowntree Foundation. The principal institutional welcome from the Irish government emerged through the Department of Foreign Affairs, the cosmopolitan common ground here being the work of the department with NGOs in Africa.[43]

The Africa Centre *Inclusive Citizenship* report depicted those surveyed, from Dublin, Dundalk and Waterford, to be strongly engaged in
community activities (63 per cent) and very strongly interested in
becoming politically active (98 per cent) but found that actual political
participation rates were much lower. That just 2 per cent of those surveyed described themselves as members of political organisations was
unsurprising given the findings of earlier research on the inability of
Irish political parties to reach out to immigrants. Some 27 per cent had
voted in the 2004 local government elections, a high turnout given various difficulties Africans faced in registering their votes.[44] Respondents
in the 2005 *Inclusive Citizenship* research identified a range of specific
barriers to civic participation including racism, language barriers and a
sense of insecurity. Immigrant identities and engagements with host
societies are inevitably complex. For example, Abel Ugba's study of
African Pentecostals in Ireland identifies religious social capital as a
basis for a limited integration, suggesting that these 'have created a
social and moral universe that is parallel to that of the majority society
as well as the ones inhabited by other sub-groups' while nevertheless
participating in the majority society in many significant ways.[45]

The emphasis on civic participation fostered by the Africa Centre is
part of a broader expansion of immigrant-led organisations. A 2005
study of these emphasised how 'civil society provides the space for the
marginalised to assert themselves and to contribute to the public sphere
– activities that embody the "stuff" of citizenship, often in the absence
of its formal acquisition'.[46] The African struggle for recognition suggests
that even where many immigrants are not citizens, a robust immigrant
civil society can do much to foster integration. African efforts at self-
integration can be seen as challenges to the dominant imagined community. Yet the risk of black Irish becoming a new category of sub-Irish
should not be ignored. This early chapter in African-Irish history might
be summarised as a pragmatic attempt by marginalised immigrants to
become embedded in a nation-state all too capable of rejecting them.

CONCLUSION

The term 'new Irish' is inclusive insofar as it opposes the Manichean
distinction at the heart of the national/non-national divide. However, a
project of integration which limits itself to 'new Irish' citizens cannot
but fail. Everything might be done to turn immigrants into citizens, to
get them to sign up as 'new Irish', but even the most liberal dispensation
of Irish passports is likely to leave an unfeasibly large proportion of the

Irish population outside the tent of social solidarity. Citizenship alone is incapable of sustaining future social cohesion. Citizens find it difficult to sustain solidarity with non-citizens. Even future naturalised immigrants may prove no more willing to do so than the citizen class of 2004.

A cosmopolitan reading of the idea of the 'new Irish' would emphasise the multiple solidarities that now need to be somehow accommodated within the Irish nation-state. It would emphasise the imaginative and normative shifts necessary to build political and institutional change. It might propose that everybody in Ireland is 'new Irish'.[47] There is, after all, a local history of such imaginative rhetoric.[48] It would counsel an adaptive nation-building response to change on the ground that would prioritise integration and social cohesion without necessarily depending on citizenship as the vehicle of inclusion. It would, for instance, build institutions and entitlements aimed at promoting the social inclusion of non-citizens and seek to promote the participation of immigrants in civil society.

One problem in the Irish case is the absence of the necessary driver of immigrant political influence to secure sufficient commitment to an expansive civil society-based integration project. In a context where the Irish state provides minimal support to immigrant organisations it is important not to lose sight of the extent to which any such civil society-based model of social cohesion is likely be an unequal one. However, as the 'African-Irish' experience demonstrates, immigrants themselves are the bearers of ideas and agency. They, no less than citizens, will seek to define what it is to belong to the new emerging Ireland. It would be foolish to view them as passive beneficiaries or losers within whatever official 'new Ireland' that emerges.

CHAPTER FOURTEEN

The Once and Future
Nation-State

The focus of a number of previous chapters has been on the exclusionary capacities of Irish institutions and how these connect to cultural rules of belonging. This final chapter does not attempt to tie up the arguments of earlier ones neatly. Any tidy conclusion would be implausible at the beginning of what will be a long-running debate about what it means to be Irish in a country so recently changed by immigration. The emphasis here is on addressing the challenges that immigration places upon the dominant ideals and practices of solidarity that influence the Irish nation-state, specifically the legacy of cultural nationalism and the developmental ideology of economic solidarity that was offered as the sole justification for Celtic-Tiger era mass immigration.

The core presumptions of the former are ones influentially articulated by J.G. Herder in the early nineteenth century. These included the belief that people can only realise themselves fully as members of an identifiable culture defined in terms of language, tradition and historical roots. Herder emphasised the multiplicity and incommensurability of the values of different cultures; different societies could have equally valid ideals but, in reality, they were incomparable.[1] These ideas served to validate both cultural nationalism and ethnic chauvinism. A nation, said James Joyce's Irish–Jewish protagonist in *Ulysses*, was the same people living in the same place. It was a definition that excluded him in other Irish eyes. Herder considered patriotism to be laudable but did not condone aggressive nationalist chauvinism; a view that many Irish who prize their nationality might concur with. Yet, the 80 per cent of nationals who voted away the immigrant birthright to citizenship are Herder's children.

Some earlier chapters have emphasised how 'nationals' will tend to see themselves in distributional conflict with 'non-nationals'. But no practical answer to problems caused by ethnic nepotism examined in earlier chapters will be found in a blanket denigration of nationalism. Nationalists forge their identities on a legacy of essentialism that keeps bubbling to the surface, the old and new variants of 'Hibernicism' discussed in the next section of this chapter being cases in point. The main communal solidarities that are practised or advocated in the Irish case remain bounded or dominated by the nation-as-ethnic-group. Irish republicanism is pretty much synonymous with Irish nationalism and suffused with the culture and religious identity of the dominant group. In such a context it may not be wise to aspire to a civic republicanism that presumes that this culture can somehow be sidelined. The analysis presented here is that cultural recognition will play a crucial role in efforts to integrate immigrant communities. But in a context where nationals get to call the shots it will be crucial to engage with nationalist ideals of belonging.

However, questions about nationalism and its discontents, for all that these preoccupy the protagonists in the debates that dominate Irish cultural politics, address just part of the modern Irish story. The Republic of Ireland is arguably one with a small 'r', reflecting a Catholic antipathy towards state worship but also the inherited nineteenth-century liberalism embedded in its institutions.[2] Social liberalism accompanied a decline in religiosity. Neo-liberalism walked hand in hand with social partnership. Rules of belonging have come to centre on human capital rather than culture, the market rather than community. Social inclusion has come to be narrowly defined as inclusion in the economy.[3] Leaving immigration aside, Ireland has undergone a social change that has arguably undermined what Robert Putnam describes as social capital: 'social networks and associated norms of reciprocity and trustworthiness'. But Putnam also emphasises that, in the short term, immigration serves to diminish social cohesion, that members of host societies tend to 'hunker down' (fall back on narrow or essentialist understandings of the ties that bind) as an immediate response to immigration.[4]

During debates about the integration of immigrants in 2004 (when Ireland hosted an EU-wide 'Reconciling Mobility and Social Inclusion' conference) Irish government ministers emphasised the role of the market.[5] As for the locals, economic competitiveness was presented as the basis for their own thin social cohesion.[6] But implicit in this debate is the premise – discussed first as it is presented by David McWilliams – that an economic downturn will unleash a nativist anti-immigrant politics. The wider analysis to be considered is that developmental nation-building expressed an uncritical modernity with multiple discontents expressed as anxieties about change, dislocation and immigration. If a thin (and perhaps now threadbare) economic integration is all that is on offer, future difficulties in coming to terms with diversity cannot simply be blamed on native tribalism.

In recent decades liberal ideas and norms about tolerance, meritocracy and individual rights have come to the fore. However, just as Irish society began to debate immigration Western liberalism was racked by a new wave of liberal intolerance towards Islam in particular and multiculturalism in general. The new muscular and relativist liberalism, which the philosopher Richard Rorty revealingly described as anti-anti-ethnocentric, emphasises the need to abandon tolerance in criticising intolerant cultures (those that do not practise its values).[7] The issue of recognition has become a stumbling block for muscular liberals. The instinct to suppress difference, to eradicate cultural identity (though not one's own) from the public sphere is quite distinct from the pluralist liberal emphasised by Isaiah Berlin in his critique of Herder. A relativist ultimately believes that there are cultural differences that cannot be bridged or reconciled. A pluralist (Berlin here is directly influenced by Herder) accepts that some values are objective to those who hold them. A pluralist understands that some differences cannot be rationally argued to a mutually agreed conclusion because the conversation is understood as a different one from the differing perspectives.[8] Pluralism therefore requires taking the cultural identities of others seriously as a basis for mutual understanding. It suggests that integration comes about through hard graft and pragmatic political engagement with the problems of recognising and addressing the consequences of difference.

Berlin's shortcoming perhaps is his preoccupation with ideas; he is an intellectual historian, not a social one. Leon Wieseltier suggests that incommensurability unravels in everyday life. In *Against Identity* he argues that all identities are porous, multifaceted and complex. But even multiculturalists represent them as if they were not. They too are Herder's children: 'If the differences between individuals and groups were as thick and as final as the multiculturalists think, then not even multiculturalism would be possible.' The multicultural model presents culture as monolithic (as do those who reject multiculturalism) but within any tradition – his example is the American Jewish community, mine include Irish nationalists and European Muslims – there are relativisms.[9] Wieseltier's assault on the policing of identity is compelling, but the problem that will not go away is that bounded identities are taken seriously by many, that they are presented as incommensurable and, as such, need to be addressed with the patience and respect that Berlin counsels. The next section examines Irish essentialist nationalism and its discontents. A later section addresses problems caused by the appeal of ethnocentric liberalism. The alternative proposed here is not that advocated by Wieseltier. It is for an approach to integration that emphasises recognition of particularistic identities and the bonding social capital these foster as necessary staging posts for successful participation in any wider society.

THE PROTOCOLS OF THE TRIBE

David McWilliams received considerable acclaim for his 2005 *The Pope's Children*, an at times brilliantly composed pop sociology of Celtic Tiger-induced social change. Its 2007 sequel, *The Generation Game*, sought to forecast the tensions and conflicts that might characterise its aftermath. McWilliams' analysis is important for what it suggests about the contours of future anti-immigrant populism. His starting place is criticism of the developmental consensus that permitted large-scale immigration in the first place or, as he puts it, the 'right wing' IBEC (Irish Business and Employers Confederation) view that only the needs of the economy should matter in immigration debates. He maintains that the debate on immigration is dominated by those not threatened by it, such as academics, journalists and politicians. Political and economic correctness, he insists, serve to shut down debate:

> If the Right have a workers-not-people view, the Left, on the other hand, have what is best described as a 'United Colours of Benetton' approach, where discussion of the wisdom of mass immigration is characterised by sanctimony. The right-on, soft-Left view appears to be that it is our role to take in as many colours, creeds and peoples as possible and that it is up to us to adapt them. This approach leads to silly censorship where any questioning of the appropriate level of immigration is immediately slapped down with accusations of racism.[10]

Undaunted, he forecasts a future immigration crisis that, he argues, can be avoided if culturally compatible immigrants are selected from the Irish Disapora rather than from the European Union and non-EU countries. He argues that immigration was accepted because economic growth ensured that there were no distributional conflicts between natives and newcomers. It was accepted as part of a social contract based on full employment and rising house prices. However, he claims this situation has left an anxious generation exposed to economic downturn looking for scapegoats:

> We are now at a turning point and people are conflicted. Everything seems rosy, but something's not quite right. We are rich but feel poor; we are strong but feel weak. Our pensions and jobs feel less secure. We are overdrawn, overtired, overworked and overstretched. There are foreigners everywhere and our neighbours' jobs are moving to the East. For sale signs are staying up longer, house prices are falling, yet the cost of living is rising. There are ten foreign children in your child's class, yet the building is falling down. No-one says hello anymore. The place is different, it's unravelling and we feel like outsiders.[11]

McWilliams described a meeting in Greystones in May 2007 where local politicians were apparently rehearsing their parts in the putative ethnocentric politics that he advocated:

> They concluded that we, the people, needed more power, more community; more us, less them; more national, less international; more Hibernian, less Cosmopolitan. This is a new version of the old conflict between Hibernianism and Cosmopolitanism which has characterised our thinking since the foundation of the State. When there are threats, perceived or actual, from outside we regroup and want to go back to a mythical Ireland that existed before all this alien transience.[12]

The conflict he presents is one between the plain people of Ireland and a cosmopolitan elite who believe in more immigration, more EU federalism and who read *The Economist*. Against this cabal stand the majority who, in the Irish case, buy the *Irish Independent* (the newspaper he writes for), want less immigration, less federalism and more local and national control. The definitions he offers of Hibernians and Cosmopolitans are crucial to understanding the populist nativist politics he goes on to advocate. The term Hibernians 'refers to those Irish people who regard themselves as Irish first, expressed by the Catholic religion, Irish culture, history and language'.[13] In *The Pope's Children* he sketched the history of the Order of Hibernians that first emerged in 1565 as a defender of the Catholic faith in Ireland through to the Ancient Order of Hibernians that was established in 1836 in New York to defend the interests of Irish Catholics both at home and abroad.[14] Cosmopolitans were defined as those people born on the island of Ireland who regard themselves first as citizens of the world and secondly as Irish – James Joyce being the supreme example – but also to encompass those who pursued a liberal social agenda, the standout figure here being Mary Robinson.[15] McWilliams presents modern Irish history as a protracted battle between both groups. For much of this the positions of both were entrenched, with the period 1916 to 1966 being the age of Hibernian hegemony when, to use the term employed elsewhere in this book, an Irish-Ireland nation-building project seemed to dominate. Cosmopolitanism became increasingly influential. Ireland joined and enthusiastically participated in the EU. Contraception and divorce became legalised. The Northern Troubles gave Hibernianism a shot in the arm but the overall impact of Northern nationalism ('a vicious nihilistic sectarian war') was to strengthen cosmopolitanism in the Republic.[16] In McWilliams' version of the end of Irish history the late 1990s saw the emergence of a new class of Irish people who instead of being one or the other, either Hibernian or Cosmopolitan, took on the best elements of both.[17]

If this was the conclusion of *The Pope's Children*, in its sequel McWilliams calls for a 'New Hibernia' nation-building project modelled to some extent on Zionism and Jewish history. This would accept all post-Famine children of the Irish Diaspora as Irish citizens and privilege them before all other guests of the nation. The Jewish Diaspora exists independently of the State of Israel but contributes its wealth, skills and influence:

> Jews from all around the world, most of whom have no traceable ancestors there, come back to Israel to recharge their Jewishness. They support Israel materially and Israel gives them a feeling of authenticity and a sense of belonging. They are part of the tribe. From an economic perspective, the Jewish Diaspora expands Israel's human capital. By granting all Jews the right of return, the right to settle there, the country has created a tangible modern link with an intangible spiritual yearning. Both sides benefit.[18]

What McWilliams proposes for Ireland is a muscular, 'almost Zionist' project. The difference is, he insists, discounting the immigrant communities that have grown over the last decade, that 'we have no Palestinians to kick out'.[19] McWilliams emphasises the necessity of tolerance as a core value, citing, for instance, Jewish communities in the past and Gay quarters more recently as proof that prosperity is a function of tolerance.[20] However, as the Dutch case suggests, sexual tolerance and ethnic tolerance do not go hand in hand. The new nativist politics promoted by Pym Fortune retained many elements of Dutch cosmopolitanism yet rejected multiculturalism.

In a section entitled 'Culture Matters' McWilliams insists that it would be easier to integrate a third-or-fourth generation Irish-American family 'who have a vested interest in this country' than a Moroccan Muslim family 'with French passports who don't speak the language, some of whom wear the veil or believe in arranged marriages'.[21] His answer is to pull out of the EU partly because of treaty requirements to accept EU migrants and, instead, recruit immigrants from the pool of 70 million global Irish who, he implies again and again, have intrinsic capabilities that make them better able than other immigrants to contribute to the economy and culture of Ireland.

He cites the authority of Pope Benedict in making his case for New-Hibernian ethnic chauvinism; Benedict, because he 'has a good handle on Catholic Europe's fears about immigration and, in particular, Islamic immigration'. In the same breath he invokes Spengler, a blogger who posts articles predicting a possible Muslim takeover of Europe.[22] But there are allusions to the original Oswald Spengler's Weimar-era *The Decline of the West* in the arguments McWilliams invokes against cosmopolitanism. The original placed the West within a millennial model of inevitable cultural rot-from-within. Springtime, for Spengler, was German-led Christendom. Summer was the Reformation. Autumn was the Enlightenment. The winter of his discontent was exemplified by the cultural modernism of the Weimar Republic.[23] Spengler's proposed 'Prussian Republic' antidote to cosmopolitan cultural rot influenced Adolph Hitler and National Socialism.[24] In a chapter titled 'Degeneration', McWilliams argues that nineteenth-century globalisation, promoted by a 'narcissistic elite', collapsed into chaos, war, racism, eugenics and Fascism. The unmentioned Irish mage of such anxieties was of course W.B. Yeats, who enthused about *The Decline of the West* at the time of its publication.[25] McWilliams emphasises the present-day appeal of such ideas in the following terms:

> The Degeneration arguments are the same now as they were then. They go to the core of the globalisation-versus-community struggle. Many Irish people believe we are being swept along on an external tide of change, from immigration, to economic downsizing, to multinationals, to foreign money, washing over us. Others claim that our culture has become too self-absorbed, celebrity-driven, narcissistic, cynical and self-serving. For some, we are even witnessing the end of civilisation.[26]

The bromide proposed by McWilliams is essentially a national front political agenda. It is couched in terms and ideas that draw upon those presented by fringe anti-immigrant nationalist groups. This can be illustrated by comparing McWilliams' 'New Hibernia' to positions advocated by *The Hibernian*, a periodical launched in 2006 as a 'forum for all those in Ireland and amongst the Irish Diaspora'. *The Hibernian* declares itself as 'both Catholic and Irish'.[27] It presents itself as a voice for those who 'wish to counter the current anti-religious, materialist trends of our society, that are geared towards the destruction of the family, the practise of abortion, contraception and the ludicrous concept of homosexual marriage'.[28] McWilliams, on the other hand, endorses a Hibernicism that selectively embraces some cosmopolitan ideas though not those concerned with culture and identity.

Various articles present the EU as a 'threat to the freedom of the Gaelic nation' and blamed it for immigration. *The Hibernian* advocates an 'Irish-Ireland' restoration using terms and arguments of previous generations of cultural essentialism ('legislated on thousands of years of tradition') made over to appeal to present-day moral conservatives ('Irish Ireland is the Fenianism that opposes sin and debauchery') and xenophobes ('our right to exist as people free from all the mild and severe forms of terrorism of alien races').[29] *The Hibernian* presents immigration as a threat to the survival of the Irish nation. Those who encourage multiculturalism and mass immigration into Ireland are 'liberal traitors'; it proclaims the duty of 'all Gaelic nationalists to oppose Europe's colonial programme with the same determination as that waged against the English occupation'.[30] A June 2006 article, 'A New Plantation?' presented multiculturalism as a policy of 'divide and conquer to the benefit of corrupt government and its sponsors'. Colonisation ensured that 'there would never in the future be accord, unity, and a common agreed upon destiny amongst those ruled'. 'God,' the article insisted, 'abhors the blending of all peoples into a single world state.' Nationhood was claimed as a principle of divine order. Readers were admonished to withstand this 'onslaught against our tradition, our culture, our Christian civilisation, and our unique way of life' and not fear being called by imbecilic critics 'racist', 'bigot', 'fascist'. Undeterred, they must assume 'the courage of Patrick Pearse and Seán South and Fr Fahy'.[31] From the late 1930s to the 1950s Fr Fahy, a member of the Holy Ghost Missionary order, published a number of anti-Semitic pamphlets. South established a branch of Fahy's organisation *Maria Duce* in Limerick in 1954 after the priest's death and disseminated his writings.[32]

An October 2006 article railed against the threat of an Islamic Ireland and criticised Peter Sutherland, the UN's special representative on migration ('another Irish-born individual not noted for his Patriotic Zeal'), for advising the Irish to adapt their sense of nationality 'in order to accommodate waves of foreigners currently establishing themselves in Ireland. In other words, stop being Irish'. Sutherland, the article insisted, was one of 'that despicable breed of self-loathing Irishmen who have plagued our Nation for centuries'.[33] Letters to the editor reflected this view. One expressed 'outrage at the dilution of the Irish nation against the wishes of the majority'.[34]

The xenophobic sectarian nationalism promoted within *The Hibernian* is hardly representative of the Irish political mainstream. But McWilliams infers that it has a real political currency that could and should be acted upon. Yet his big idea – immigration-without-foreigners – has already perhaps been fully tested. In *Cherry-picking the Diaspora* Katy Hayward and Kevin Howard examine the Jobs Ireland campaign that ran from the late 1990s. Its slogans included 'Returning Home?', 'Coming Home?', 'Ag Teacht Abhaile?' and even 'Wild Geese Come Home'. Jobs Ireland road shows visited Newfoundland, Boston, Sydney, Liverpool, Munich and Berlin. But by early 2000 it was believed that the pool of potential returning expatriates in Britain and America was becoming exhausted; there was consequently a shift in emphasis towards a wider definition of the Irish abroad.[35] Returned Irish as a proportion of overall immigration reduced from just below 70 per cent in 2000 to below 30 per cent of those who arrived in 2004. By the time Ireland opened its doors to the new EU countries in May 2004 the Diaspora was already, in a sense, fished out.

What then of the seventy million Irish invoked by McWilliams? Many of these would not fit the narrow (Catholic) Hibernian template. Ever since the election of John F. Kennedy, the first and only Catholic American president, it has been customary for his successors to find Irish roots, a trend lampooned on the YouTube video 'there's no-one more Irish than Barack O'Bama'.[36] American surveys have found that slightly over 50 per cent of those who said their primary ethnic identity was Irish were Protestant.[37] The identities of many of the seventy million global Irish are likely to be multiple ones of a kind that essentialist nationalists cannot conceive of as viable. Those who most closely fit the Hibernian template are of course the Catholics of Northern Ireland who possess an automatic right to Irish citizenship. Kevin Howard suggests that these too might be considered as part of the Diaspora, displaced as they were after 1922 by a new border.[38] But here too McWilliams' inference that the Irish everywhere are intrinsically the same misses the social distance that comes from living in different societies. For decades ideological aspirations for a united Ireland were core tenets of Southern politics. In practice, affinity with Northern Catholics remained mostly abstract.[39] Northern nationalists came to be perceived as culturally different by their Southern brethren and even to have more in common with unionists. As exaggerated by a Southern respondent in a 2004 survey, 'Northern Ireland is just different. Everything about it – the people, the infrastructure, even *their* clothes, *their* way of life, *they are different people*.'[40] Somewhat similarly, unionists who define themselves as British have had an uneasy relationship with the mainland British. The real lessons of the Diaspora are ones that essentialists are incapable of grasping. Place matters as well as culture in defining how we think of ourselves. Difference is inevitable. However, belonging can be defined by the necessity of living together in a shared space as well as in terms of cultural particularism. The culturally homogenous societies commended by Herder are not viable options for diverse twenty-first-century nation-states. 'New Hibernia' is a dangerous fantasy insofar as the Ireland without immigrants it proposes is unattainable. To place immigrant communities irrevocably outside the nation is unsustainable. There is no Madagascar to send 'non-nationals' to.[41]

If nationalists are to reject ethnocentrism they will most likely do so in terms that make sense to them rather than those proposed by outside critics. For this to occur there needs to be engagement with and empathy towards how nationalists think of themselves. In a 2001 essay, 'Strangers in their own country: Multiculturalism in Ireland', Declan Kiberd proposes an alternative inclusive nationalism. This recalls Isaiah Berlin's conclusion from his reading of Herder that pluralism requires mutual recognition. Kiberd emphasises the need to engage with Irish nationalism's 'fear of hybridity' and an Irish cultural 'jeopardised sense of identity'.[42] He would promote a reading of Irish history as being one of successful past assimilation, whereby newcomers were folded into the nation to become, as the cliché has it, 'more Irish than the Irish themselves'. The approach he describes as civic nationalism differs considerably from both the hardcore ethnocentric *The Hibernian* and the airbrushed anti-immigrant populism of 'New Hibernia'. As a political project it has possibilities that are addressed in the next section of this chapter. In intellectual terms what Kiberd advocates might be summarised as Herder tempered by Joyce; the dominant imagined Ireland rebalanced by how it was depicted in *Ulysses*, where the Irish protagonist of the greatest novel of the twentieth century was a Jew. Here Kiberd exemplifies an Irish intellectual tradition of seeking pluralism through green on green dialogue.[43] If it cannot be found always in history, find it then in the novels and other artefacts of Irish culture. The Irish, he argues, need to reinvent the once and future Irish nation as 'always multi-cultural, in the sense of being eclectic, open, assimilative' and by affirming the nation not as a legacy of the past but 'the site of the future, a zone of pluralisms which will prove its durability precisely by the success with which it embraces refugees, exiles and newcomers'.[44]

CULTURAL RECOGNITION AND THE BOUNDED NATION

The need for a post-tribal political project is emphasised by *The Republic*, a journal launched in 2001 by the Ireland Institute. The institute is symbolically headquartered in the former Pearse family home in Dublin. Its patrons include leading figures in post-colonial Irish Studies from the Field Day collective such as Seamus Deane, Brian Friel and Declan Kiberd. An editorial article in the first issue, 'Beyond nationalism: Time to reclaim the republican ideal' by Finbar Cullen, observed that republicanism was a term equated by many with militant and armed nationalism. More generally, Ireland's republican heritage had become overwhelmed by nationalism.[45] As imagined communities go, or as Cullen put it 'acts of self-imagination', nationalism had the advantage over republicanism in that it sprang from a sense of nation that pre-existed the state as a concrete reality. It would be naïve to dismiss nations as forms of imagined community that could be easily re-imagined. They acquired a concrete existence as cultural entities and had become the basis of political organisation and of rights:

> Nationalism proposes that the state should be based upon the nation and rights derive simply from nationality ... It is in this sense that nationalism is a form of identity politics: political questions are addressed in terms of nationality, i.e. identity. But even in areas where politics based on identity seem useful, there is much that is problematic. Questions of culture constitute such an area. If identity in the shape of nationality is to be the arbitrator of cultural issues, then culture will be divided into culture that is an expression of the nation and culture from without. Culture from outside the nation will seem alien and to some degree will be interpreted as threatening to the national culture. Two further points are worth considering. Firstly, while such politics based on identity are familiar to all of us, they are at such odds with life and experience that they cannot stifle the impulses for openness and democracy that are everywhere. And secondly, the placing of culture in the national

sphere, responsible for the expression of national identity, can
lead to a narrowing down of democratic space, and an exclusion
of identities that cross national boundaries.[46]

Cullen argued that nationalism has swallowed up all kinds of political
programmes that have sought to make use of it, including republican
ones.[47] A reply article in the second issue revealed the scale of the challenge of selling a pluralist republicanism to nationalists. In
'Republicanism and nationalism: An imagined conflict' Daltún Ó
Ceallaigh argued that a republic could not emerge except through nationalism: 'Properly speaking, in Ireland, all republicans were nationalist,
even if not all nationalists were republican.'[48] He argued, making a point
anticipated and rejected by Cullen, that there were inclusive as well as
exclusionary nationalisms. As for the question of cultural intolerance he
offered the following maxim: 'In culture, treasure quality in your own
and augment it with quality from others. At the same time, if external culture is that of an imperial power and being imposed on a nation while
that nation's culture is being extirpated, resistance to attempted substitu-
tion, as distinct from worthwhile addition, is only natural.'[49] In effect the
caveat inserted here serves to licence ethnic chauvinism up to and including the xenophobic nationalism of *The Hibernian*. As put in a reply by
Cullen to Ó Ceallaigh, the essential problem of Irish nationalism is that
it bases the political organisation of society on ethnicity.[50]

In 2005 *The Republic* addressed head-on these intellectual challenges with coming to terms with immigration. An editorial argued that
easy assumptions about Ireland's sense of itself had not stood well in
the face of immigration:

> If we believed that Ireland's experience of colonisation and emi-
> gration had given us a special and benign outlook on the world,
> the great difficulties that have been encountered in making space
> for a relatively small number of immigrants have disabused us of
> our illusions … Far from Irish society finding itself in solidarity
> with others who find themselves in predicaments that are familiar
> in the story that we tell ourselves about ourselves, there has
> instead been a willingness to turn our backs, block off loopholes,
> close doors, and wish 'they' would go away.[51]

In a 2005 article T.J. Matthews challenged the twin parochialisms of
both camps within Irish intellectual politics:

> If 'revisionism' and post-colonialism defined the extremes of cul-

tural debate in Ireland over the past three decades or so, it is clear that these critical models have become outdated with the drawing of the new century. Traces of the old ideological squabble linger on, of course, and will continue to be heard for some time to come. But the fact remains that the standard revisionist analysis does not have much potency in post-Good-Friday-Agreement Ireland, where Irish nationalism has been well and truly revised, republican guns are silent, and cultural identity is now vested in the people rather than the territory. In a similar way, the classic post-colonial analysis of Irish under achievement is under strain in an Ireland now securely positioned as one of the most successful economies in the developed world. [52]

Matthews argued that the Hibernian model of Irish identity misunderstood both the twenty-first-century Irish at home and the Irish of the Diaspora; a better understanding of the complex identities of the global Irish could inform a positive debate about what it means to be Irish that would include immigrants. Irish people, he insisted, experience being Irish differently in different places; being Irish in Boston is not the same as being Irish in Dublin. Similarly, being Vietnamese in Ireland is not the same as being Vietnamese in Vietnam. In each case place played a key role in the evolution of a person's cultural identity; Irishness properly defined was the sum total of the cultural lives of all inhabitants of a place, indigenous and immigrant. This, he describes as a 'Hibernocentric' approach. It emphasised shared spatial dynamics rather than shared cultural bonds. Rather than draw on essentialist ideal types, cultural politics needed to refer to society, the diverse people living in the same place.[53] What Matthews proposed was a notion of hyphenated identity. Just as there could be Irish-Americans in the United States, so too could there be Filipino-Irish or Vietnamese-Irish whose own cultures of origin now fed into and therefore would ultimately redefine Irish culture. In essence he proposed a challenge to Herder's legacy of cultural pessimism, namely the ethnocentric fear of contamination of one's own essential cultural identity by outsiders.

This amalgam of essentialism and pessimism is exemplified by the account of Lithuanian immigrants presented by David McWilliams. By 2007 Ireland had the biggest Lithuanian immigrant community in the world; as McWilliams put it: 'One per cent of Irish people are Lithuanian.' He depicted the Lithuanians as exemplary immigrants ('They are going to make it') but it was inconceivable to him that they could ever become Irish:

If you want to see why the insidious, creeping use of the term the
'New Irish' is entirely inaccurate and nonsensical, come to the
Lithuanian School in Inchicore on a Saturday. Here you will see a
people intent on preserving their culture and language. The
Russians couldn't wipe it out, and certainly living in Ireland won't.
These people are as much New Irish as I was New English when I
lived in London.

It will take a lot to deflect these people. While we complain on
'Liveline' about under-funding in education, every Saturday morning over 150 Lithuanian children who have already done five days
in school come here to learn Lithuanian language, culture and
maths. They obviously don't rate our maths. Their parents pay for
this. There is no State hand-out, nor are they looking for one. This
is a volunteer effort by Lithuanian parents keen to make sure that
their children get the best education possible, while at the same
time being able to write in their own language when they go home
to Granny for the summer.[54]

In 'New Hibernia' even model immigrants should not be welcomed
because they could never become Irish enough. Even if Lithuanians
took out Irish citizenship they would still be 'non-nationals'. Learning
Lithuanian was presented as a threat to social cohesion. However, the
need for a Saturday school came about because Lithuanian children are
being successfully educated in English. Matthews, on the other hand,
proposed the Gaelscoil system of Irish language schools as a model for
future multicultural recognition. His example was the Tagalog-speaking
Filipino community: allowing children to learn Tagalog as well as
English would enrich the Irish linguistic mix rather than threaten Irish
distinctiveness; the expatriate Filipino identity that resulted would also
be an Irish one.[55]

Republicans propose that citizenship should be configured in civic
rather than cultural terms. In *The Republic* two articles inconclusively
examined the dilemmas here for Travellers. Colm Walsh's proposals in
'Between rhetoric and reality: Travellers and the unfinished republic'
for recognition of Traveller ethnicity and for a communal right to self-
determination were not on the republican menu.[56] Paul Delaney advocated a civic nationalism that sided with Ó Ceallaigh in dismissing
Cullen's concerns about nationalist chauvinism.[57] Delaney presented
the difference between civic nationalism and ethnic nationalism in the
following terms:

This distinction can be summarised briefly; ethnic nationalism has been defined as a collective form of identification that is based on the significance of an almost mystical ethnic – that is to say, a racial essence, which grounds identity in exclusive and inherited characteristics. Civic nationalism, by contrast, has been thought to stress the importance of fluidity and self-awareness in the make-up of any populace and to understand the basic idea of the nation in terms of an imagined community of citizens living in a pre-scribed geographical space.[58]

Ethnic nationalism, he continued, inevitably leads to states of exclusion and paralysis while civic nationalism is alive to change and allows, he claims, 'for expansive conditions of citizenship and cultural exclusivity'. The proofs offered here were hermeneutic ones. Delaney is a literary critic. His focus was on literature by and about Travellers that, as con-sidered in Chapter 2, would write them in or out of existence. Here, somewhat similarly, he instanced the argument of *Travellers: Citizens of Ireland* that they are fellow-citizens, with a distinct cultural identity and a legitimate ethnic inheritance that 'if accepted' would ensure their rights as citizens were respected.[59] But Travellers are denigrated, to use a phrase quoted by Delaney from a Traveller's memoir, as 'ghosts of an earlier form of existence'.[60] Delaney's limited proposal was that Irish artists, commentators and critics should critically engage with homoge-neous conceptions of Irish identity and Irish culture. However, he did not address the political rejection of Traveller ethnic recognition.

A 2004 article by Tariq Modood emphasised the shortcomings of the republican presumption of cultural neutrality. The ideal republic, he noted, does not recognise group identities among the citizenry. Instead it seeks to mould all citizens into civic community. This community may be based upon subscription to universal principles such as liberty, equal-ity and fraternity; upon the promotion of a national culture, or, as in the case of France, both.[61] In the Irish case the latter dominates; repub-licanism is subordinated by nationalism. The French experience sug-gests that even with a strong emphasis on civic republicanism the state plays cultural favourites. Denial of cultural diversity renders obscure the slighting and discrimination experienced by minority cultures.[62] Modood's emphasis here on the necessity of cultural recognition was one shared by Kiberd from an inclusive nationalist perspective:

> For this to work properly in a multi-cultural society, it will be nec-essary to abolish the old distinction between the public sphere as the zone of reason and the private area as a place of emotion. The pub-lic sphere should now be able to project the diversity of cultures

within it, rather than suppress them. In Ireland this would involve not just showing respect for Muslims, Hindus, Jews and Buddhists, but also for Catholics and Protestants – and *that* would entail a reversal of many recent trends, which have worked to make even southern Catholicism a matter of more private than public symbolism.[63]

The civic nationalism advocated by Kiberd reflects the principle of communitarian subsidiary advocated within Catholic social thought. It is already enshrined in Article 44 of Bunreacht na hÉireann, the 1937 Constitution. The core principle is that of subsidiarity; the state should not encroach unnecessarily on the autonomy of the community, understood principally in terms of Catholic institutions but also those of other denominations. What this amounts to is provision for multiculturalism institutionalised within the nation-state. The Irish state funds Muslim schools. These, like Catholic, Protestant and Jewish ones, are allowed to hire teachers and select students according to faith-based criteria but provide education in accordance with a national curriculum.

If in the past education has been the key driver of nation-building, so too will it play such a role in twenty-first-century adaptive nation-building. Here future problems are likely to centre on the capacity of the existing system to reject immigrant children. In 2007 rising numbers of non-Catholic immigrant children were unable to secure school places. At that time the overwhelming majority of primary schools in the Republic of Ireland were faith-based; 3,032 Catholic, 183 Church of Ireland, fourteen Presbyterian, two Muslim, one Jewish, one Jehovah's Witness, one interdenominational and one Religious Society of Friends (Quakers).[64] Just forty were multidenominational. The rest could invoke, as did some Dublin Catholic schools in 2007, an exemption from the 2000 Equality Act. The Act was designed to prohibit discrimination in the provision of goods and services on religion and eight other grounds. However, it specifically allowed faith schools (more than 98 per cent of all 'state' primary schools) to discriminate on the basis of religious affiliation in cases where there was competition for school places.[65] In a 2006 address the Catholic primate of Ireland, Archbishop Diarmuid Martin, outlined an inclusive Catholic ethos that contrasted with that of *The Hibernian*:

> ... in debates about education today, far too little attention is given to the extraordinary work that is being done in Catholic schools in welcoming children of many nationalities into one school community. When I look at the situation in the diocese of Dublin, it is

most often the Catholic school in an area which is the most representative in terms of nationalities and religious denominations, while still maintaining its Catholic ethos, also in the wide sense of the word catholic, which gives rise to openness and welcome.[66]

Yet something close to a worst-case scenario was observed at a September 2007 meeting in Dublin 15. Those present included more than seventy parents who had not found primary school places for their children because, in the face of competition for places, Catholic children were prioritised while immigrant children were shunted towards two new Educate-Together schools. A journalist in attendance wrote: 'As they take their seats, one thing becomes startlingly clear: apart from the organisers, myself and five or six others, everyone else in the room is black.'[67] These immigrant parents were non-Catholics who had moved into a predominately Catholic and predominantly white community. They were members of the putative 'New Irish' community who had, since the birth of their Irish-born children, run the gauntlet of hostility towards asylum seekers, fear of deportation, direct provision, being the focus of racism during the Citizenship Referendum campaign and now unwitting and potentially permanent educational apartheid. Another new emergency primary school in Dublin 15, Scoil Choilm, admitted eighty-three junior infants in 2007, 'the vast majority of whose parents come from Nigeria, Colombia, Romania, Poland and Moldova'.[68]

The need to prevent such segregation has been emphasised in subsequent debates about education. In January 2008 the Irish Primary Principals' Network called on the Minister for Education to work harder to prevent ghettoisation and Archbishop Martin announced that two new west Dublin Catholic schools would have one-third of places allocated to non-Catholic pupils.[69] At its best the denominational model works to recognise plural identities as the basis of a broader social cohesion. This potential found expression in 2007 with the piloting of the first tri-religious intercultural interdenominational primary school in County Kildare. This has as its patrons the Catholic Church, the Progressive Jewish Congregation and the Islamic Cultural Centre of Ireland.

CULTURAL RECOGNITION AND ADAPTIVE NATION-BUILDING

The emerging Irish institutional model will most likely be one where something short of French-style republicanism is practised in some spheres while particularistic identity is formally recognised in others. The parameters of this new identity settlement were sketched out in 2007 when Conor Lenihan, the Minister of State for Integration, backed the decision of the Garda commissioner to refuse a Sikh garda permission to wear a turban as part of his uniform.[70] Shortly after, the minister announced that one plank of his integration programme would consist of faith-based initiatives.

The 2007 prohibition on turbans was justified in terms of a 'tradition' of cultural neutrality that dated back to the Civil War. Arguably the refusal was about avoiding setting a precedent for future multicultural symbolic recognition. However, as the historian John A. Murphy observed disapprovingly, this presumed neutrality broke down when it came to the dominant ethnic group:

> The Garda Síochána, like all other agencies and organs of the State, must be neutral and secular. And the logic of this position should be faced unflinchingly – no Pioneer badges or *fáinnes* on uniforms. And no sporting of ashes on Ash Wednesdays – a protocol which should also extend to the chambers of the Oireachtas. The Taoiseach should take up the lead here rather than wait for the Ceann Comhairle to politely request the removal of the ostentatious pietistic smudge, growing larger by the year. But I won't hold my breath.[71]

During the turban debate Conor Lenihan suggested that there would be further secularisation of the public sphere, 'but not overnight'. He argued that the state should invest in an egalitarian small 'r' republican ethos.[72] The main initiative to date that could be called a civic republican one has been the replacement in 2006 of the Irish language requirement for membership of the Gardaí by proficiency in any second language other than English. However, similar reforms have yet to be introduced for teachers and civil servants.

Debates about national identity have yet to be asserted in relation to integration. For all the stridency of some nationalists, it seems that many Irish are unsure about how to define their national identity. At a 2007 conference organised by the Office of Integration under the title 'The Chance to Get it Right', a debate was held as to whether Ireland should follow the example of other countries by introducing a citizenship examination. None of the civil servants, academics, NGO representatives or immigrants present supported such a move. When asked what was it immigrants were expected to integrate into, respondents favoured civic values over cultural ones as the basis of integration. The guiding norms were those 'best practices' outlined in the EU *Handbook on Integration* that was used to frame the conference.[73] Here integration was defined in terms that made no reference to culture. The handbook identified EU-wide antipathy to the term 'multiculturalism'. The emphasis was upon social policy, political and civic participation, education and social mobility; the view being that these, but the latter in particular, were important for future social cohesion. Vulnerable immigrants, in the language of *The Handbook on Integration*, lacked the necessary 'competences' to achieve social mobility.[74]

Multiculturalism is now a much-maligned term, one slighted to project anxieties about Muslims in particular. For all its problems it needs to be reclaimed if only because Western nation-states *are* multicultural, because the identities that dominate nation-states like Ireland *are* particularistic, as are those of immigrants. For all his scepticism, Leon Wieseltier insists that it is impertinent to address the criticism of identity to those whose existence is threatened.[75] This holds too for those who feel threatened. But the current received wisdom, reflected in *The Handbook on Integration*, is that immigrant cultural difference should not be recognised. The argument has two components. The first is that when minority communities are allowed to hive themselves off from the mainstream this generates future conflict. What is missing here is the pushing out due to racism and discrimination that generally precipitates the pulling away. The second is the 'clash of civilisations' argument directed specifically against Muslims. This presumes that their integration is impossible so should not be attempted in the first place. However, this argument licenses a wider rejection of cultural recognition within the nation-state, one that appeals to nationalist essentialists as well as ethnocentric liberals.

In the face of such received wisdom it is necessary to directly address the presumption that Muslims cannot be successfully integrated. At a February 2007 conference the Reception and Integration Agency commended Dutch rejection of multiculturalism as an example for Ireland.[76] The Dutch experience is pertinent to the Irish case but full account needs to be taken of the different context in each case. The Netherlands has a tradition of institutional subsidiarity; a framework for the practice of cultural recognition that existed before large-scale integration. The different religious pillars created their own institutions. These structured the lives of their members to a considerable extent. Each had their own ideologically sensitive organisations; political parties, youth movements, hospitals, newspapers, housing associations, even associations of stamp collectors. Many were either full or partly state-funded. These pillars were the milieu through which people participated in Dutch society. They allowed groups with incompatible moral or religious doctrines to create their own worlds within a climate of overall co-operation. But from the 1970s the indigenous pillars went into decline, the victims of their own success. They are credited with having contributed to the social 'emancipation' of different communities and such emancipation, especially in the case of Calvinists and Catholics, accelerated the collapse of pillars. For example, the Roman Catholic and Dutch Reform political parties merged into a single Christian party that subsequently declined.[77] A Muslim pillar of sorts eventually emerged (comprising by 2005 forty-one elementary schools, just two secondary schools and two university faculties of Islamic Theology) but by then the native Dutch had become less communal and more individualistic; sexual and social liberalism became core social values against which integration into Dutch society came to be judged.[78]

What at face value looked like a functional mechanism for social integration, the emergence of a putative Muslim pillar in keeping with Dutch tradition was now an anachronism out of step with the ways the Dutch now integrated themselves into society. The first Islamic primary schools did not open until 1988. By 2005 just forty-one out of 7,000 were Muslim. These served some 8,400 mostly Moroccan or Turkish children. They are far from universally popular with Moroccan and Turkish parents; a series of studies in 2000 found that not more than 30 to 40 per cent would send their children to such schools if they had the choice to do so. Muslim isolation from the Dutch mainstream tends to be both overstated and understated. Many Islamic schools vary only slightly from the mainstream curriculum. Many are 'liberal' when it comes to the observation of Islamic rules of behaviour by staff and students. However, in 2001 some 94.5 per cent of pupils attending Islamic schools were classified as disadvantaged. Ian Buruma argues in his account of the disintegration of Dutch multiculturalism that it is lazy and inaccurate to assert that Islam is incompatible with secular Western democracy.[79] Laissez-faire multiculturalism, allowing the marginalisation of Dutch Turks and Dutch Moroccans to go unheeded, letting things drift – if this was multicultural tolerance, no wonder it failed.

A 2008 *Time* article charted the rise of a Euro-Muslim middle class. It suggested that some Muslim expressions of cultural distinctiveness are manifestations of confidence rather than an impulse to self-ghettoise ('By 25, Kaddouri was doing well enough at work that she dared to start wearing a headscarf'); though often some assertions came at considerable cost ('Suspended for five weeks for breaking the rule' of the Parisian hospital where she worked).[80] The transferable cautionary lessons that can be extracted from Dutch and French experiences include the dangers to social cohesion of failing to plan for linguistic integration of immigrants; in the Irish case this means fluency in English, the consequences of economic marginalisation and the inadequacy of integration that is restricted to the economy. The Dutch conclusion that Muslim religious identity caused multiculturalism to fail was specifically one drawn by a society that insistently rooted its social as well as political identity in liberalism. While Muslims have pushed for an Islamic pillar, they have not been able to achieve the kind of mechanism that previously enabled other religious groups to integrate within Dutch society.

For all that they have modernised, the Irish still rely on denominational education as their principal nation-building engine. Whereas the Dutch presumed that liberal multiculturalism would work without a politics of recognition (support structures that would enable Muslims to integrate into Dutch society from their specific starting places), the Irish institutional starting place is one that emphasises recognition. In the Irish case Muslim culture has been formally respected within the nation-state. For example, the president of the Republic attended the opening of the Dublin Islamic Cultural Centre in 1996. On issues such as wearing the hijab and dress code for girls the general trend has been towards flexibility, notwithstanding opposition by leading figures in some political parties (Fine Gael and Labour) during 2008 debates.[81] What these objected to was the wearing of the headscarf in 'state schools', a category made up mostly of denominational schools. An *Irish Times* poll in June 2008 identified 48 per cent support for the wearing of headscarves or hijabs in 'state schools' with 39 per cent of respondents maintaining that these should be prohibited.[82] But bodies such as the Joint Management Body for Secondary Schools (JMB) and the Association of Management of Catholic Secondary Schools (AMCSS) advise schools not to make an issue of school uniform rules where these conflict with a child's religion. This, according to the JMB secretary, 'points towards a typically Irish solution to the problems of Islamic integration', where the only issue is that the headscarf should match the colour of the school uniform.[83] As put in 2008 by one Catholic school principal who exemplified this perspective: 'Muslim children are free to wear the headscarf and the other children don't even notice. They see the child, not the headscarf.'[84] Such recognition cannot be accurately depicted as allowing Muslims to create their own society within a society. It exists as part of a broader system that allows for cultural recognition that could now be expanded; for example, the Gaelscoil model offers a potential template for other linguistic communities within a national curriculum that emphasises English language fluency. The recognition advocated here could not be more different from laissez-faire multiculturalism. Culture and identity are not understood as ends in themselves but as means to ends.

Robert Putnam makes an emphatic distinction between bonding and bridging forms of social capital. Some bonding social capital can be bad for wider society for all the benefits it confers upon a group; his worst-case examples here include the Mafia and Al-Qaeda; the consequences of bonding social capital can include ethnic nepotism (practised below the level of the state) and sectarianism. His evidence here supports to a limited extent the claims of liberal anti-multiculturalists. But Putnam emphasises the benefits of many forms of bonding social capital. For example, Christian or Islamic groups may bond along religious lines but bridge across ethnic ones. As such the question for policy makers is how to minimise the exclusionary consequences of bonding social capital and to maximise the positive consequences of bridging social capital.[85] There has not yet been a substantive study of the integration of Irish Muslims. However, Abel Ugba's research on religious social capital among African Pentecostals in Ireland suggests that even 'conservative' Islam is likely to foster some integration into Irish society. Like Islam, Pentecostalism promotes an almost essentialist identity among its members. Religious identity is presented as different from and superior to other identity markers like nationality, skin colour and immigrant status. Pentecostals repudiate many of the practices of the wider Irish society. They do not endorse alcohol consumption, sex outside marriage, homosexuality or listening to non-Christian music. Like Muslims or the conservative Catholic readers of *The Hibernian* they can be presented as having created their own parallel social and moral universe. However, they are nevertheless connected to the Irish social mainstream in many significant ways. African Pentecostals interviewed by Ugba emphasised how church membership and activities helped give them the confidence and skills to cope with the demands of living and working in Irish society; a bonding social capital that nevertheless helped them to overcome barriers to participating in the wider world. Ugba's account depicts the identities of individual Pentecostals as fluid and nuanced, as reflecting the realities of their experiences in Ireland as well as religious devotion.[86]

The extent to which African Pentecostals, Muslims or other immigrants integrate will by no means depend on cultural recognition alone.

The Irish education system has failed many Irish people generation after generation on the basis of social class.[87] Almost certainly this 'underclass' who deserve better will come to include some immigrants. Almost inevitably, such exclusions will be interpreted as the result of cultural conflict rather than – here the experience of Northern Catholics resonate as much as those of Muslims in Bradford, Paris or Amsterdam – as having much to do with economic exclusion and discrimination. Putnam makes no bones about the challenges of integrating immigrants within twenty-first-century nation-states. His findings are that immigration and increased diversity reduce trust, social solidarity and social capital in the short term. But immigration, he concludes, is good for host countries in the long run. As Ireland comes to the end of its mass immigration honeymoon, as it hunkers down in the face of diversity, native-born citizens are 'unnerved' by what they perceive as new and different.[88] These are Putnam's phrases but they echo David McWilliams' account of Irish disquiet. These decreases in trust and solidarity are partly the result of barriers produced by anxiety and partly due to the real challenges of addressing social complexity. Putnam suggests that, in the long run, successful immigrant societies overcome such fragmentation by building new forms of social-solidarity and extending existing ones such as citizenship and national identity.

It is in this context that the Republic of Ireland has perhaps entered its third uncertain phase of cultural-economic nation-building. Post-independence 'Irish-Ireland' emphasised culture as the basis of solidarity. The task it set itself was the intergenerational reproduction of Catholicism and Gaelic culture. Post-1950s developmental nation-building de-emphasised the cultural reproduction of Irish society in favour of economic growth, social liberalism and the individualisation of Irish life. While this fostered a generic modernisation, as discussed in the previous chapter, that allows for cosmopolitan acceptance of immigrants, it does not provide for their integration into the Irish nation-state. The effect of the 2004 Referendum on Citizenship was to narrow the empirical definition of what it meant to be Irish, inventing the conundrum of the Irish-born non-Irish child as a perverse twenty-first-century civics lesson. If citizenship without recognition is not always enough to ensure integration, the absence of both renders integration very difficult indeed. The problem is not too many immigrants seeking Irish nationality but that many of those living here are unlikely to naturalise. Citizenship is a prerequisite of many forms of bridging social capital. Without a critical mass of 'new nationals' essentialist distinctions between 'nationals' and 'non-nationals' will remain something of a dead hand at the tiller. The challenge is to come up with ways of binding the Irish to their diverse nation-state was well as integrating the new guests of the nation.

CHAPTER FIFTEEN

Endnote on Ethnic Nepotism

The closing focus is on the concept of ethnic nepotism that has influenced the analysis presented in a number of preceding chapters. The value of the concept is its capacity to address twenty-first-century political responses to immigration that do not lend themselves to being depicted as racism. The focus on ethnic nepotism in this book seeks to adjust for the shortcomings of theories of racism to explain Irish responses to immigrants and, more broadly, to account for what David Goodhart depicts as a pragmatic or realist post-multicultural turn in Western debates about immigration. In the Irish case racism alone cannot explain the outcome of the 2004 referendum promoted by the government as commonsense citizenship, even if (as Chapter 9 considers) racism in Irish society was exploited to achieve that specific end. The argument of *New Guests of the Irish Nation* is that ethnic nepotism presents a considerable risk to future social cohesion.

First, this endnote explains ethnic nepotism as a socio-biological concept focusing particularly on the work of Frank Salter. Here the socio-biological debate about ethnic nepotism offers a theoretical account of why rights and entitlements of new migrants to Western countries are being undermined. Second, the advocacy of ethnic nepotism as a political and ideological response to immigration is discussed. Here a parallel can be seen with essentialist understandings of national identity developed by J.G. Herder in the nineteenth century. Herder's argument that cultures were incommensurable translated into a pessimism about cultural mixing that is similar to the fatalism about ethnic mixing that emerges from Salter's account of genetic interests. Here the blood and soil territorial imperative of romantic nationalism is repackaged as a selfish gene territorial imperative.

Salter's definition of and case for ethnic nepotism informs how the term is used in various chapters even if there are crucial distinctions between the tooth and claw ethnic nepotism that he advocates and lesser degrees of ethnic chauvinism characteristic of mainstream political responses to immigration. Ethnic nepotism theory maintains that members of an ethnic group tend to favour members of their group over others because they are more related to the former. It emphasises a disposition to favour kin over outsiders especially where people and groups have to compete for scare resources.[1] Here ethnicity is ultimately defined in terms of common descent: ethnic and racial sentiments are understood as extensions of kinship sentiments; ethnocentricism and racism are thus extended forms of nepotism.[2]

Salter describes his work as 'political ethology', meaning the study of political phenomena from a biological perspective. He presents ethnic nepotism as a neo-Darwinism socio-biological theory of inclusive fitness:

> In neo-Darwinian theory, genes are the basic unit of selection and humans are 'survival machines' evolved to perpetuate them into succeeding generations. Conversely, for humans and all other organisms, reproductive interest consists of perpetuating their distinctive genes. Humans like other organism(s) are so evolved that their 'interests' are reproductive. Said differently, the interests of an individual human (i.e. the directions of its striving) are expected to be toward ensuring the indefinite survival of its genes and their copies, wherever these are resident in the individual, its descendents or its collateral relatives. Thus genetic interests are the number of copies of our distinctive genes carried by reproducing individuals. Individual genetic interest is carried by close kin, and ethnic interests by one's ethnic group.[3]

Salter proposes that ethnic genetic interest accounts for warfare and genocide. It finds spatial expression in the struggle for the control of territory and the establishment of nation-states dominated numerically by an ethnic nation where their interests can find expression: 'Not to control a territory creates risks of subjugation, displacement and marginalisation. For all past human experience territory is a resource for maintaining ethnic genetic interests in the long run.'[4] The default presumption of his model is that zero-sum conceptions of interest are rational. From Salter's perspective ethnic altruism tends to be self-sacrificial. The biological interests of a given ethnic prioritise the welfare of its children but under certain circumstances self-sacrificial altruism *can* be adaptive where it preserves 'the genetic interest of a population of genetically similar individuals'.[5] Salter proposes that altruism towards ethnic outsiders can only be justified when it is in the genetic interests of the dominant ethnic group. One example he gives relevant to the Irish case is of the trade-off between economic growth that benefits the host ethnic and the, in his view, detrimental consequences of immigrants and their descendents for the genetic interest of the host group.

As presented by Salter, ethnic nepotism is more a political theory of human interests than a socio-biological theory of human behaviour. It proposes a calculus for ascertaining ethnic genetic interest (in copies of their own genes) in different relational situations that Salter uses to argue how ethnic groups ought to act in specific circumstances. Here ethnic kinship is presented as relative to the population chosen for comparison. Salter's calculus defines the degree of ethnic interest competition in terms of genetic difference between groups. Furthermore, his model prioritises genetic reproduction over any individual motivation. Salter gives the example that it would be more adaptive for an Englishman to risk life or property resisting the immigration of two Bantu immigrants in England than his taking the same risk to rescue one of his own children from drowning. Salter argues that the genetic difference between English and Bantu is so great that 'on the face of it, competition between them would make within-group altruism amongst random English (or amongst random Bantu) almost as adaptive as parent-child altruism.'[6] Chapter 9 recounts how a member of Fine Gael defected from the party to campaign against the Referendum on Citizenship. Her motivation in doing so was as the grandmother of a 'mixed race' child. Salter would argue that in thinking about the kind of Ireland she wanted for her family she had acted against her ethnic genetic interest; people, he argues, ought to 'perceive' their genetic interests and then 'be motivated to pursue them'.[7]

Salter's conception of ethnic genetic interests presumes that humans who ignore their genetic duty are derelict in doing so. He acknowledges that they are often unaware of their genetic interests outside of immediate kin.[8] That Salter's theory fails to explain human motivation is unsurprising. As one scientist critic put it, Salter's concept is itself an attempt to base individual interests in the metaphorical interest of genes:

> 'Life' does not have an 'interest', anymore than water had an 'interest' in flowing downhill. And even if 'life' or 'genes' did have an 'interest', so what? Why should we as individuals put the interests of our genes before our personal wants and needs, or even

give it any weight at all? Salter does not recognise the 'so what?' objection, but his answer to it is just the same old flapdoodle about genes as 'fundamental' to our existence. Ultimately Salter's attitude towards the genes is more mystical than scientific.[9]

Salter's work presents ethnicity in biological rather than cultural terms. In effect it recalls nineteenth-century depictions of nations as races, the story of the Irish race as examined in Chapter 2 being an example of this. It adds a new layer of metaphysics to older strata of romantic nationalism and historicist conceptions of national destiny. Salter's calculus of ethnic genetic interest leads him to advocate genetic nationalism: 'Group spirit,' he quotes, 'tribal spirit or tribalism, national spirit or nationalism are one and the same thing.' Members of the same ethnic nation have a particular affection for their native land: 'They would give their lives freely to preserve the integrity of the land and the liberty of its people ... They are sharers in a common interest and a common destiny; they hope and believe that their stock will never die out. They inhabit a sharply delimited territory and claim to own it.'[10] Ethnic nepotism theory strips the poetry from romantic nationalism. It also offers a theory of political behaviour that purports to explain why ethnic nationalists such as Patrick Pearse might want to die childless for Ireland's unborn generations.

Unsurprisingly, Salter's gene calculus has been enthusiastically endorsed by racist organisations.[11] While Goodhart does not cite ethnic nepotism theory per se, his political arguments are similarly drawn. As put in his influential 2004 essay, *Discomfort of Strangers*:

> Thinking about the conflict between solidarity and diversity is another way of asking a question as old as human society itself; who is my brother, with whom do I share mutual obligations? The traditional conservative, Burkean view is that our affinities ripple out from our families and localities to the nation, and not very far beyond. That view is pitted against a liberal universalist one that sees us in some sense equally obligated to all human beings, from Bolton to Burundi – an idea that is associated with the universalist aspects of Christianity and Islam, with Kantian universalism and left-wing internationalism. Science is neutral in this dispute, or rather it stands on both sides of the argument. Evolutionary psychology stresses both the universality of most human traits and – through the notion of kin selection and reciprocal altruism – the instinct to favour our own. Social psychologists also argue that the tendency to perceive in-groups and out-groups, however

ephemeral, is innate. In any case, Burkeans claim to have common sense on their side. They argue that we feel more comfortable with, and readier to share with and sacrifice for, those with whom we have shared histories and similar values. To put it bluntly – most of us prefer our own kind.[12]

Goodhart purports to challenge 'the rhetoric of the liberal state' where the glue of ethnicity ('people who look and talk like us') has become replaced with the glue of values ('people who think and behave like us'). He argues that such liberalism discounts the historical context from which shared values emerge. He criticises it for promoting a politically unsustainable ideal of solidarity. In more strident language but along the same lines, Salter is a trenchant critic of 'anti-nationalists' such as Jurgen Habermas whose intellectual project ('constitutional patriotism' detached from ethnic-nationalism) is to reconcile 'ethnic majorities to their own demise':

> According to this formula a country would lose nothing if the founding ethnic group were peacefully replaced so long as some set of values – democracy, equality, non-discrimination, minority rights – were retained. The combination of constitutional patriotism and multiculturalism is, as one would expect, subversive of the ethnic interests of the majority.[13] Goodhart, like Salter, argues that there is an inevitable conflict or trade-off between social solidarity and diversity, though he presents this in cultural rather than genetic terms.[14] Salter, like Goodhart, argues that diversity undermines the moral consensus on which social solidarity rests.[15]

In the United Kingdom the influence of Goodhart's arguments can be seen in the green paper, *The Path to Citizenship* (2008).[16] Using, as Goodhart put it, 'a rhetoric that would have been unthinkable 10 years ago', the British Home Secretary advocated restricting certain welfare benefits to those who had achieved full citizenship, after six years 'probation'.[17] Rather than emphasise their positive contributions, *The Path to Citizenship* proposed that newcomers incur additional taxes to 'pay their way' in order, as the Minister for Integration put it, to 'win an emotional argument about immigration'.[18] Goodhart argues that this political shift has little to do with racism ('the average Briton is more comfortable with difference – consider the rise of interracial marriage') and much to do with pragmatism. As he stated in a 2008 article 'The baby-boomers finally see sense on immigration':

> The justification for giving priority to the interests of fellow

citizens boils down to the pragmatic claim about the value of the nation-state. Without fellow-citizen favouritism, the nation-state ceases to have much meaning. And most of the things liberals desire – democracy, redistribution, welfare states, human rights – only work when one can assume the shared norms and solidarities of national communities.[19]

So what changed in the minds of the liberal baby boomer generation that promoted gender and racial equality? According to Goodhart, they came to grasp that a belief in universal moral equality did not mean having the same obligations to all humans: 'We do not consider our families to be on a different moral plane, yet would not hesitate to put their interests first.'[20]

The crucial difference between Salter and Goodhart is that the latter promotes cultural rather than genetic nepotism, making the distinction in the following terms: 'Until a few decades ago, the basis of national "specialness" would have been ethnicity-shared ancestry, history, sacrifice. In multi-ethnic and multiracial societies, the basis of specialness is citizenship itself.'[21] Goodhart, a liberal who disapproves of racism, envisages solidarity in terms of a British nation-state that has already come to consist of an ethnically diverse population. Here is a fundamental difference to the Irish case where the interests of the dominant ethnic group dominate the nation-state. British politicians and intellectuals pit their 'nationals' against 'non-nationals' in a context where the former were at least now demonstrably diverse. Ireland began its immigration politics not having recalibrated what it means to be Irish for more than a century.

Ireland's history of sectarian ethnic conflict might be interpreted as vindicating theories of ethnic nepotism but this history, especially its most recent reconciliatory phase, suggests that competing ethnic groups can respectively conclude that ethnic nepotism is not in the interest of themselves or their children (as distinct from their ethnic genetic interests). Salter's advocacy of ethnic nationalism as a response to immigration finds its closest Irish equivalent in the arguments of David McWilliams as described in Chapter 14. Many expressions of ethnic chauvinism are not harmful to other groups. Irish government lobbying on behalf of undocumented Irish migrants in the United States is one such example of ethnic solidarity. Yet, the same Irish politicians who lobby the White House on their behalf do not demonstrate similar empathy towards 'non-nationals' in equivalent circumstances under their jurisdiction.

Accepting the need for a realistic account of the limits of solidarity and empathy is not the same as maintaining that ethnic nepotism is functional. What matters considerably here is which understandings of interests prevail. Arguments for multi-ethnic altruism (extending the same rights and support to immigrants and their children that we would give to ourselves and our children) are emphasised in a number of chapters. In summary, such altruism is presented as an investment in the future of the Irish nation, a necessary adaptation in the face of trans-ethnic interdependencies. Without an adaptive nation-building that allows immigrants to become part of the Irish nation, ethnic nepotism is likely to undermine such investment.

Notes

CHAPTER ONE

1. B. Cowen, 'The soul of Ireland is in good shape', in J. Mullholland (ed.), *The Soul of Ireland: Issues of Society, Culture and Identity. Essays from the 2006 McGill Summer School* (Dublin: Liffey Press, 2006), pp.3–4.
2. H. Arendt, *The Jew as Pariah: Jewish Identity and Politics in the Modern Age*, edited by R.H. Feldman (New York: Grove Press, 1978), p.242.
3. A number of Irish academic analyses of the Irish politics of immigration have imported Goldberg's notion of the 'racial state'. D.T. Goldberg, *The Racial State* (Oxford: Blackwell, 2002). These have concluded that the Republic of Ireland is a 'racial state' on its way to becoming a 'racist state'. Examples here include R. Lentin and R. McVeigh, *After Optimism: Ireland, Racism and Globalisation* (Dublin: Metro Éireann, 2006); R. Lentin, 'Ireland: racial state and crisis racism', *Ethnic and Racial Studies*, 30, 4 (2007), pp.610–27; A. Christie, 'From racial to racist state: questions for social work professionals working with asylum seekers', *Journal of Applied Social Studies*, 7, 2 (2006), pp.35–49.
4. The Republic of Ireland along with the Netherlands, Belgium, Luxembourg, the Scandinavian countries and some of the new EU member states allow for local enfranchisement based on residence rather than citizenship. J. Shaw, *The Transformation of Citizenship in the European Union* (Cambridge: Cambridge University Press, 2007), p.77.

CHAPTER TWO

1. Census figures put the population of Ireland at 8,175, 224 in 1841, 6,553,290 in 1851 and 5,764, 543 in 1861. The population continued to decline. The 1961 census reported a population of 2,800,000 for the Republic of Ireland.
2. R. MacSharry and P.A. White, *The Making of the Celtic Tiger: The Inside Story of Ireland's Boom Economy* (Cork: Mercier Press, 2000), p.361.
3. S. Sassen, *Guests and Aliens* (New York: The New Press, 1999), p.140.
4. See C. Coulter and S. Coleman (eds), *The End of Irish History? Critical Reflections on the Celtic Tiger* (Manchester: Manchester University Press, 2003).
5. A. Jackson, *Ireland: 1798–1998* (London: Blackwell, 1999), p.415.
6. T. Garvin, 'National identity in Ireland', *Studies*, 95, 379 (2006), pp.241–50.
7. C. McCarthy, *Modernisation: Crisis and Culture in Ireland 1969–1992* (Dublin: Four Courts Press, 2000), pp.17–18.
8. B. Fanning, *The Quest for Modern Ireland: The Battle of Ideas 1912–1986* (Dublin: Irish Academic Press, 2008), pp.19–20.
9. In the preface to the English edition of *Das Kapital*, vol 1: 'A country that is more developed industrially only shows, to the less developed, the image of its own future', cited in F. Fukuyama, *The End of History and the Last Man* (London: Penguin, 1992), p.68.
10. D. O'Sullivan, *Cultural Politics and Irish Education since the 1950s* (Dublin: Institute of Public Administration, 2006).

11. E. Gellner, *Culture, Identity and Politics* (Cambridge: Cambridge University Press, 1987), pp.15–16.
12. The Young Irelander newspaper, *Nation* (9 September 1943) cited by E. Crooke, *Politics, Archaeology and the Creation of a National Museum of Ireland* (Dublin: Irish Academic Press, 2000), p.17.
13. Gellner, *Culture, Identity and Politics*, p.16.
14. The final paragraph of Haverty's last chapter reads: 'While these pages are going through the press, the revolution has actually begun. Minor risings have taken place in various parts of Ireland; the great English arsenal at Chester has well nigh fallen into Fenian hands; English troops are pouring into Ireland, and hurrying from point to point. It is too soon for the pen of History to begin to chronicle these movements. They will form a new chapter of the History of Ireland.' M. Haverty, *The History of Ireland from the Earliest Period to the Present Time Derived from Native Annals and from the Researches of Dr O'Donovan, Professor Eugene Curry, The Rev. C.P. Meehan, Dr R.R. Madden and other Eminent Scholars and from All Resources of Irish History Now Available* (New York: Thomas Fannell and Son, 1967).
15. But one adopted from the chronology of the Septuagint and the Greeks which dated the world as 5,200 years old at the beginning of the Christian Era; an improbable chronology, Haverty accepted. Ibid., pp.10–15.
16. Ibid., p.2.
17. Ibid., p.11.
18. Ibid., p.88. For an account of the characteristic integration of early histories into European nationalisms see Crooke, *Politics, Archaeology and the Creation of a National Museum*, p.19.
19. Crooke, *Politics, Archaeology and the Creation of a National Museum*, p.41.
20. Garvin, 'National Identity in Ireland', pp.241–50.
21. S. McCall, *And So Began the Irish Nation* (Dublin: Talbot Press, 1930), p.xiii.
22. Ibid., p.451.
23. Ibid., p.452.
24. T. Cahill, *How the Irish Saved Civilisation* (London: Hodder and Stoughton, 1995), p.130.
25. Haverty, *History of Ireland*, p.70.
26. Cahill, *How the Irish Saved Civilisation*, p.3.
27. Haverty, *History of Ireland*, p.70.
28. D. Corkery, *The Hidden Ireland: A Study of Gaelic Munster in the Eighteenth Century* (Dublin: Gill and Macmillan, 1970), p.10.
29. M. Tierney, 'Politics and culture: Daniel O'Connell and the Gaelic past', *Studies*, 27, 107 (1938), pp.353–81.
30. Ibid., p.354.
31. E. Gellner, *Nations and Nationalism* (Oxford: Blackwell, 1983), p.57.
32. Gellner's argument about the role of collective amnesia drew on E. Renan, *Qu'est-ce, qu'un nation?* (Paris, 1882), cited in ibid, p.6.
33. 'Foreword' to P. Loughrey (ed.), *The People of Ireland* (Belfast: Appletree Press/BBC Northern Ireland), p.7.
34. H. Butler, *Ten Thousand Saints* (Kilkenny: Wellbrook Press, 1972), p.24.
35. Ibid., p.81.
36. Fr John Ryan, *Irish Monasticism: Origins and Early Development* (London: Longmans, 1931). Ryan's claim that the '(Irish) race ... has shown itself capable of producing in unique abundance the very highest type of which humanity is capable, the saint. Therein lies our chief claim to recognition and to glory as a nation.' Cited in Butler, *Ten Thousand Saints*, p.24.
37. For an account of genealogical making of saints and ancestors within Irish folklore see Butler, *Ten Thousand Saints*, pp.44–62.
38. Published scholarship cataloguing Shelta and Traveller Cant dates from 1886. S. MacAlister, *The Secret Languages of Ireland with Special Reference to the Origins and Nature of the Shelta Language Partly Based upon Collections and Manuscripts of the Late John Sampson Litt.D.* (Cambridge: Cambridge University Press, 1939), p.134.
39. But borrowed from Karl Marx: 'Geschichtlose Volke'. E. Wolf, *Europe and the People without History* (Berkeley: University of Berkeley, 1982).
40. F. O'Toole, 'Travellers as real people', *Irish Times*, 1 December 2007.
41. Cited in J. Helleiner, *Irish Travellers: Racism and the Politics of Culture* ((Toronto: University of Toronto Press, 2000), p.44.

42. The claim that black people were racially inferior because it said so in the Bible (the curse of Ham) was commonplace before the advent of scientific racisms (e.g. eugenics) and claims about cultural inferiority of racialised groups. For a contestation of the use of Scripture see F. Douglass, *Narrative of the Life of Fredrick Douglass* (London: Penguin, 1986), p.50.

43. N. Joyce and A. Farmer, *Traveller* (Dublin: Gill and Macmillan, 1985), p.1.

44. For example, Sinéad Ní Shuinear, 'Irish Travellers, ethnicity and the origins question', in M. McCann, S. Ó Síocháin and J. Ruane (eds), *Irish Travellers: Culture and Ethnicity* (Belfast: Institute of Irish Studies, 1994), pp.62–3; J. Helleiner, 'Gypsies, Celts and Tinkers: Colonial antecedents of anti-Traveller racism in Ireland,' *Ethnic and Racial Studies*, 18, 3 (1995), pp.532–54; M. Hayes, *Irish Travellers: Representations and Realities* (Dublin: Liffey Press, 2006), p.124.

45. C. Clear, *Social Change and Everyday Life in Ireland, 1850–1922* (Manchester: Manchester University Press, 2007), p.129.

46. M. Hayes, *Irish Travellers: Representations and Realities* (Dublin: Liffey Press, 2006), p.31.

47. A. Bhreatnach, *Becoming Conspicuous: Irish Travellers, Society and the State 1922–70* (Dublin: University College Dublin, 2007).

48. The case for describing what occurred in Limerick in 1904 as a pogrom is that the hostility whipped up by Fr Creagh and the accompanying boycott of Jewish businesses resulted in the community leaving the city in their entirety. The Jews were successfully driven out of Limerick.

49. *United Irishman*, 13 January 1904.

50. R. Foster, *Modern Ireland 1600–1972* (London: Allen Lane, 1988).

51. The caption reads: 'A tribe within a tribe, the travelling people are an alienated minority in Irish society, the victims of greater discrimination than ethnic groups like the Indians or Chinese.' P. Loughrey (ed.), *The People of Ireland* (Belfast: Appletree Press/BBC Northern Ireland).

52. D. Keogh, *Twentieth-Century Ireland: Nation and State* (Dublin: Gill and Macmillan, 1994).

53. D. Ferriter, *The Transformation of Ireland 1900–2000* (London: Palgrave, 2005), pp.594–5, 725–6.

54. R. Foster, *Luck and the Irish: A Brief History of Change 1970–2000* (London: Allen and Lane, 2007).

55. J.J. Lee, *Ireland: Politics and Society 1912–1985* (Cambridge: Cambridge University Press, 1986).

56. B. Graham (ed.), *In Search of Ireland: A Cultural Geography* (London: Routledge, 1997); W. Crotty and D.E. Schmitt, *Ireland and the Politics of Change* (London: Longman, 1998).

57. R. Foster, *Paddy and Mr Punch* (London: Penguin, 1993), p.29.

58. For an overview see McCann, Ó Síocháin and Ruane, *Irish Travellers: Culture and Ethnicity*.

59. Notably, P. Sayers (1873–1958), *Machtnamh Seana Mhná (An Old Woman's Reflections)*, trans. from the Irish by Seamus Ennis (London: Oxford University Press, 1962). The Traveller memoirs contrasted with these are S. Gmelch (ed.), *Nan: The Life of a Travelling Woman* (New York: Norton, 1986) and N. Joyce, *Traveller: An Autobiography* (Dublin: Gill and Macmillan, 1985).

60. M. MacGréil, *Prejudice in Ireland Revisited* (Maynooth: Survey and Research Unit, 1996), p.334.

61. Ibid., p.326.

62. Beginning with G. Gmelch and S. Gmelch, 'The emergence of an ethnic group: The Irish tinkers', *Anthropological Quarterly*, 49, 4 (1976), pp.225–38.

63. S. Cornell and P. Hartmann, *Ethnicity and Race: Making Identities in a Changing World* (Thousand Oaks, CA: Pine Forge Press, 1998), p.17.

64. Travellers were defined as an ethnic group in a seminal 1983 ruling by the Law Lords, the United Kingdom's de facto supreme court. The qualifying essential criteria for ethnic group status included 'a cultural tradition of its own, including family and social customs and manners, often, but not necessarily associated with religious observance'. *Mandla v. Dowell Lee* cited in K. Boyle and B. Watt, *International and United Kingdom Law Relevant to the Protection of the Rights and Cultural Identity of the Travelling Community in Ireland: Paper commissioned by the Task Force on the Travelling Community* (Colchester: Human Rights Centre, University of Essex, 1995).

65. Government of Ireland, *Report of the Task Force on the Travelling People* (Dublin: Stationery Office, 1995).

66. For example, Niall Crowley, the first director of the Equality Authority, was previously the director of Pavee Point which also employed Philip Watt who became the first director of the NCCRI.

67. For a comprehensive analysis of the politics of Traveller ethnicity see R. McVeigh, 'Ethnicity denial and racism: The case of the government of Ireland against Irish Travellers', *Translocations*, 2,1 (2007), pp.90–133, www.translocations.ie

68. Irish government submission to CERD, cited in ibid., p.98.

69. J. Coakley, 'Religion, ethnic-identity and the Protestant minority in the Republic', in W. Crotty and D.E. Schmitt, *Ireland and the Politics of Change* (London: Longman, 1998), p.182.

70. H. Butler, 'The Bell: An Anglo-Irish view', in *Independent Spirit: Essays* (New York: Farrar, Straus and Giroux, 1996), p.85.

71. J. White, *Minority Report: The Protestant Community in the Irish Republic* (Dublin: Gill and Macmillan, 1975); C. Murphy and L. Adair, *Untold Stories: Protestants in the Republic of Ireland 1912–2002* (Dublin: Liffey Press, 2002).

72. For example, Pavee Point, www.paveepoint.ie and The Irish Traveller Movement, www.itm-trav.com

73. The National Consultative Committee on Racism and Interculturalism (NCCRI) arose out of policy commitments set out as Ireland's response to the European Year Against Racism (1997), www.nccri.ie

74. The justification made by the Garda commissioner and backed by the government referred directly to the Civil War era origins of the force and the need then to avoid displays of sectarian political affiliation.

75. Cited by C. Reilly, 'Gardaí "backtracking" on turban issue', *Metro Éireann*, 23 August 2007.

76. Garvin, 'National identity in Ireland', p.249.

77. In a recent summary: 'In the last 50 years Ireland changed from being a very isolated, insular, Catholic rural society revolving around agriculture to a more open, liberal-individualist, secular, urban society revolving around business, commerce and high-tech, trans-national corporations. In the last 15 years, the pace of change became more dramatic and Ireland is now identified as one of the most globalised societies in the world.' T. Inglis, *Global Ireland: Same Difference* (London: Routledge, 2007), p.7.

78. P. Bourdieu, 'The schools as a conservative force', in J. Eggleston (ed.), *Contemporary Research in the Sociology of Education* (London: Methuen, 1974).

CHAPTER THREE

1. 7 December 1963.

2. The accounts of the views or statements of councillors, officials, residents and Travellers in this chapter are referenced by the date of the issue of the *Clare Champion* within which these appeared. As such, these generally occurred in the preceding week. Hereafter, these are referred to by date.

3. *Young Travellers: Many Voices, One Community* (Ennis: Ennis Travellers Training Centre, 1984).

4. 14 June 1991, 10 October 1997, 19 October 1998.

5. *Report of the Commission on Itinerancy* (Dublin: Stationery Office, 1963).

6. 6 December 1964.

7. It was agreed that Clare County Council, in conjunction with Limerick County Council, Limerick City Corporation and Tipperary North Riding Council would request the Minister for Defence to make the site available and that costs should be shared between the four local authorities. 18 June 1966.

8. 6 December 1964.

9. 18 June 1966.

10. Senator D.P. Honan.

11. 9 December 1967.

12. 9 December 1967.

13. 22 February 1969.

14. *Tigíns*, from the Irish for 'little houses', were envisaged as the principal form of accommodation to be used in the initial settlement of Travellers. The tigín featured in the logo of the settlement movement.

15. *Clare Champion*, 1963 to 1999.
16. 9 January 1971.
17. 18 January 1969.
18. 15 February 1969.
19. 2 February 1969.
20. Ibid.
21. 3 May 1969.
22. 11 October 1969.
23. 17 June 1972.
24. 7 November 1970.
25. The committee ran a campaign in 1972 which began with a newspaper advertisement than ran for three months: 'Wanted urgently: shelter for fifty children born in Ennis, living in sub-human conditions on the roadside. Do you care enough to help?'
26. 17 October 1970.
27. 17 June 1972.
28. 5 December 1970.
29. 22 February 1969, 17 November 1970.
30. 4 June 1972.
31. 17 July 1972.
32. 8 November 1969.
33. 16 June 1972.
34. 17 July 1972.
35. 4 June 1972, 14 July 1972.
36. 26 June 1971.
37. 29 March 1974, 11 June 1976, 9 December 1977, 7 August 1982, 9 March 1984.
38. 13 February 1971.
39. 5 February 1974.
40. 4 June 1996.
41. 2 July 1982.
42. 20 January 1984.
43. In 1984 an official reported that the local authorities were responsible for twenty unaccommodated indigenous families in the area. 7 December 1984.
44. 13 May 1988.
45. 11 June 1976.
46. 31 October 1970.
47. 21 October 1977.
48. 7 August 1982.
49. 29 March 1974.
50. Travellers have been noted to avoid places where deaths of family members occurred. In common with many Gypsy and Traveller cultures, 'the standard way of coming to terms with a bereavement is to move away'. See A. Binchy, 'Travellers' Language: A Sociolinguistic Perspective', in M. McCann, S. Ó Síocháin and J. Ruane (eds), *Irish Travellers: Culture and Ethnicity* (Belfast: Institute of Irish Studies, 1994), pp.134–54.
51. 17 May 1985.
52. 24 May 1984.
53. 13 May 1985.
54. 13 May 1985.
55. The lack of a site management agreement was cited by the county manager as the reason why various disruptions and vandalism had occurred. 20 May 1994.
56. This was explained as the result of a feud between Traveller families dating back more than thirty years. 13 December 1996.
57. 21 January 1997.
58. 4 January 1997.
59. This included picketing of county council offices and alleged intimidation of council staff seeking to inspect a proposed site. 23 March 1996.
60. 1 March 1996, 22 March 1996, 16 May 1997.
61. 27 February 1987.
62. 25 September 1981.
63. 2 January 1998.

64. Report by the chairman of the National Council of Settlement Committees. 5 March 1976.
65. 12 November 1982.
66. 15 November 1985.
67. Statement by Ennis Committee for Travelling People, 20 February 1987.
68. 20 February 1987
69. Ibid.
70. Letter quoted in the *Clare Champion*, 27 February 1987.
71. 8 July 1988.
72. 13 May 1988.
73. For example, both councillors stated that they opposed allowing further families to be housed on Cloughleigh in Ennis. 13 May 1988.
74. 4 October 1991.
75. 18 March 1994.
76. 25 April 1997.
77. 4 July 1997.
78. 27 June 1997.
79. 27 June 1997.
80. 9 January 1998.
81. 2 May 1997.
82. 20 June 1997.
83. 4 July 1997.
84. 1 August 1997.
85. 4 July 1997.
86. 16 May 1997.
87. 4 July 1997, 10 October 1997.
88. A prediction that the plan would be deferred pending the 1999 local government elections was made by a councillor who was a member of the Traveller Accommodation Advisory Committee following newspaper coverage of the threat of hostility by residents to such a plan. The view that it should be deferred was shared by a number of councillors. 19 September 1998.
89. 17 September 1999.
90. 17 September 1999.
91. 29 October 1999.
92. 8 January 1999.
93. 29 September 1997.
94. 3 April 1987.
95. B. Fanning, 'Asylum seekers, travellers and racism', *Doctrine and Life*, 50, 6 (2000), pp.358–66.
96. 25 September 1981.
97. An article prior to the 1991 local elections noted that approximately 100 Travellers were registered voters in Ennis. The article commented that Travellers were unlikely to vote for two candidates. Both of these 'had taken hard-line attitudes on the Traveller Question'. One topped the poll on a number of occasions; both have served as chairperson of Ennis UDC. 14 June 1991.
98. 20 July 1984, 12 June 1987.
99. *Young Travellers: Many Voices, One Community.*
100. Buffer, a Traveller term for settled people.
101. These invariably appeared on the Ennis news page and contrasted vividly with lengthy, more prominent and usually front-page articles reporting the anti-Traveller statements of councillors, officials and residents.
102. 29 March 1985.
103. 24 May 1985.
104. 26 April 1985.
105. 16 March 1984, 10 May 1991.
106. 11 May 1991.
107. 26 September 1998.
108. 20 October 1998.
109. 9 May 1991.
110. In February 1989 the Catholic bishop, Dr Harty, gave a sermon which urged greater acceptance of minority groupings like Travellers. A number of councillors interpreted this as a criticism of

the urban district council (UDC). One councillor said at a UDC meeting that she had squirmed in her seat during the sermon. Another councillor stated that he found the bishop's remarks personally insulting and ill-informed. 3 February 1989.

111. 3 November 1995.
112. *Clare Champion*, 14 July 1972, 26 June 1982, 1 March 1996 and 12 December 1997.
113. Ennis CDP, *Roadside Travellers, Ennis: A Profile*, 2002–2004 (Ennis: Ennis CDP, 2004).

CHAPTER FOUR

1. Fianna Fáil councillor at a Waterford County Council meeting, *Sunday Independent*, 14 April 1996.
2. For example, headlines such as 'Patience runs thin when uncivilised Travellers spill blood', *Sunday Independent*, 25 May 1997.
3. Notably the *Report of the Task Force on the Travelling People* (1995) which set the tone of an Irish state project of promoting the integration of Travellers into Irish society. The report was critical of past failed policies of assimilation. It made some 400 recommendations aimed at addressing inequalities and discrimination encountered by Travellers.
4. The campaign began in Westport, County Mayo when publicans collectively decided to refuse to serve Travellers who had come to the area as tourists undertaking an annual pilgrimage to Croagh Patrick. It was endorsed by the Clare branch of the Vintners' Federation of Ireland. 'Clare publicans defend right to refuse', *Clare Champion*, 11 February 2000, p.3.
5. B. Fanning, *Racism and Social Change in the Republic of Ireland* (Manchester: Manchester University Press, 2002), pp.122–51.
6. Ibid., pp.131–2.
7. For example, *Clare Champion*, 12 November 1982 and 12 December 1997.
8. This could be seen in the headlines of *Clare Champion* newspaper articles. Examples such as 'Fifteen houses for itinerants amid angry objections by residents', 'Itinerant problem heading for explosive situation', 'Outrage over plans for halting site' and 'Halting site to spark residents' revolt' illustrate the longstanding permissibility of hostility to Travellers in local politics. See *Clare Champion*, 14 July 1972, 26 June 1982, 1 March 1996 and 12 December 1997.
9. G. Gmelch, *The Irish Tinkers: The Urbanisation of an Itinerant People* (Long Grove, IL: Waveland Press, 1985); J. MacLaughlin, 'Nation-building, social closure and anti-Traveller racism in Ireland', *Sociology*, 33, 1 (1999), p.128.
10. S. Gmelch and G. Gmelch, 'The itinerant settlement movement: Its policies and effects on Irish Travellers', *Studies*, 63, 249 (1974), p.1.
11. Structural functionalist theories, derived from the sociology of Talcott Parsons, understand social order as the product of consensual social norms that serve a functional purpose. This implied that as society changed the functional necessities for social order changed too. See G. Ritzer, *Sociological Theory* (New York: McGraw-Hill, 1992), pp.233–9, 271–4.
12. J. MacLaughlin, *Travellers in Ireland: Whose Country, Whose History?* (Cork: Cork University Press, 1995), pp.24–5.
13. Fanning, *Racism and Social Change*, p.51.
14. Ibid., p.117.
15. S. Ní Shuinear, 'Irish Travellers, ethnicity and the origins question', in M. McCann, S. Ó Síocháin and J. Ruane (eds), *Irish Travellers: Culture and Ethnicity* (Belfast: Institute of Irish Studies, 1994), p.50.
16. Commission on Itinerancy, *Report of the Commission on Itinerancy* (Dublin: Official Publications, 1963).
17. P. McCarthy, 'The sub-culture of poverty reconsidered', in M. McCann, S. Ó Síocháin and J. Ruane (eds), *Irish Travellers: Culture and Ethnicity*, p.122. Portrayals of Travellers as a sub-culture of poverty predominated in Irish academic literature until the 1980s. See, for instance, the main state policy document of that era, the *Report of the Travelling People Review Body* (Dublin: Official Publications, 1983).
18. S. Hall, 'Gramsci's relevance for the study of race and ethnicity', *Journal of Communication Inquiry*, 10, 2 (1986), pp.5–27.
19. F. Engels, *The Condition of the Working Class in England* (Oxford: Blackwell, 1971 [1844]), p.122.
20. L. Curtis, *Apes and Angels: The Irishman in Victorian Caricature* (Newton Abbot: David and Charles, 1971), p.21.

21. K. Howard, 'From Group to Category: The Emergence of the Irish in Britain as an Ethnic Minority', Unpublished PhD thesis, University College Dublin, 2003.

22. R. Swift, 'The Irish in Britain', in P. O'Sullivan (ed.), *The Irish in the New Communities* (Leicester: Leicester University Press, 1997), p.66.

23. M. Hickman, *Religion, Class and Identity: The State, the Catholic Church and the Education of the Irish in Britain* (Aldershot: Avebury, 1995), p.73.

24. M. Preston, 'Race and class in the language of charity in nineteenth-century Dublin', in T. Foley and S. Ryder (eds), *Ideology and Ireland in the Nineteenth Century* (Dublin: Four Courts Press, 1998), p.108.

25. Ibid. As suggested by Preston, 'The training of women as laundresses might be considered as a metaphor for the spiritual and bodily cleansing of the poor.'

26. This he describes in the strongest possible terms: 'As a result of the emergence of what are little short of Ku-Klux-Klan-type delegations that are not averse to employing the tactics of urban gangs, isolated Traveller families in many part of the country are now literally living in fear of their lives', MacLaughlin, *Travellers and Ireland*, p.3.

27. See J. O'Connell, 'Travellers in Ireland: An examination of discrimination', in R. Lentin and R. McVeigh (eds), *Racism and Anti-Racism in Ireland* (Belfast: Beyond the Pale, 2002), p.54.

28. From an article entitled 'Time to get tough on tinker terror culture' by Mary Ellen Synon, *Sunday Independent*, 28 January 1996.

29. O'Connell, *Travellers in Ireland*, p.58.

30. M. MacGréil, *Prejudice and Tolerance in Ireland Revisited* (Maynooth: Survey and Research Unit, 1996), pp.330, 447.

31. Citizen Traveller, *Information* Pack (Dublin: Citizen Traveller, 1999)

32. MacLaughlin, *Travellers and Ireland*, p.3.

33. Ní Shuinear, 'Irish Travellers, ethnicity and the origins question', p.50.

34. F. Fanon, *The Wretched of the Earth* (New York: Grove Press, 1968), p.42; L. Greenslade, 'White skin, white masks', in O'Sullivan (ed.), *The Irish in the New Communities*, p.213.

35. Greenslade, 'White skin, white masks', pp.214–15.

36. Examples include segregation in the provision of social services, state benefits and segregation in schools. See National Consultative Committee on Racism and Interculturalism (2003), *Travellers in Ireland: An Examination of Discrimination and Racism*, www.nccri.com/travellr2.html

37. G.W. Allport, *The Nature of Prejudice* (Cambridge, MA: Addison-Wesley, 1966), p.14.

38. Ibid., p.57.

39. P.E. Taguieff, *The Force of Prejudice: On Racism and Its Doubles* (Minneapolis, MN: University of Minnesota Press, 2001), p.327.

40. The functionalist school maintains that the 'final solution' of genocide emerged through a rational process of attempting and then discarding other means to exclude Jews from the Reich. Bauman describes Nazi efforts to get rid of the Jews in functionalist terms, whereby the 'final solution' emerged not as a considered choice made at the start by ideologically motivated leaders: 'It did, rather, emerge, inch by inch, pointing at each stage to a different destination, shifting in response to ever-new crises, and pressed forward with a "we will cross that bridge once we come to it" philosophy.' See Z. Bauman, *Modernity and the Holocaust* (New York: Cornell, 1989), p.15.

41. Hart, in his study of violence in Cork between 1916 and 1923, concluded that disproportionately high numbers of Travellers and Protestants were murdered by the IRA. He confirmed that eight so-called 'tinkers or tramps' were killed as 'spies or informers' out of a total of 122 so-called persons. He identified four further accounts of killings of tramps which could not be fully verified. The specific targeting of Protestant landowners and Travellers arguably suggests that a degree of ethnic cleansing occurred during the War of Independence and the Civil War. P. Hart, *The IRA and its Enemies: Violence and Community in Cork 1916–1923* (Oxford: Oxford University Press, 1998), p.304.

42. J. Helleiner, *Irish Travellers: Racism and the Politics of Culture* (Toronto: University of Toronto Press, 2000), p.74.

43. See Fanning, *Racism and Social Change*, p.133. By way of example, on 16 June 2000 the *Clare Champion* published a letter from Travellers asking that the council provide temporary water, refuse collection facilities and temporary toilets 'which would ease many of the problems identified as concerns of residents'.

44. *Clare Champion*, 2 August 1985.

45. A Garda stated in court that he had begged and implored the crowd to go home. He asked one person in the crowd who he knew to be a sensible man and to get the people to go home. The man replied: 'No, let ye go home and we'll deal with them.' *Clare Champion*, 9 January 1987.

46. *Clare Champion*, 6 February 1987.

47. For example, *Clare Champion*, 13 November 1992.

48. *Clare Champion*, 13 November 1992.

49. An advertisement by Citizen Traveller described the 2002 Act as racist. The Minister for Justice, Equality and Law Reform announced an immediate review of the funding of the group which was subsequently disbanded.

50. Fanning, *Racism and Social Change*, p.188.

51. The views of Travellers about over-policing were endorsed by some senior Garda interviewees in the same study. F. O'Brien, 'What are the perspectives of senior police managers and members of the Traveller community in the context of implementation of Traveller rituals?' (Templemore: Garda Síochána College, unpublished, 2002).

52. W. Macpherson, *The Stephen Lawrence Inquiry: Report of an Inquiry by Sir William Macpherson of Cluny* (London: The Stationery Office, 1999).

53. A number of studies of nineteenth-century Britain discuss the targeting of the Irish by new police forces, disproportionate prosecutions and specific ordinances that criminalised the consumption of alcohol in Irish areas. See Hickman, *Religion, Class and Identity*, p.78.

54. *Clare Champion*, 12 October 2001.

55. 'Travellers have made life hell In Cloughleigh', *Clare Champion*, 19 October 2001, p.1.

56. 'Vigilante threat for Clare drug dealers', *Clare Champion*, 21 January 2001, p.1.

57. Notably Operation Dóchas. See statement by Minister for Justice, Equality and Law Reform, Written answers: Garda Deployment, Dáil Éireann vol. 471, 21 November 1996.

58. 'Minister warns against vigilante action', *Clare Champion*, 5 February 2002.

59. 'Traveller accommodation crisis could spark racist attacks', *Clare Champion*, 10 March 2000, p.1.

60. 'Judge slams council over Traveller accommodation', *Clare Champion*, 22 September 2000, p.1.

61. 'Council rejects Traveller accommodation figures', *Clare Champion*, 30 August 2002, p.1.

62. 'High Court moves in Traveller accommodation showdown', *Clare Champion*, 7 April 2000.

63. 'Travellers move in on the council', *Clare Champion*, 14 April 2000.

64. 'Council "disgusted" by presence of Travellers', *Clare Champion*, 17 November 2000; 'Travellers force councillors to move', *Clare Champion*, 21 April 2000; 'Council unveil emergency halting sites behind closed doors', *Clare Champion*, 28 April 2000.

65. 'Breakthrough in Ennis Traveller accommodation crisis', *Clare Champion*, 9 March 2001, p.1.

66. 'Jail threat forces Traveller movement', *Clare Champion*, 1 March 2002, p.1.

67. Editorial, *Clare Champion*, 21 July 2001.

68. 'Chamber calls for action on halting site', *Clare Champion*, 21 September 2001.

69. 'Children protest over school halting site', *Clare Champion*, 19 October 2001.

70. 'Petrol bomb attack on Travellers', *Clare Champion*, 22 February 2002.

71. 'Bishop calls for action on Traveller problem', *Clare Champion*, 26 July 2002.

72.   For instance, it cited the case of a family made homeless because of intimidation from neighbours being offered the same house that they had already vacated. They accused the council of ignoring allegations of intimidation. Now the family were 'staying in an inadequate leaking caravan outside Tesco's' (supermarket) pending prosecution and eviction. 'Traveller group criticises council', *Clare Champion*, 9 June 2000.

73. B. Rolston, 'Bringing it all back home: Irish emigration and racism',*Race and Class*, 45, 2 (2003), pp.39–53, at p.48.

74. Allport, *The Nature of Prejudice*, p.12.

75. Taguieff, *The Force of Prejudice*, p.327.

CHAPTER FIVE

1. A. Lively, *Masks: Blackness, Race and the Imagination* (London: Chatto and Windus), pp.13–52.

2. J. Solomos and L. Back, *Racism and Society* (London: Routledge, 1996), pp.18–19.

3. M. Barker, *The New Racism* (London: Junction Books, 1981).
4. A. Brown, '"The other day I met a constituent of mine": a theory of anecdotal racism', *Ethnic and Racial Studies*, 22, 1 (1999), pp.23–55.
5. B. Fanning, *Racism and Social Change in the Republic of Ireland* (Manchester: Manchester University Press, 2002), p.47.
6. 3,883 asylum seekers arrived in Ireland in 1997.
7. *Irish Independent*, 5 May 1997.
8. *Sunday World*, 25 May 1997.
9. *Irish Independent*, 7 June 1997.
10. *Sunday World*, 13 June 1997.
11. Fanning, *Racism and Social Change*, p.101.
12. Nora Owen TD, Dáil Debates, col 835, 28 February 1996.
13. 'Just why Nora Owen did her successor the favour of introducing the measure when her sell-by date was already up is unclear.' See P. Cullen, 'Refugees, Asylum and Race on the Borders', in E. Crowley and J. MacLaughlin (eds), *Under the Belly of the Tiger* (Dublin: Irish Reporter Publications, 1997), p.103.
14. See *Irish Times*, 18 October 1997 and Cullen, 'Refugees , Asylum Seekers and Race on the Border', p.105.
15. Address to the Irish Business and Employers Confederation, 30 September 1999.
16. B. Fanning and P. Mac Éinrí *Regional Resettlement of Asylum Seekers: A Strategic Approach* (Cork: Irish Centre for Migration Studies, 1999).
17. *Irish Times*, 24 November 1999.
18. *Irish Times*, 27 April 2000.
19. B. Fanning and A. Veale, 'Child Poverty as Public Policy: Direct Provision and Asylum Seeking Children in the Republic of Ireland', *Child Care in Practice*, 10, 3 (2004), pp.241–52.
20. *Irish Times*, 29 February 1998.
21. *Clare Champion*, 14 November 1997.
22. B. Fanning, 'Asylum seekers, Travellers and racism', *Doctrine and Life*, 50, 6 (2000).
23. *Clare Champion*, 14 July 1972, 26 June 1982, 1 March 1996 and 12 December 1997.
24. R. Boyd, 'Politicians use code-words to defy anti-racist election pact', *Metro Éireann*, April 2002.
25. *Irish Times*, 2 March 1999.
26. Fanning, *Racism and Social Change*, pp.111–46.
27. From a survey by Action from Ireland (AFRI) in 2002. A questionnaire was distributed to candidates for the 2002 general election. Members of some political parties were instructed not to respond individually. Most individual responses came from smaller parties such as Sinn Féin, the Green Party, the Socialist Party and the Workers Party. See www.activelink.ie/thecommitments
28. *Irish Times*, 15 July 2002.

CHAPTER SIX

1. Irish Refugee Council, *Regional Reception of Asylum Seekers in Ireland: Policy Recommendations* (Dublin: Irish Refugee Council, 2001), pp.11–13.
2. Child benefits form the main plank of Irish state policies against child poverty. Their removal from asylum seeker families comes as a serious blow on top of the freeze on direct provision rates from 2000 onwards that reduced their value in real terms year on year. In 2005 child benefits were €141.60 per month for each of the first two children. For an overview of asylum policy see E. Quinn and G. Hughes, *Reception systems, their capacity and the social situation of asylum applicants within the reception system* (Dublin: Economic and Social Research Institute, 2005).
3. United Nations Educational Scientific and Cultural Organisation (UNESCO) General Conference, 27 November 1978.
4. W. Macpherson, *The Stephen Lawrence Inquiry: Report of an Inquiry by Sir William Macpherson of Cluny* (London: HMSO, 1999), p.22.
5. C. Joppke, 'The legal-domestic sources of immigrant rights: The United States, Germany and the European Union', *Comparative Political Studies*, 34, 4 (2001), p.345.
6. B. Humphries, 'From welfare to authoritarianism: The role of social work in immigration controls', in S. Cohen, B. Humphries and E. Mynott (eds), *From Immigration Controls to Welfare Controls* (London: Routledge, 2002), p.121.

7. Z. Bauman, *Modernity and Ambivalence* (Cambridge: Polity Press), cited in A. Christie, 'Responses of the social work profession to unaccompanied children seeking asylum in the Republic of Ireland', *European Journal of Social Work*, 5, 2 (2002), pp.187–98, at p.188.
8. A. Christie, 'Asylum seekers and refugees in Ireland: Questions of racism and social work', *Social Work in Europe*, 9, 1 (2002), pp.10–17.
9. L. Dominelli, 'An uncaring profession? An examination of racism in social work', in P. Braham, A. Rattansi and R. Skellington (eds), *Racism and Anti-Racism* (London: Sage, 1992), p.170.
10. A. Moroney, 'Negotiating an island culture', *Irish Social Worker*, 16, 3 (1999), pp.4–5.
11. Lord Laming, *The Victoria Climbie Inquiry: Report of an Inquiry by Lord Laming* (London: The Stationery Office, 2003), www.victoria–climbie–inquiry.org.uk
12. Ibid., p.12.
13. Ibid., p.345.
14. Ibid.
15. Ibid.
16. M. Lipsky, 'Street-level bureaucracy', in M. Hill (ed.), *The Policy Process* (London: Harvester Wheatsheaf, 1993), p.381.
17. B. Hudson, 'Michael Lipsky and street-level bureaucracy', in Hill (ed.), *The Policy Process*, p.339.
18. P. Kennedy and J. Murphy-Lawless, *The Maternity Care Needs of Refugee and Asylum-Seeking Women* (Dublin: Northern Area Health Board, 2002), p.120.
19. Ibid., p.120.
20. Ibid. Also see Comhlámh, *Refugee Lives: The Failure of Direct Provision as a Social Response to the Needs of Asylum Seekers in Ireland* (Dublin: Comhlámh Refugee Solidarity Group, 2001); B. Fanning, A. Veale and D. O'Connor, *Beyond the Pale: Asylum-Seeking Children and Social Exclusion* (Dublin: Irish Refugee Council, 2001).
21. Kennedy and Murphy-Lawless, *Refugee and Asylum Seeking Women*, p.62.
22. M. Horgan and F. Douglas, 'Some aspects of quality in early childhood education', in A. Cleary, M. Nic Ghiolla Phádraig and S. Quin (eds), *Understanding Children. Volume 1: State, Education and Economy* (Dublin: Oak Tree Press, 2001), p.139.
23. Department of Health and Children, *National Standards for Children's Residential Centres* (Dublin: Stationery Office, 2002), p.2.
24. Ibid., p.12.
25. Cited from a study by E. Ross, *How the needs of unaccompanied minors are being met in Ireland* (unpublished, 2003).
26. J. Rylands, 'Findings of a research project on psychological need, social support and estimates of psychological distress amongst unaccompanied minors', Conference on Unaccompanied Minors, Dublin Castle, June 2001.
27. A. Rea, 'Psychosocial needs, social support and estimates of psychological distress amongst unaccompanied refugee minors in Ireland', Conference on Unaccompanied Minors, Dublin Castle June 2001.
28. Department of Social Community and Family Affairs, *Building an Inclusive Society: Review of the National Anti-Poverty Strategy under the Programme for Prosperity and Fairness* (Dublin: Stationery Office, 2002), p.17.
29. Christie, 'Responses of the social work profession to unaccompanied children seeking asylum in the Republic of Ireland', p.187.
30. Ibid., pp.191–2.
31. P. Conroy, *Trafficking in Unaccompanied Minors in Dublin* (Dublin: International Organisation of Migration, 2003).
32. P. Conroy cited, *Irish Examiner*, 5 January 2005.
33. Conroy, *Trafficking in Unaccompanied Minors*, p.48.
34. Irish Refugee Council, etc in an article by E. Browne, H. Curley and C. Murphy, 'The scandal of missing children', *Village*, 28 January 2005.
35. Irish Refugee Council, 'Post-Afghan hunger strike reflections on Ireland's asylum system', 24 May 2006, www.irishrefugeecouncil.ie/presso6/afghan.htm
36. RTE interview with Denis Naughton TD, Fine Gael (opposition) health spokesman, 21 April 2008.
37. Government of Ireland, *The National Children's Strategy: Our Children – Their Lives* (Dublin: Stationery Office, 2000), p.10.
38. E. Quinn and G. Hughes, *Illegally Resident Third Country Nationals in Ireland: State Approaches to their Situation* (Dublin: Economic and Social Research Institute, 2005), p.25.

39. The 2005 policy discussion document states the following: 'At present much legislation under which Departments operate are largely silent as regards non-nationals (other than nationals of other EU or EEA Member States) as they were written at a time when immigration was not a significant issue in Ireland. There may be provisions for universal entitlements which apply to all residents regardless of nationality. While such universal-type provisions have advantages in terms of social equity and simplicity of administration, in recent times it has been clear that they also potentially present attractions to persons entering the State illegally ... consideration should be given as to what extent a prohibition on providing public services to non nationals who are not legally resident in the State and the extent of such prohibition. For example, such migrants might be allowed to access emergency medical treatment, but not social housing or publicly funded third level courses.' See Quinn and Hughes, ibid., pp.26–7. Department of Justice, Equality and Law Reform, *Immigration and Residence in Ireland: Outline Policy Proposals for an Immigration and Residence Bill* (Stationery Office, 2005), p.19.

CHAPTER SEVEN

1. These, in the order reproduced here, first appeared as B. Fanning, 'Internal exiles', *Asyland*, no. 5 (summer 2003); B. Fanning, 'On beasts of burden (and their children)', *Asyland*, no. 10 (winter 2004); B. Fanning, 'New guests of the nation', *Studies*, 93, 369 (2004).
2. The 2004 Social Welfare (Miscellaneous Provisions) Act removed rights from new immigrants to Unemployment Assistance, Old Age (Non-Contributory) and Blind Pensions, Widow(er)'s and Orphan's (Non-Contributory) Pensions, One Parent Family Payment, Carer's Allowance, Disability Allowance, Supplementary Welfare Allowance (other than once-off exceptional and urgent needs payments) and Children's Allowances. The Act was a political feint aimed at countering anxiety about the decision to allow immigrants from the ten new European Union states to work in Ireland. Something similar happened in the United Kingdom. In February 2006 the government acknowledged that EU law (EU 1408 of 1971) imposed reciprocal obligations on EU states to recognise the entitlements of citizens from other EU countries resident in their own countries. This means that the removal of entitlements set out under the 2004 Act could never have applied to immigrants arriving from the new EU member states.
3. Before, during and after the Holocaust the Department of Justice had a policy of overt discrimination against Jewish refugees. A 1953 memorandum stated that: 'In the administration of the alien laws it has always been recognised in the Departments of Justice, Industry and Commerce and External Affairs that the question of the admission of aliens of Jewish blood presents a special problem and the alien laws have been administered less liberally in their case.' National Archives, Department of An Taoiseach. NAI, D.T., S11007, 23 September 1953.
4. See Chapter 4 on Ireland and the Holocaust. B. Fanning, *Racism and Social Change in the Republic of Ireland* (Manchester: Manchester University Press, 2002).
5. R. Hilberg, *The Politics of Memory: The Journey of a Holocaust Historian* (Chicago: Ivan R. Dee, 1996).
6. In a 1938 article the chairman of the Irish Co-ordinating Committee for the Relief of Christian Refugees advocated a policy of admitting Christian refugees considered as non-Aryan 'hybrids' or *Mischlinge* (those, he explained, with Jewish ancestry who had converted to Christianity) under the Nuremburg Laws, but not unconverted Jews. Dillon argued that the plight of these 'Christian Jews' exceeded that of the unconverted Jews because they could not turn to wealthy Jews in America for assistance. This position became the official policy of the Department of Justice. T.W.T. Dillon, 'The refugee problem and Ireland', *Studies*, 28, 4 (1939), pp.409–10.
7. D.E. Schmitt, *The Irony of Irish Democracy: The Impact of Political Culture on Administrative and Democratic Political Development in Ireland* (Lexington: Lexington Books, 1973).
8. Fanning, *Racism and Social Change*, p.92.
9. J. Rawls, *A Theory of Justice* (Oxford: Oxford University Press, 1973).
10. *Irish Independent*, 3 March 2004.
11. J. Quadango, *The Color of Welfare* (Oxford: Oxford University Press, 1994).
12. *Irish Times*, Friday 12 March 2004. Two of the masters have contested the minister's claims that they pressed for measures to stem the arrival of non-national women as distinct from asking for more resources, *Irish Times*, 13 March 2004.
13. J.S. Mill, *On Liberty* (London: Routledge, 1991).
14. Rawls, *A Theory of Justice*.

15. D. McCrone, *The Sociology of Nationalism* (London: Routledge, 1998), p.54.

16. Max Weber cited in Z. Bauman, *Modernity and the Holocaust* (London: Sage, 1996), p.22.

17. M. Peillon, 'Strangers in our midst', in É. Slater and M. Peillon (eds), *Memories of the Present: A Sociological Chronicle of Ireland 1997–1998* (Dublin: Institute of Public Administration, 2000), p.111.

18. Article 40 of the Irish Constitution sets out the personal rights of citizens. Article 41 sets out the rights of the family (notably 41.1.1. 'The state recognises the family as the natural primary and fundamental unit group of society, and as a moral institution possessing inalienable ... rights, antecedent and superior to all positive law.'). Article 42 refers to the rights (and duties) of parents to provide for the religious and moral, intellectual, physical and social education of their children.

19. G. Ritzer, *Sociological Theory* (New York: McGraw-Hill, 1996), pp.116, 126, 208, 271–4.

20 A. Hess, *Concepts of Social Stratification: European and American Models* (London: Palgrave, 2001), p.121.

21. Fanning, *Racism and Social Change*, pp.30–56.

22. T. Inglis, *Moral Monopoly* (Dublin: University College Dublin Press, 1998), p.172.

CHAPTER EIGHT

1. Castles and Davidson distinguish between three understandings of nation-building processes: (i) a sovereignty perspective whereby an ethnic group that controls a bounded territory becomes a nation; (ii) the *Kulturnation* (cultural nation, also known as the ethnic nation); and (iii) the *Staatnation* (state nation also known as civic nation). The first and second of these are explicitly grounded in the dominance of some majority ethnic group. The third presumes universalism but in practice (e.g. France) is grounded in presumptions about cultural homogeneity. S. Castles and A. Davidson, *Citizenship and Migration: Globalisation and the Politics of Belonging* (London: Macmillan, 2000), pp.13–15.

2. Mary Robinson described her presidency in terms of a symbolic fifth province that included 'the 70 million or so people of Irish descent around the world'. L. Siggins, *Mary Robinson: The Woman Who Took Power in the Park* (London: Mainstream, 1997), p.149.

3. J.J. Lee, *Ireland 1912–1985: Politics and Society* (Cambridge: Cambridge University Press, 1989), p.227.

4. Ibid., p.647.

5. Walker describes Bismarck's exhortation to the German people, over the heads of their particular political leaders, to 'think with your blood' as an attempt to 'activate a mass psychological vibration predicated upon an intuitive sense of consanguinity'. C. Walker, 'A nation is a nation, is a state, is an ethnic group, is a ...', *Ethnic and Racial Studies*, 1, 4 (1988), pp.379–88, at p.380.

6. O'Hearn argues that neo-liberalism has taken much credit for growth and prosperity at the expense of an emphasis on the role of welfare goods and services, notably the expansion of free secondary education from the 1960s. The 1990s economic boom tends to be attributed in popular discourse to neo-liberal policies such as privatisation and to 'responsible' fiscal policies. D. O'Hearn, *The Atlantic Economy: Britain, the US and Ireland* (Manchester: Manchester University Press, 2001), p.190.

7. W.K Roche and T. Craddon, 'Neo-corporatism and social partnership', in M. Adshead and M. Millar (eds), *Public Administration and Public Policy in Ireland: Theory and Practice* (London: Routledge, 2003), p.73; G. Taylor, 'Hailing with an invisible hand: A "cosy" political dispute amid the rise of neoliberal politics in modern Ireland', *Government and Opposition*, 37, 4 (2002), pp.501–23, at p.521.

8. P. Kirby, 'Globalisation', in B. Fanning, P. Kennedy, G. Kiely and S. Quin (eds), *Theorising Irish Social Policy* (Dublin: University College Dublin Press, 2004), pp.37–8.

9. National Consultative Committee on Racism and Interculturalism, *Anti-Racism Protocol for Political Parties*, www.nccri.ie

10. The Africa Solidarity Centre was established in 2001. Its goals included a 'focus on the medium and long-term issues of concern to African immigrants in Ireland, especially issues relating to community development' and to 'work in solidarity with like-minded organisations to address the needs of African immigrant communities in Ireland'. Africa Solidarity Centre, *Annual Report 2002*, www.africacentre.ie

11. See A Rushanara and C. Ó Cinnéide, *Our House? Race and Representation in British Politics* (London: Institute of Public Policy Research, 2002).

12. B. Fanning, F. Mutwarasibo and N. Chadamoyo, *Positive Politics: Participation of Immigrants and Ethnic Minorities in the Electoral Process* (Dublin: Africa Solidarity Centre, 2004), p.16.
13. The category of persons entitled to vote in the local elections in Ireland is broader than for any other poll. There are no citizenship requirements and any national of any country ordinarily resident in the local electoral area, who is over 18 and is on the register, is entitled to vote. N. Whelan, *Politics, Elections and the Law* (Dublin: Blackhall, 2000).
14. 1992 Electoral Act.
15. The campaign included the Refugee Project of the Irish Bishops' Conference, various asylum seeker support groups and the Irish Refugee Council.
16. Rule 1.3 of Fianna Fáil's Corú and Rialacha (Constitution and Rules).
17. Editorial, *Irish Examiner*, 2 December 2003.
18. Fanning et al., *Positive Politics*, p.13.
19. The rule was changed by the party's National Executive at its meeting on 4 December 2003.
20. *Irish Independent*, 14 April 2004.
21. Joint statement by Integrating Ireland and the Irish Refugee Council, 13 April 2004.
22. Statutory Instrument 175.2004 (Dublin: Stationery Office).
23. D O'Connell and C Smyth, 'Citizenship and the Irish Constitution', in U. Fraser and C. Harvey (eds), *Sanctuary in Ireland: Perspectives on Asylum Law and Policy* (Dublin: Institute of Public Administration, 2003), p.265.
24. P. Weil, 'The transformation of immigration policies, immigration control and nationality laws in Europe', *European University Institute Working Paper*, eui. no. 5 (1998), pp.40–7, www.eui.it
25. Statement by Brian Lenihan, Minister of State for Children, 24 May 2005.
26. J. Coakley, 'Northern Ireland and the British dimension', in J. Coakley and M. Gallagher, *Politics in the Republic of Ireland* (London: Routledge, 2005), pp.418–26.
27. M. McDowell, *Sunday Independent*, 14 March 2004.
28. Ibid.
29. www.Irishhealth.com, 'Referendum to deal with "baby tourists"', 11 March 2004.
30. 'Two of the Masters have contested the Minister's claims that they pressed for measures to stem the arrival of non-national women as distinct from asking for more resources', *Irish Times*, 13 March 2004.
31. As described in Chapter 7. See also P. Kennedy and J. Murphy-Lawless, *The Maternity Care Needs of Refugee and Asylum-Seeking Women* (Dublin: Northern Area Health Board, 2002).
32. *Irish Times*, 22 April 2004.
33. A. Ruddock, *Sunday Independent*, 11 April 2004; Editorial, *Irish Times*, 18 April 2004.
34. Speech by Minister Mary Coughlan at the launch of the Fianna Fáil referendum campaign, 25 May 2004.
35. M. McDowell, *Sunday Independent*, 14 March 2004.
36. www.Irishhealth.com, 'Referendum to deal with "baby tourists"', 11 March 2004.
37. *Sunday Business Post*, 6 June 2004.
38. Councillor Pat O'Connor, letter to editor, *Irish Times*, 10 April 2004.
39. Debate on Senator John Minihan's private member's motion on the Referendum on Citizenship in the Seanad, 8 April 2004.
40. Debate on Senator John Minihan's private member's motion on the Referendum on Citizenship in the Seanad, 8 April 2004.
41. This view is based upon the structure, tone and content of a number of radio debates on flagship RTÉ programmes ('Morning Ireland', 'Today with Pat Kenny') in which the minister participated in the weeks prior to the referendum.
42. The 2001 Irish Nationality and Citizenship Act superseded the 1935 Aliens Act.
43. R. Lentin, 'Who ever heard of an Irish Jew? Racialising the intersection between "Irishness" and "Jewishness"', in R. Lentin and R. McVeigh (eds), *Racism and Anti-Racism in Ireland* (Belfast: Beyond the Pale, 2002), p.153.
44. H. Arendt, *The Origins of Totalitarianism* (London: George Allen and Unwin, 1961), p.229.
45. In Powell's case this backfired. S. Heffer, *Like A Roman: The Life of Enoch Powell* (London: Phoenix, 1998), p.453.
46. A. Brown, '"The other day I met a constituent of mine": A theory of anecdotal racism', *Ethnic and Racial Studies*, 22, 1 (1999), pp.23–55, at p. 23.
47. National Consultative Committee on Racism and Interculturalism, *Reported Incidents Related to Racism May to October 2004*, www.nccri.com/publications.html

48. Article 45.1 of the Constitution states: 'The State shall strive to promote the welfare of the whole people by securing or protecting as effectively as it may a social order in which justice and charity inform all the institutions of the national life.'

49. B. Fanning, 'Integration and social policy', in B. Fanning (ed.), *Immigration and Social Change in the Republic of Ireland* (Manchester: Manchester University Press, 2007).

50. Joppke contrasts immigration practices of states with 'thin' social citizenship, such as the United States, with those with well developed rights to welfare. In the US citizens have few additional rights above and beyond those conferred upon immigrants with legal permanent residence. The US Constitution emphasises residence and personhood rather than citizenship. Formal citizenship was only introduced with the fourteenth amendment in 1868. See C. Joppke, 'How immigration is changing citizenship: A comparative view', *Ethnic and Racial Studies*, 22, 4 (1999), pp.629–32.

51. Under the 2004 Irish Nationality and Citizenship Act non-national parents of children born on or after 1 January 2005 must prove that they have 'a genuine link with Ireland'. This will be evidenced by being resident legally in Ireland for three out of the previous four years immediately after the birth of the child. The Act specifies that time spent in Ireland as students or asylum seekers will not be included in calculating non-parents' period of residence in Ireland.

CHAPTER NINE

1. P. Pearse, 'The Coming Revolution' in S. Regan (ed), *Irish Writing: An Anthology of Irish Literature in English 1789–1939* (Oxford: Oxford University Press, 2004).

2. R. Kearney, Editorial, *The Crane Bag: Art and Politics*, 1, 1 (1977).

3. A. Sen, *Identity and Violence: The Illusion of Destiny* (London: Norton, 2006), p.11.

4. P. Hart, *The IRA and its Enemies* (Oxford: Oxford University Press, 1998).

5. B. Fanning, *Racism and Social Change in the Republic of Ireland* (Manchester: Manchester University Press, 2002), p.81.

6. R. Rorty, *Objectivism, Relativism and Truth* (New York: Cambridge University Press, 1994), p.203.

7. Ibid., p.29.

8. B. Allen, 'What was epistemology', in R. Brandom (ed.), *Rorty and his Critics* (London: Blackwell, 2000), p.224.

9. T.S. Adorno, E. Frenkel-Brunswick, D.J. Levinson and R.N. Sanforo, *The Authoritarian Personality* (New York: Harper and Row, 1950).

10. S. Body-Gendrot, 'Now you see it, now you don't', *Ethnic and Racial Studies*, 21, 5 (1998), p.849.

11. I. Berlin, *The Power of Ideas* (London: Chatto and Windus, 2000).

12. Ibid., p.13.

13. H. Arendt, *The Origins of Totalitarianism* (London: George Allen and Unwin, 1961), p.294.

14. Ibid., p.299.

15. Cited by E. Longley, 'Multiculturalism and Northern Ireland', in E. Longley and D. Kiberd, *Multiculturalism: The View From the Two Irelands* (Armagh: Centre for Cross-Border Studies, 2001), p.9.

CHAPTER TEN

1. S. Deane, *Foreign Affections: Essays on Edmund Burke* (Cork: Cork University Press, 2005).

2. C. Cruise O'Brien, *The Great Melody: A Thematic Biography of Edmund Burke* (London: Sinclair Stevenson, 1992).

3. S. Deane, 'Unhappy at home: Interview with Seamus Heaney', *The Crane Bag*, 1, 1 (1977), p.69.

4. Ibid.

5. See S. Deane, 'An Example of Tradition', *The Crane Bag*, 3, 1 (1978), p.377.

6. Ibid., p.378.

7. K. Galbraith, *A History of Economics: The Past as the Present* (London: Penguin, 1991), p.64.

8. C. McCarthy, *Modernisation: Crisis and Culture in Ireland 1969–1992* (Dublin: Four Courts Press, 2000), p.213.

9. E. Gellner, 'The sacred and the national', *LSE Quarterly*, 3 (1989), pp.357–69.

10. J. Cleary, *Outrageous Fortune: Capital and Culture in Modern Ireland* (Dublin: Field Day Publications, 2007), p.15.
11. D. Kiberd, *Inventing Ireland* (London: Jonathan Cape, 1995), and L. Gibbons, *Transformations in Irish Culture* (Cork: Cork University Press, 1996).
12. Cleary, *Outrageous Fortune*, pp.17–19.
13. 'Such theories tend to see colonial power as an all-embracing, trans-historical force, controlling and transforming every aspect, every tiny detail of colonised societies. The writings and attitudes of those involved with empire are seen as constituting a system, a network, a discourse in the sense made famous by Michel Foucault. It inextricably combines the production of knowledge with the exercise of power. It deals with stereotypes and polar antitheses. It has both justificatory and repressive functions. And perhaps above all *it* is a singular 'it': colonial discourse and by extension the categories in which it deals (the coloniser, the colonised, the subject people, etc) can meaningfully be discussed in unitary, abstract and unsituated terms.' S. Howe, *Ireland and Empire: Colonial Legacies in Irish History and Culture* (Oxford: Oxford University Press, 2000), p.108.
14. C. Cruise O'Brien, *Memoir: My Life and Themes* (London: Profile, 1998), p.6.
15. S. Deane, *Reading in the Dark* (London: Vintage, 1997).
16. C. Cruise O'Brien, *Neighbours: The Ewart Biggs Memorial Lectures* (London: Faber and Faber, 1980), p.29.
17. Both quotes are cited from Kiberd. The second is from Seamus Heaney's poem 'Station Island': 'Raking dead fires/ a waster of time for someone your age/That subject people stuff is a cod's game ...' See Kiberd, *Inventing Ireland*, pp.559, 597.
18. D. Corkery, *The Hidden Ireland* (Dublin: Gill and Macmillan, 1970).

CHAPTER ELEVEN

1. D. Lyons S.J., 'The Negro in America', *Studies*, 40, 157 (1951), pp.69–80, at pp.70–7.
2. N. Ignatiev, *How the Irish Became White* (London: Routledge, 1995), p.179.
3. R. Lentin and R. McVeigh, *After Optimism: Ireland, Racism and Globalisation* (Dublin: Metro Éireann, 2006), p.4.
4. D.T. Goldberg, *The Racial State* (Oxford, Blackwell, 2002), p.4.
5. Ibid., p.16.
6. Ibid., p.44.
7. Lord Acton 1862 cited ibid, p.67
8. Lentin and McVeigh, *After Optimism*, p.18.
9. Ibid., p.162.
10. S.J. Brown S.J., 'What is a nation?', *Studies*, 1, 3 (1913), pp.496–510; S.J. Brown S.J., 'The question of Irish nationality', *Studies*, 1, 4 (1913), pp.634–55.
11. T.M. Kettle, *The Open Secret of Ireland* (London: W.J. Ham-Smith, 1912), cited in *Studies*, 1, 4 (1913), p.496.
12. Original italics, ibid., p.499.
13. Ibid., p.498
14. B. Fanning, *Racism and Social Change in the Republic of Ireland* (Manchester: Manchester University Press, 2002), p.10.
15. Brown, 'What is a nation?', p.503.
16. Ibid.
17. Ibid., p.505.
18. Ibid.
19. Ibid., p.509.
20. S.J. Brown S.J., 'Recent studies in nationality', *Studies*, 9, 35 (1920), pp.20–46.
21. Ibid., pp.458–9.
22. Ibid., p.463.
23. E. Gellner, *Encounters with Nationalism* (Oxford: Blackwell, 1994), p.63.
24. For discussion of their cover image see B. Rolston and M. Shannon, *Encounters: How Racism Came to Ireland* (Belfast: Beyond the Pale, 2002), p.64.
25. Ibid., p.8.
26. Ibid., p.88.
27. Fanning, *Racism and Social Change*, p.42.

28. P. Hart, *The IRA and its Enemies: Violence and Community in Cork 1916–1923* (Oxford: Clarendon Press, 1998), p.311.
29. Hart uses a single heading for tinkers and tramps in tabulating those shot by the IRA. Bhreatnach in her history of Travellers criticises this conflation of two quite different out-groups but suggests that they were so lumped together by the settled population at the time. Hart cites a description of one Mick O'Sullivan ('a very raggedy individual, a kind of tinker and a hard nail') by the volunteer who shot him in May 1921. See A. Bhreatnach, *Becoming Conspicuous: Irish Travellers, Society and the State 1922–70* (Dublin: University College Dublin Press, 2007), p.30 and Hart, *IRA and its Enemies*, pp.309–10.
30. L. Gibbons, 'Memory without walls: From Kevin Barry to Osama bin Laden', *Village*, 20 October 2005
31. Hart states that of 113 private homes burned by the guerrillas in Cork, ninety-six (or 85 per cent) belonged to Protestants. None of the more than two dozen farms seized from 'spies' in 1921 and 1922 was owned by a Catholic. By the end of 1922 Cork's Protestant community was almost half its pre-revolutionary size. Hart, *IRA and its Enemies*, p.313.

CHAPTER TWELVE

1. These resulted in the *Towards 2016* social partnership agreement.
2. These transitory restrictions do not apply to Malta and Cyprus, the two new 'Western' EU member states.
3. European Commission, *Report on the Functioning of the Transitional Arrangements set out in the 2003 Accession Treaty* (Brussels: COM/2006/0048, 2006).
4. K. Allen, 'Neo-liberalism and immigration', in B. Fanning (ed.), *Immigration and Social Change in the Republic of Ireland* (Manchester: Manchester University Press, 2007), pp.89–90.
5. 'Ferries row could sink the social partnership', *Irish Times*, 16 November 2005.
6. R. Erne, 'A contentious consensus', in T. Schulten, R. Bispinck and C. Schäfer (eds), *Minimum Wages in Europe* (Brussels: ETUI, 2006), pp.65–83.
7. SIPTU, *EU Services Directive: The Frankenstein Directive* (Dublin: SIPTU, 2006).
8. Ibid.
9. Erne, 'A contentious consensus', pp.65–83.
10. 'Has Labour's Pat Rabbitte lost the plot?', *Waterford News and Star*, 13 January 2006.
11. In the TNS poll, a third of those surveyed had a firm opposition to immigration and immigrants. Roughly 20 per cent had a very positive position; 53 per cent believed that migrant labour was making it harder to for Irish people to get jobs; 63 per cent believed that immigration was pushing down wages but 59 per cent and 52 per cent considered that migrants were good for the economy and society respectively. *Irish Times*, 22 January 2006.
12. Indymedia Ireland, www.indymedia.ie/article/72660, accessed 1 April 2006.
13. Ibid.
14. *Irish Times*, 23 January 2006.
15. Labour Party, *A Fair Place to Work and Live* (Dublin: The Labour Party, 2006).
16. Ahern stated that the allowance of €1,000 would be payable only to children in receipt of children's allowances under the age of six. At the time, child benefit claims were currently being made in respect of some 4,000 children under the age of eighteen by EU nationals with children resident in other member states. Ahern estimated that one quarter of these were under the age of six. M. Brennock, *Irish Times*, 1 February 2006.
17. *Irish Times*, 1 February 2006.
18. B. Fanning, 'Integration and social policy', in B. Fanning (ed.), *Immigration and Social Change in the Republic of Ireland* (Manchester: Manchester University Press, 2007), p.252.
19. Government of Ireland, *Reconciling Mobility and Social Inclusion* (Dublin: Stationery Office, 2005), p.6.
20. Fanning, 'Integration and Social Policy', pp.251–2.
21. Emphasising, for instance, how research in the United States indicates that racial considerations are the single most important factor shaping whites' views on welfare. M. Gilens, '"Race coding" and white opposition to welfare', *American Political Science Journal*, 90, 3 (1996), p.601.
22. D. Goodhart, 'Discomfort of Strangers', *Prospect* (June 2004).
23. F.K. Salter, 'Introduction', in F.K. Salter (ed.), *Welfare, Ethnicity and Altruism: New Findings and Evolutionary Theory* (London: Frank Cass, 2004), p.5.

24. Government of Ireland, *Reconciling Mobility and Social Inclusion*, p.6.
25. M. Rhodes, 'Globalisation, Labour Markets and Welfare States: A Future of "Competitive Corporatism"?' EUI Working Papers, RSC 97/36.(Florence: European University Institute, 1997). Also see R. Erne, *European Unions: Labour's Quest for Transnational Democracy* (Ithaca: Cornell University Press, 2008).
26. The publication of T.K. Whitaker's report *Economic Development* in 1958 formally inaugurated a developmental nation-building report. See B. Fanning, *The Quest for Modern Ireland* (Dublin: Irish Academic Press, 2008), pp.8--9.
27. D. Begg, 'Managing migration and cultural change', in J. Mullholland (ed.), *The Soul of Ireland: Issues of Society, Culture and Identity. Essays from the 2006 McGill Summer School* (Dublin: Liffey Press, 2006), pp.43–5.
28. Government of Ireland, *Towards 2016: Ten-Year Framework Social Partnership Agreement 2006–2015* (Dublin: Stationery Office, 2006).
29. Begg, 'Managing migration', p.46.
30. A caveat is warranted. The experience of other countries is that membership and inclusiveness are by no means one and the same. Like other institutions unions face challenges in integrating minorities. See R. Milkman and K. Wong, 'Organising immigrant workers', in L. Turner, H.C. Katz and R.W. Hurd (eds), *Rekindling the Movement* (Ithaca: Cornell University Press, 2001); R. Penninx and J. Roosblad, (eds), *Trade Unions, Immigration and Immigrants in Europe*, 1960–1993 (New York: Berghahn Books, 2000).
31. Source: Central Statistics 2008, *Quarterly National Household Survey*, Union Membership Q2 2007, 10 April 2007. Available at: www.cso.ie/releasespublications/documents_labourmarket/current/qhnsunionmembership.pdf

CHAPTER THIRTEEN

1. 'Portlaoise elects Ireland's first black mayor', *Irish Times*, 29 June 2007.
2. 'Ireland looks beyond race – Adebari', *Irish Times*, 6 July 2007.
3. B. Fanning, J. Shaw, J.A. O'Connoll and M. Williams, *Irish Political Parties, Immigration and Integration in 2007* (Dublin: Migration and Citizenship Research Initiative, 2007), p.4, www.ucd.ie/mcri
4. As put by one respondent: 'It will obviously take time for such communities to become established members of society and of the party and it will most likely require a few election cycles before such members find themselves in a position to contest an election or propose themselves for election.' Ibid., p.9.
5. Since 1 January 2005, under the 2004 Irish Citizenship and Nationality Act, Irish-born child non-citizens are only entitled to take out Irish citizenship if they comply with the relevant statutory requirements, including being resident in the state for five years. Consequently, no such children will be eligible to apply under that provision before 1 January 2010. Response to parliamentary question, Dáil Éireann, 3 May 2006.
6. Kant's *Perpetual Peace* was promoted by the signing in March 1795 of the Treaty of Bael by Prussia and revolutionary France. This, he argued, was an illegitimate kind of treaty because it was based on a balance of power rather than a moral willingness to create binding international law. See O.A. Payrou Shabani, 'Cosmopolitan justice and immigration: A critical theory perspective', *European Journal of Social Theory*, 10, 1 (2007), pp.87–98, at p.89.
7. See R. Fine and W. Smith, 'Jurgen Habermas's theory of cosmopolitanism', *Constellations*, 10, 4 (2003), pp.469–87; U. Beck, 'The cosmopolitan perspective: Sociology of the second age of modernity', *British Journal of Sociology*, 51, 1 (2000), pp.79–105.
8. I. Kant, *Groundwork of the Metaphysics of Morals*, edited by Mary Gregor (Cambridge: Cambridge University Press, 1997), pp.4, 421.
9. J. Rawls, *A Theory of Justice* (Oxford: Oxford University Press, 1973), p.137.
10. Ibid., pp.253–4.
11. R. Fine and V. Boon, 'Cosmopolitanism: Between past and future', *European Journal of Social Theory*, 10, 1 (2007), pp.5–16, at p.6.
12. Ibid.
13. Here the idea of a Cosmopolitan Europe is promoted to get past the veto-driven zero-sum politics of an enlarged EU through an emphasis on new forms of cosmopolitan agreement to pursue differentiated EU integration. What Beck and Grade call 'cosmopolitan realism'

accepts that political action is interest-based but insists on an approach to the pursuit of one's own interests that is compatible with those of a larger community. U. Beck and E. Grande, 'Cosmopolitanism: Europe's way out of crisis', *European Journal of Social Theory*, 10, 1 (2007), pp.67–85, at pp.71–2.

14. I.E. Carvalhais 'The cosmopolitan language of the state: Post-national citizenship and the integration of non–nationals', *European Journal of Social Theory*, 10, 1 (2007), pp.99–111, at p103.

15. The ECRE is a pan-European network of refugee-assisting NGOs whose stated objectives include the promotion of 'humane, generous, coherent response by the international community to refugee movements', 'strengthening networking between refugee-assisting NGOs and developing their "institutional capacity" in Europe'. ESRE mission statement, www.ecre.org.

16. Notably the *National Action Plan Against Racism* following the UN-sponsored World Conference on Racism, Racial Discrimination, Xenophobia and Related Intolerance in Durban, South Africa in 2001 (The Durban Declaration).

17. Ibid., p.299.

18. B. Anderson, *Imagined Communities: Reflection on the Origins and Spread of Nationalism* (London: Verso, 1983), p.15.

19. The 2002 Housing Miscellaneous Provisions Act. See U. Crowley, 'Boundaries of citizenship: The continued exclusion of Travellers', in K. Hayward and M. Mac Carthaigh (eds), *Recycling the State: The Politics of Adaptation in Ireland* (Dublin: Irish Academic Press, 2007), p.89.

20. R. McVeigh, '"Ethnicity denial" and Racism: The case of the government of Ireland against Travellers', *Translocations*, 2, 1 (2007), pp.99–133.

21. See www.paveepoint.ie

22. *Irish Times*, 27 July 2007.

23. In a 1764 essay Kant ended an account of a reported encounter between a priest and 'Negro carpenter' by dismissing a point supposedly expressed by the latter by saying: 'It might be that there were something in this which perhaps deserved to be considered; but in short, this fellow was quite black from head to foot, a clear proof that what he said was stupid.' I. Kant (1764), 'Observations on the feeling of the beautiful and sublime', in I. Kramnick (ed.), *The Portable Enlightenment Reader* (London: Penguin, 1995), p.639.

24. K. Hayward, 'Introduction: The Politics of Adaptation in Ireland', in K. Hayward and M. Mac Carthaigh (eds), *Recycling the State*, pp.6–13.

25. E. Gellner, *Nations and Nationalism* (Oxford: Blackwell, 1983), p.57.

26. The term used in the Fianna Fáil campaign in support of the 2004 referendum.

27. Ireland's first Minister of State for Integration backed the Garda commissioner in prohibiting a Sikh Garda reservist from being allowed to wear a turban on duty.

28. Under the 2004 Social Welfare (Miscellaneous Provisions) Act immigrants not habitually resident in Ireland for years were deemed not entitled to Unemployment Assistance, Old Age (Non-Contributory) and Blind Pensions, Widow(er)'s and Orphan's (Non-Contributory) Pensions, One-Parent Family Payment, Carer's Allowance, Disability Allowance, Supplementary Welfare Allowance (other than once-off exceptional and urgent needs payments) and Children's Allowances. The removal of welfare safety nets and the loss of entitlement to children's allowances place immigrants at disproportionate risk of poverty. In February 2006 the government acknowledged that EU law (EU 1408 of 1971) imposed reciprocal obligations on EU states to recognise the entitlements of citizens from other EU countries resident in their own countries.

29. The Ninth Amendment to the Constitution, which led to the 1985 Electoral (Amendment) Act, extended suffrage for Dáil elections to cover British citizens and created a power for a minister to extend this on the basis of reciprocity in the event that other EU member states conferred the right to vote in their parliamentary elections on Irish citizens. See Fanning, Shaw, O'Connell and Williams, *Irish Political Parties*, p.x.

30. Beck and Grande, *Cosmopolitanism: Europe's Way out of Crisis*, pp.71–2.

31. A post-national concept of citizenship incorporates a regime of rights working on a global or trans-national level (such as the EU) and/or as a higher stage of inclusion of non-nationals within the national social, civic and political rights. I.E. Carvalhais, 'The cosmopolitan language of the state: Post-national citizenship and the integration of non-nationals', *European Journal of Social Theory*, 10, 1 (2007), pp.99–111, at p.100.

32. After five years legal residence migrant workers can apply for Irish citizenship. Most of those who naturalised between 2000 and 2004 were from outside the European Union. Out of a total of just 5,387 who acquired Irish citizenship the largest cohorts were Pakistani (653), Bosnian (578), Indian (299), Somali (257), Iraqi (229) and Sudanese (200). Note: the Bosnian cohort included those admitted as programme refugees. Somali, Iraqi and Sudanese cohorts seem to predominantly consist of former asylum seekers who obtained refugee status or leave to remain. Pakistani and Indian cohorts are more likely to have been labour migrants (e.g. working in the health system). Data from the Department of Justice, Equality and Law Reform cited in NESC, *Managing Migration in Ireland* (Dublin: National Economic and Social Council, 2006), p.37.

33. O'Donoghue made no reference to this. Instead he spoke of Adebari's voluntary work in Portlaoise, 'doing everything from setting up a support group for the unemployed to joining the Abbeyleix Tennis Club'. *Irish Times*, 6 July 2007.

34. Adebari received residency status on the basis of having an Irish-born child. 'Hail the chieftain', *Irish Independent*, 25 August 2007

35. S. Mullally, 'Children, citizenship and constitutional change', in B. Fanning (ed.), *Immigration and Social Change in the Republic of Ireland* (Manchester: Manchester University Press, 2007), p.28.

36. *Irish Times*, 15 March 2005.

37. Neltah Chadamoyo cited in 'I didn't know what racism was until I came to Ireland', *Irish Times*, 4 November 2006.

38. Theophilus Ejorah cited in 'Political activism and the Irish African community', Indymedia Ireland, 22 July 2006, www.indymedia.ie/article/77404

39. R. Doyle, *The Deportees* (London: Jonathan Cape, 2007).

40. See F. Mutwarasibo and S. Smith, *Africans in Ireland: Developing Communities* (Dublin: African Cultural Project, 2000); A. Ugba, 'African pentecostals in twenty-first-century Ireland: Identity and integration', in Fanning (ed.), *Immigration and Social Change in the Republic of Ireland*; B. Fanning, F. Mutwarasibo and N. Chadamoyo, *Positive Politics: Participation of Immigrants and Ethnic Minorities in the Electoral Process* (Dublin: Africa Solidarity Centre, 2003); T. Ejorh, *Inclusive Citizenship in 21st-Century Ireland: What Prospects for the African Community?* (Dublin: Africa Centre, 2006).

41. Africa Centre, *Strategic Plan 2005–2008* (Dublin: Africa Centre, 2005), p.5, www.africacentre.ie

42. Ibid., p.7.

43. T. Ejorh, 'Immigration and citizenship: African immigrants in Ireland', *Studies*, 96, 381 (2007), pp.47–53, at p.48.

44. In the run-up to the 2004 election many non-citizen residents, asylum seekers and those with leave to remain were illegally refused their right to register because their Department of Justice identification cards were not deemed acceptable. N. Chadamoyo, B. Fanning and F. Mutwarasibo, 'Breaking into politics', in Fanning (ed.), *Immigration and Social Change in the Republic of Ireland*, p.193.

45. A. Ugba, 'African Pentecostals in Ireland', in Fanning (ed.) *Immigration and Social Change in the Republic of Ireland*, p.182.

46. A. Feldman, D.I. Ndakengerwa, A. Nolan and C. Fresse, *Diversity, Civil Society and Social Change in Ireland: A North–South Comparison of the Role of Immigrant/'New' Minority Ethnic-Led Community and Voluntary Sector Organisations* (Dublin: Migration and Citizenship Research Initiative, 2005), p.10.

47. A. Feldman, *The New Irish Lecture Series 2007–8*, Boston College Centre for Irish 48.

48. Notably, President Mary Robinson's emphasis on Diasporic Irishness.

CHAPTER FOURTEEN

1. I. Berlin, *The Proper Study of Mankind* (London: Pimlico, 1998), pp.369–70, at p.393.

2. B. Fanning, *The Quest for Modern Ireland: The Battle of Ideas 1912–1986* (Dublin: Irish Academic Press, 2008), p.224.

3. National Social and Economic Council, *The Developmental Welfare State* (Dublin: Stationery Office, 2005).

4. R.D. Putnam, 'E pluribus unum: Diversity and community in the twenty-first century', *Scandinavian Political Studies*, 30, 2 (2007), pp.137–67, at p.137.

5. Office for Social Inclusion, *Reconciling Mobility and Social Inclusion: The Role of Employment and Social Policy* (Dublin: Stationery Office, 2004), p.27.
6. Ibid., p.6
7. See B. Fanning and T. Mooney, 'Pragmatism and intolerance', *Philosophy and Social Criticism*, vol. 35 (2009), pp. [page numbers to be inserted in at proof stage] R. Rorty, *Objectivism, Relativism and Truth* (New York: Cambridge, 1994).
8. I. Berlin, *The Power of Ideas* (London: Chatto and Windus, 2000), p.12.
9. L. Wieseltier, *Against Identity* (New York: William Drenttel, 1996).
10. D. McWilliams, *The Generation Game* (Dublin: Gill and Macmillan, 2007), p.60.
11. Ibid., p.209.
12. Ibid., p.210.
13. D. McWilliams, *The Pope's Children* (Dublin: Gill and Macmillan, 2005), p.216.
14. Ibid., pp.216–17.
15. Ibid., p.216.
16. Ibid., p.219.
17. Ibid., p.223.
18. McWilliams, *Generation Game*, p.243.
19. Ibid., p.242.
20. Ibid., p.256.
21. Ibid., p.255.
22. McWilliams cites a website rather than Spengler's *Decline of the West*, www.asiantimes.com/pengler. Ibid., p.224.
23. See Table One: 'Contemporary Spiritual Epochs' in the appendix to O. Spengler, *The Decline of the West: Form and Actuality* (New York: Knoff, 1947).
24. R.A. Pois, 'Spengler', in R. Turner (ed.), *Thinkers of the Twentieth Century* (London: St James Press, 1987), pp.725–7.
25. On Yeats' reading of Spengler see R. Foster, *W.B. Yeats: A Life Vol. II* (Oxford: Oxford University Press, 2003), pp.312–13 and p.398. As portrayed acerbically in Frank O'Connor's 1941 obituary essay, Yeats 'was a fascist and an authoritarian, seeing in world crises only the break-up of the "dammed liberalism" he hated; an old IRB man, passionate nationalist, lover of tradition; hater of reason, popular education and "mechanical logic"'. F. O'Connor, 'The old age of a poet', *The Bell*, 1, 5 (February 1941), pp.7–9.
26. McWilliams, *Generation Game*, p.211.
27. *The Hibernian* is edited by Gerry McGeough, a breakaway member of Sinn Féin and a former IRA volunteer. He was extradited to the United States where he was convicted of attempting to buy surface-to-air missiles in 1983.On release from prison in 1996 he was deported.
28. 'Editorial', *The Hibernian*, May 2006, www.hibernianmedia.com
29. 'Irish Ireland', *The Hibernian*, March 2007, www.hibernianmedia.com
30. 'Save our National Birthright', *The Hibernian*, July 2006, www.hibernianmedia.com
31. 'A New Plantation?', *The Hibernian*, June 2006, www.hibernianmedia.com
32. M. O'Riordan, 'The Sinn Féin tradition of anti-Semitism from Arthur Griffith to Seán South', in P. Feely (ed.), *The Rise and Fall of Irish Anti-Semitism* (Dublin: Labour History Workshop, 1984), pp.22–4.
33. 'An Islamic Ireland?', *The Hibernian*, October 2006, www.hibernianmedia.com
34. Letters to editor, *The Hibernian*, December 2006, www.hibernianmedia.com
35. K. Hayward and K. Howard, 'Cherry-picking the Diaspora', in B. Fanning (ed.), *Immigration and Social Change in the Republic of Ireland* (Manchester: Manchester University Press, 2007), pp.47–62.
36. YouTube, June 2008, www.youtube.com
37. B. Walker, 'Diaspora made up of many shades of green', *Irish Times*, 3 January 2008.
38. K. Howard, 'Accidental Diasporas: A perspective on Northern Ireland's nationalisms', in A. Ni Éigeartaigh, K. Howard and D. Getty, *Rethinking Diasporas: Hidden Narratives and Imagined Borders* (Newcastle: Cambridge Scholars Publishing, 2007), pp.78–9.
39. Fanning, *Quest for Modern Ireland*, p.173.
40. British Council, *Through Irish Eyes: Irish Attitudes toward the UK* (Dublin: British Embassy, 2004), cited in Howard, 'Accidental Diasporas', p.88.
41. The reference to Madagascar here is metaphorical. An unfeasible plan to expel Germany's Jews to Madagascar emerged as the penultimate solution. Their genocide was promoted as the final solution. See Z. Bauman, *Modernity and the Holocaust* (London: Sage, 1996), p.15.

42. D. Kiberd, 'Strangers in their own country: Multiculturalism in Ireland', in E. Longley and D. Kiberd, *Multiculturalism: The View from the Two Irelands* (Cork: Cork University Press, 2001), p.52.
43. Fanning, *Quest for Modern Ireland*, p.39.
44. Kiberd, 'Strangers in their own country', p.66.
45. F. Cullen, 'Beyond nationalism: Time to reclaim the republican ideal', *The Republic*, vol. 1 (2001), p.7.
46. Ibid., p.10.
47. Ibid., pp.12–13.
48. D. Ó Ceallaigh, 'Republicanism and nationalism: An imagined conflict', *The Republic*, vol. 2 (2001), pp.141–2.
49. Ibid., p.139.
50. F. Cullen, Postscript to Ó Ceallaigh, *An Imagined Conflict*, p.144.
51. F. Cullen and A. Ó Snodaigh, 'Editorial', *The Republic*, vol.4 (2005), p.5.
52. T.J. Matthews, 'In praise of "Hibernocentrism": Republicanism, globalisation and Irish culture', *The Republic*, vol. 4 (June 2005), pp.7–14, at p.8.
53. Ibid., p.12.
54. www.cso.ie, cited in McWilliams, *Generation Game*, p.152.
55. Matthews, 'In praise of "Hibernocentrism"', p.13.
56. C. Walsh, 'Between rhetoric and reality: Travellers and the unfinished republic', *The Republic*, vol. 2 (2001), pp.82–6.
57. P. Delaney, 'Travellers, representation and Irish culture', *The Republic*, vol. 3 (2002), p.81.
58. Ibid., p.81.
59. Ibid., p.86.
60. Cited from S. Maher, *The Road to God Knows Where: A Memoir of a Travelling Boyhood* (Dublin: Veritas, 1998), p.164.
61. T. Modood, 'Multiculturalism, secularism and the state', *The Republic*, vol. 4 (2005), pp.15–30, at p.19.
62. P. Mac Éinrí, 'Integration models and choices', in Fanning (ed.), *Immigration and Social Change*, p.219.
63. Kiberd, 'Strangers in their own country', p.68.
64. Source: Department of Education, 2007.
65. Section 7.3c of the 2000 Equal Status Act states that faith-based primary and post-primary schools (the overwhelming majority) are permitted to discriminate against persons from outside their faith: 'Where the establishment is a school providing primary or post-primary education to students and the objective of the school is to provide education in an environment which promotes certain religious values, it admits persons of a particular religious denomination in preference to others or it refuses to admit as a student a person who is not of that denomination and in the case of a refusal, it is proved that the refusal is essential to maintain the ethos of the school.'
66. Archbishop Diarmuid Martin, 'Hope of a different, more mature, more lively church', in J. Mullholland (ed.), *The Soul of Ireland. Issues of Society, Culture and Identity: Essays from the 2006 McGill Summer School* (Dublin: Liffey Press, 2006), p.171.
67. E. O'Kelly cited by R. Boland, 'Faith before fairness', *Irish Times*, 8 September 2007.
68. Ibid.
69. *Irish Times*, 2 February 2008.
70. Address by Conor Lenihan, Minister of State for Integration, UCD, 14 September 2007.
71. J.A. Murphy, 'The time to separate faith from the fatherland is now', *Sunday Independent*, 2 September 2007.
72. *Irish Times*, 4 January 2008.
73. As put in the EU handbook circulated at the 2007 'Integration: The Chance to Get it Right' conference: 'What does integration mean? The question might be expected to trigger familiar debates about assimilation or multiculturalism, but participants at the technical seminars preparing the handbook hardly used these terms. As policy makers and practitioners working with immigrant integration on a day-to-day basis they took a rather more practical approach, focusing on outcomes in terms of social and economic mobility, education, health, housing, social services, and societal protection'. Directorate-General Justice, Freedom and Security, *Handbook on Integration for Policy–makers and Practitioners* (Luxembourg: European Community Publications Office, 2007), p.8.

74. Ibid., p.7.
75. Wieseltier, *Against Identity*, p.14.
76. The 'Integration Policy: Strategies for a Cohesive Society' conference organised by the Irish Naturalisation and Immigration Service of the Department Of Justice, Equality and Law Reform at Dublin Castle, 1 February 2007.
77. Here I draw mostly on a 2001 article that anticipated the Dutch political rejection of multiculturalism. B. Spiecker and J. Steutel, 'Multiculturalism, pillarisation and liberal civic education in the Netherlands', *International Journal of Educational Research*, 35, 3 (2001), pp.293–304, at pp.296–7. Also see M.P. Vink, 'Dutch "multiculturalism" beyond the pillarisation myth', *Political Studies Review*, vol. 5 (2007), pp.337–50, at p.344.
78. Exemplified by the video produced by Dutch immigration authorities to convey to newcomers the 'quintessence of "Dutchness"'. This included naked sunbathers and a gay wedding along with footage of tulips, windmills and William of Orange. M. Burleigh, *Sacred Causes: Religion and Politics from the European Dictators to Al Qaeda* (London: Harper, 2006), p.476.
79. I. Buruma, *Murder in Amsterdam: The Death of Theo Van Gogh and the Limits of Tolerance* (London: Atlantic Books, 2006).
80. C. Power, 'Breaking through', *Time*, 11 February 2008, p.30.
81. Labour Party education 'spokesman' Ruairi Quinn and his Fine Gael counterpart Brian Hayes stated their opposition to the wearing of the headscarf in state schools. *Irish Times*, 6 June 2008.
82. The poll sampled 1,000 voters across all forty-three constituencies. Some 48 per cent supported the wearing of headscarves or hijabs, 39 per cent considered that the wearing of headscarves or hijabs should not be allowed, and 13 per cent had no opinion. *Irish Times*, 9 June 2008.
83. K. Flynn, 'Understanding Islam in Ireland', *Islam and Christian–Muslim Relations*, 17, 2 (2006), pp.223–38 at p.231. Joint Management Board secretary Ferdia Kelly cited in 'Schools backing Muslim headscarf', *The Irish Catholic*, 22 May 2008.
84. Ibid., *The Irish Catholic*, 22 May 2008.
85. R.D. Putnam, *Bowling Alone: The Collapse and Revival of American Community* (New York: Touchstone, 2000), p.23; Putnam, 'E pluribus unum' p.138.
86. A. Ugba, 'African Pentecostals in Ireland', in Fanning (ed.) *Immigration and Social Change*, pp.180-2.
87. T. McVeigh, 'Educational Disadvantage', in B. Fanning and M. Rush (eds), *Care and Social Change in the Republic of Ireland* (Dublin: University College Dublin Press, 2006).
88. Putnam, 'E pluribus unum', p.138.

CHAPTER FIFTEEN

1. T. Vananen, 'Domestic ethnic conflict and ethnic nepotism: A comparative analysis', *Journal of Peace Research*, 36, 1 (1999), pp.55–73, at p.73.
2. Ibid., p.56.
3. F. K. Salter, 'Estimating ethnic genetic interests: Is it adaptive to resist replacement migration?', *Population and Environment*, 24, 2 (2002), pp.111–140, at pp.112–13.
4. Ibid., p.115.
5. Ibid., pp.111–12.
6. Ibid., pp.123–4.
7. F. K. Salter, *Genetic Interests: Family, Ethny and Humanity in an Age of Mass Migration* (Frankfrurt: Transaction, 2003), p.188.
8. Ibid.
9. Gene Expression, www.gnxp.com/MT2/archieves/003501.html.
10. Cited by Salter from A. Keith, *A New Theory of Human Evolution* (New York: Philosophical Library, 1968), pp.317–19. See in Salter, *Estimating Ethnic Genetic Interest*, p.114.
11. A review essay posted by *American Renaissance* depicted Salter's views as 'in almost perfect harmony' with its justifications for 'racial consciousness and activism'. J. Taylor, 'What we owe our people: A scientist explains the genetic basis of nationalism', www.amren.co/newstore/genetic_interest_review.html
12. D. Goodhart, 'Discomfort of Strangers', *Prospect*, June 2004
13. Salter, 'Estimating genetic interests', p.134.

14. Goodhart, 'Discomfort of Strangers'.
15. F.K. Salter, 'Introduction', in F.K. Salter (ed.), *Welfare, Ethnicity and Altruism: New Findings and Evolutionary Theory* (London: Frank Cass, 2004), p.5.
16. Border and Immigration Agency, *The Path to Citizenship: Next Steps in Reforming the Immigration System* (London: Home Office, 2008).
17. Cited from D. Goodhart, 'The baby-boomers finally see sense on immigration', *The Observer*, 24 February 2008.
18. L. Byrne, UK Minister for Integration, press release, 20 February 2008.
19. Goodhart, 'The baby-boomers finally see sense on immigration'.
20. Ibid.
21. Ibid.

Bibliography

Adorno, T.S., Frenkel-Brunswick, E., Levinson, D.J. and Sanforo, R.N. *The Authoritarian Personality* (London: Harper and Row, 1950).

Allen, K. 'Neo-liberalism and immigration', in B. Fanning (ed.), *Immigration and Social Change in the Republic of Ireland* (Manchester: Manchester University Press, 2007).

Allport, G.W. *The Nature of Prejudice* (Cambridge, MA: Addison-Wesley, 1966).

Anderson, B. *Imagined Communities: Reflection on the Origins and Spread of Nationalism* (London: Verso, 1983).

Arendt, H. *The Origins of Totalitarianism* (London: George Allen and Unwin, 1961).

Arendt, H. *The Jew as Pariah: Jewish Identity and Politics in the Modern Age*, edited by R.H. Feldman (New York: Grove Press, 1978).

Barker, M. *The New Racism* (London: Junction Books, 1981).

Bauman, Z. *Modernity and the Holocaust* (New York: Cornell, 1989).

Beck, U. 'The cosmopolitan perspective: Sociology of the second age of modernity', *British Journal of Sociology*, 51, 1 (2000), pp.79–105.

Beck, U. and Grande, E. 'Cosmopolitanism: Europe's way out of crisis', *European Journal of Social Theory*, 10, 1 (2007), pp.67–85.

Berlin, I. *Proper Study of Mankind* (London: Pimlico, 1998).

Berlin, I. *The Power of Ideas* (London: Chatto and Windus, 2000).

Bhreatnach, A. *Becoming Conspicuous: Irish Travellers, Society and the State 1922–70* (Dublin: University College Dublin Press, 2007).

Border and Immigration Agency, *The Path to Citizenship: Next Steps in Reforming the Immigration System* (London: Home Office, 2008).

Boyle, K. and Watt, B. *International and United Kingdom Law Relevant to the Protection of the Rights and Cultural Identity of the Travelling Community in Ireland: Paper commissioned by the Task Force on the Travelling Community* (Colchester: Human Rights Centre, University of Essex, 1995).

Brown, A. '"The other day I met a constituent of mine": a theory of anecdotal racism', *Ethnic and Racial Studies*, 22, 1 (1999), pp.23–55.

Brown, S.J. 'Recent studies in nationality', *Studies*, 9, 35 (1920), pp.20–464.

Burleigh, M. *Sacred Causes: Religion and Politics from the European Dictators to Al Qaeda* (London: Harper, 2006).

Buruma, I. *Murder in Amsterdam: The Death of Theo Van Gogh and the Limits of Tolerance* (London: Atlantic Books, 2006).

Butler, H. *Ten Thousand Saints* (Kilkenny: Wellbrook Press, 1972).

Butler, H. *Independent Spirit: Essays* (New York: Farrar, Straus and Giroux, 1996).

Cahill, T. *How the Irish Saved Civilisation* (London: Hodder and Stoughton, 1995).

Carvalhais, I.E. 'The cosmopolitan language of the state: Post-national citizenship and the integration of non-nationals', *European Journal of Social Theory*, 10, 1 (2007), pp.99–111.

Castles, S. and Davidson, A. *Citizenship and Migration: Globalisation and the Politics of Belonging* (London: Macmillan, 2000).

Christie, A. 'Responses of the social work profession to unaccompanied children seeking asylum in the Republic of Ireland', *European Journal of Social Work*, 5, 2 (2002), pp.187–98.

Christie, A. 'Asylum seekers and refugees in Ireland: Questions of racism and social work', *Social Work in Europe*, 9, 1 (2002), pp.10–17.

Clear, C. *Social Change and Everyday Life in Ireland, 1850–1922* (Manchester: Manchester University Press, 2007).

Cleary, J. *Outrageous Fortune: Capital and Culture in Modern Ireland* (Dublin: Field Day Publications, 2007).

Coakley, J. and Gallagher, M. *Politics in the Republic of Ireland*, (London: Routledge, 2005).

Cohen, S., Humphries, B. and Mynott, E. *From Immigration Controls to Welfare Controls* (London: Routledge, 2002).

Comhlámh, *Refugee Lives: The Failure of Direct Provision as a Social Response to the Needs of Asylum Seekers in Ireland* (Dublin: Comhlámh Refugee Solidarity Group, 2001).

Commission on Itinerancy, *Report of the Commission on Itinerancy* (Dublin: Stationery Office, 1963).

Conroy, P. *Trafficking in Unaccompanied Minors in Dublin* (Dublin: International Organisation of Migration, 2003).

Corkery, D. *The Hidden Ireland: A Study of Gaelic Munster in the Eighteenth Century* (Dublin: Gill and Macmillan, 1970).

Cornell, S. and Hartmann, P. *Ethnicity and Race – Making Identities in a Changing World* (Thousand Oaks, CA: Pine Forge Press, 1998).

Coulter, C. and Coleman, S. (eds), *The End of Irish History? Critical Reflections on the Celtic Tiger* (Manchester: Manchester University Press, 2003).

Crooke, E. *Politics, Archaeology and the Creation of a National Museum of Ireland* (Dublin: Irish Academic Press, 2000).

Crotty, W. and Schmitt, D.E. *Ireland and the Politics of Change* (London: Longman, 1998).

Crowley, U. 'Boundaries of citizenship: The continued exclusion of Travellers', in K. Hayward and M. Mac Carthaigh (eds), *Recycling the State: The Politics of Adaptation in Ireland* (Dublin: Irish Academic Press, 2007).

Cruise O'Brien, C. *Neighbours: The Ewart Biggs Memorial Lectures* (London: Faber and Faber, 1980).

Cruise O'Brien, C. *The Great Melody: A Thematic Biography of Edmund Burke* (London: Sinclair Stevenson, 1992).

Cruise O'Brien, C. *Memoir: My Life and Themes* (London: Profile, 1998).

Cullen, F. 'Beyond nationalism: Time to reclaim the republican ideal', *The Republic*, vol. 1 (2001).

Curtis, L. *Apes and Angels: The Irishman in Victorian Caricature* (Newton Abbot: David and Charles, 1971).

Deane, S. 'Unhappy at Home: Interview with Seamus Heaney', *The Crane Bag*, 1, 1 (1977), p.69.

Deane, S. 'An example of tradition', *The Crane Bag*, 3, 1 (1978).

Deane, S. *Reading in the Dark* (London: Vintage, 1997).

Deane, S. *Foreign Affections: Essays on Edmund Burke* (Cork: Cork University Press, 2005).

Delaney, P. 'Travellers, representation and Irish culture', *The Republic*, vol. 3 (2002).

Department of Health and Children, *National Standards for Children's Residential Centres* (Dublin: Stationery Office, 2002).

Department of Social Community and Family Affairs, *Building an Inclusive Society: Review of the National Anti-Poverty Strategy under the Programme for Prosperity and Fairness* (Dublin: Stationery Office, 2002).

Directorate-General Justice, Freedom and Security, *Handbook on Integration for Policy-makers and Practitioners* (Luxembourg: European Community Publications Office, 2007).

Douglass, F. *Narrative of the Life of Fredrick Douglass* (London: Penguin, 1986).

Ejorh, T. *Inclusive Citizenship in 21st-Century Ireland: What Prospects for the African Community?* (Dublin: Africa Centre, 2006).

Ejorh, T. 'Immigration and citizenship: African immigrants in Ireland', *Studies*, 96, 381 (2007), pp.47–53, at p.48.

Engels, F. *The Condition of the Working Class in England* (Oxford: Blackwell, 1971 [1844]).

Erne, R. 'A contentious consensus', in T. Schulten, R. Bispinck and C. Schäfer (eds), *Minimum Wages in Europe* (Brussels: ETUI, 2006), pp.65–83.

Fanning, B. 'Asylum seekers, travellers and racism', *Doctrine and Life*, 50, 6 (2000), pp.358–66.

Fanning, B. *Racism and Social Change in the Republic of Ireland* (Manchester: Manchester University Press, 2002).

Fanning, B. (ed.), *Immigration and Social Change in the Republic of Ireland* (Manchester: Manchester University Press, 2007).

Fanning, B. *The Quest for Modern Ireland: The Battle of Ideas 1912–1986* (Dublin: Irish Academic Press, 2008).

Fanning, B. and Mac Éinrí, P. *Regional Resettlement of Asylum Seekers: A Strategic Approach* (Cork: Irish Centre for Migration Studies, 1999).

Fanning, B. and Mooney, T. 'Pragmatism and Intolerance', *Philosophy and Social Criticism*', vol. 35 (forthcoming, 2009).

Fanning, B. and Veale, A. 'Child poverty as public policy: Direct provision and asylum-seeking children in the Republic of Ireland', *Child Care in Practice*, 10, 3 (2004), pp.241–52.

Fanning, B., Veale, A. and O'Connor, D. *Beyond the Pale: Asylum-Seeker Children and Social Exclusion* (Dublin: Irish Refugee Council, 2001).

Fanning, B., Mutwarasibo, F. and Chadamoyo, N. *Positive Politics: Participation of Immigrants and Ethnic Minorities in the Electoral Process* (Dublin: Africa Centre, 2003).

Fanning, B., Shaw, J., O'Connell, J.A. and Williams, M. *Irish Political Parties, Immigration and Integration in 2007* (Dublin: Migration and Citizenship Research Initiative, 2007), www.ucd.ie/mcri

Fanon, F. *The Wretched of the Earth* (New York: Grove Press, 1968).

Feldman, A., Ndakengerwa, D.I., Nolan, A. and Fresse, C. *Diversity, Civil Society and Social Change in Ireland: A North–South Comparison of the Role of Immigrant/'New' Minority Ethnic-Led Community and Voluntary Sector Organisations* (Dublin: Migration and Citizenship Research Initiative, 2005).

Ferriter, D. *The Transformation of Ireland, 1900–2000* (London: Profile, 2005).

Fine, R. and Boon, V. 'Cosmopolitanism: Between past and future', *European Journal of Social Theory*, 10, 1 (2007), pp.5–16.

Fine, R. and Smith, W. 'Jurgen Habermas's theory of cosmopolitanism', *Constellations*, 10, 4 (2003), pp.469–87.

Flynn, K. 'Understanding Islam in Ireland', *Islam and Christian–Muslim Relations*, 17, 2 (2006), pp.223–38.

Foley, T. and Ryder, S. (eds), *Ideology and Ireland in the Nineteenth Century* (Dublin: Four Courts Press, 1998).

Foster, R. *Modern Ireland 1600–1972* (London: Allen Lane, 1988).

Foster, R. *Paddy and Mr Punch* (London: Allen Lane, 1993).

Foster, R. *W.B. Yeats: A Life, Vol. II* (Oxford: Oxford University Press, 2003).

Foster, R. *Luck and the Irish: A Brief History of Change 1970–2000* (London: Allen Lane, 2007).

Fraser, U. and Harvey, C. *Sanctuary in Ireland: Perspectives on Asylum Law and Policy* (Dublin: Institute of Public Administration, 2003).

Fukuyama, F. *The End of History and the Last Man* (London: Penguin, 1992).

Galbraith, J.K. *A History of Economics: The Past as the Present* (London: Penguin, 1991).

Garvin, T. 'National identity in Ireland', *Studies*, 95, 379 (2006), pp.241–50.

Gellner, E. *Nations and Nationalism* (Oxford: Blackwell, 1983).

Gellner, E. *Culture, Identity and Politics* (Cambridge: Cambridge University Press, 1987).

Gellner, E. 'The sacred and the national', *LSE Quarterly*, 3 (1989), pp.357–69.

Gellner, E. *Encounters with Nationalism* (Oxford: Blackwell, 1994).

Gibbons, L. *Transformations in Irish Culture* (Cork: Cork University Press, 1996).

Gmelch, G. and Gmelch, S.B. 'The emergence of an ethnic group: The Irish tinkers', *Anthropological Quarterly*, 49, 4 (1976), pp.225–38.

Gmelch, S.B. and Gmelch, G. 'The itinerant settlement movement: Its policies and effects on Irish Travellers', *Studies*, 63, 249 (1974).

Gmelch, G. *The Irish Tinkers: The Urbanisation of an Itinerant People* (Long Grove, IL: Waveland Press, 1985).

Goldberg, D.T. *The Racial State* (Oxford: Blackwell, 2002).

Government of Ireland, *Report of the Task Force on the Travelling People* (Dublin: Stationery Office, 1995).

Government of Ireland, *The National Children's Strategy: Our Children – Their Lives* (Dublin: Stationery Office, 2000).

Government of Ireland, *Towards 2016: Ten-Year Framework Social Partnership Agreement 2006–2015* (Dublin: Stationery Office, 2006).

Graham, B. (ed.), *In Search of Ireland: A Cultural Geography* (London: Routledge, 1997).

Hart, P. *The IRA and its Enemies: Violence and Community in Cork 1916–1923* (Oxford: Oxford University Press, 1998).

Haverty, M. *The History of Ireland from the Earliest Period to the Present Time Derived from Native Annals and from the Researches of Dr O'Donovan, Professor Eugene Curry, The Rev. C.P. Meehan, Dr R.R. Madden and other Eminent Scholars and from All Recourses of Irish History Now Available* (New York: Thomas Fannell and Son, 1967).

Hayes, M. *Irish Travellers: Representations and Realities* (Dublin: Liffey Press, 2006).

Hayward, K. 'Introduction: The politics of adaptation in Ireland', in K. Hayward and M. Mac Carthaigh (eds), *Recycling the State: The Politics of Adaptation in Ireland* (Dublin: Irish Academic Press, 2007).

Hayward, K. and Howard, K. 'Cherry-picking the Diaspora', in B. Fanning (ed.), *Immigration and Social Change in the Republic of Ireland* (Manchester: Manchester University Press, 2007).

Heffer, S. *Like A Roman: The Life of Enoch Powell* (London: Phoenix, 1998).

Helleiner, J. 'Gypsies, Celts and Tinkers: Colonial antecedents of anti-Traveller racism in Ireland', *Ethnic and Racial Studies*, 18, 3 (1995), pp.532–54.

Helleiner, J. *Irish Travellers: Racism and the Politics of Culture* (Toronto: University of Toronto Press, 2000).

Hickman, M. *Religion, Class and Identity: The State, the Catholic Church and the Education of the Irish in Britain* (Aldershot: Avebury, 1995).

Howard, K. 'Accidental Diasporas: A perspective on Northern Ireland's nationalisms', in A. Ni Éigeartaigh, K. Howard and D. Getty (eds), *Rethinking Diasporas: Hidden Narratives and Imagined Borders* (Newcastle: Cambridge Scholars Publishing, 2007).

Howe, S. *Ireland and Empire: Colonial Legacies in Irish History and Culture* (Oxford: Oxford University Press, 2000).

Hillburg, R. *The Politics of Memory: The Journey of a Holocaust Historian* (Chicago, Ivan R. Dee, 1996).

Ignatiev, N. *How the Irish Became White* (London: Routledge, 1995).

Inglis, T. *Global Ireland: Same Difference* (London: Routledge, 2007).

Jackson, A. *Ireland: 1798–1998* (London: Blackwell, 1999).

Joppke, C. 'The legal-domestic sources of immigrant rights: The United States, Germany and the European Union', *Comparative Political Studies*, 34, 4 (2001), p.345.

Joppke, C. 'How immigration is changing citizenship: A comparative view', *Ethnic and Racial Studies*, 22, 4 (1999), pp.629–32.

Joyce, N. and Farmer, A. *Traveller* (Dublin: Gill and Macmillan, 1985).

Kant, I. *Groundwork of the Metaphysics of Morals*, edited by Mary Gregor (Cambridge: Cambridge University Press, 1997).

Kant, I. 'Observations on the feeling of the beautiful and sublime', in I. Kramnick (ed.), *The Portable Enlightenment Reader* (London: Penguin, 1995).

Kennedy, P. and Murphy-Lawless, J. *The Maternity Care Needs of Refugee and Asylum-Seeking Women* (Dublin: Northern Area Health Board, 2002).

Keogh, D. *Twentieth-Century Ireland: Nation and State* (Dublin: Gill and Macmillan, 1994).

Kiberd, D. *Inventing Ireland* (London: Vintage, 1995).

Kiberd, D. 'Strangers in their own country: Multiculturalism in Ireland', in E. Longley and D. Kiberd, *Multiculturalism: The View From the Two Irelands* (Cork: Cork University Press, 2001).

Kirby, P. 'Globalisation', in B. Fanning, P. Kennedy, G. Kiely and S. Quin (eds), *Theorising Irish Social Policy* (Dublin: University College Dublin Press, 2004).

Lee, J.J. *Ireland: Politics and Society 1912–1985* (Cambridge: Cambridge University Press, 1989).

Lentin, R. 'Ireland: Racial state and crisis racism', *Ethnic and racial Studies*, 30, 4 (2007), pp.610–27.

Lentin, R. and McVeigh, R. (eds), *Racism and Anti-Racism in Ireland* (Belfast: Beyond the Pale, 2002).

Lentin, R. and McVeigh, R. *After Optimism: Ireland, Racism and Globalisation* (Dublin: Metro Éireann, 2006).

Lipsky, M. 'Street-level bureaucracy', in M. Hill (ed.), *The Policy Process* (London: Harvester Wheatsheaf, 1993).

Lively, A. *Masks: Blackness, Race and the Imagination* (London: Chatto and Windus, 1998).

Longley, E. and Kiberd, D. *Multiculturalism: The View From the Two Irelands* (Armagh: Centre for Cross-Border Studies, 2001).

Lord Laming, *The Victoria Climbie Inquiry: Report of an Inquiry by Lord Laming* (London: The Stationery Office, 2003), www.victoria–climbie–inquiry.org.uk

Loughrey, P. (ed.), *The People of Ireland* (Belfast: Appletree Press, 1988).

MacAlister, S. *The Secret Languages of Ireland with Special Reference to the Origins and Nature of the Shelta Language Partly Based upon Collections and Manuscripts of the late John Sampson Litt.D.* (Cambridge: Cambridge University Press, 1939).

Mac Éinrí, P. 'Integration models and choices', in B. Fanning (ed.), *Immigration and Social Change* (Manchester: Manchester University Press, 2007).

MacGréil, M. *Prejudice and Tolerance in Ireland Revisited* (Maynooth: Survey and Research Unit, 1996).

MacLaughlin, J. *Travellers in Ireland: Whose Country, Whose History?* (Cork: Cork University Press, 1995).

MacLaughlin, J. 'Nation-building, social closure and anti-Traveller racism in Ireland', *Sociology*, 33, 1 (1999).

Macpherson, W. *The Stephen Lawrence Inquiry: Report of an Inquiry by Sir William Macpherson of Cluny* (London: The Stationery Office, 1999).

MacSharry, R. and White, P.A. *The Making of the Celtic Tiger: The Inside Story of Ireland's Boom Economy* (Cork: Mercier Press, 2000).

McCall, S. *And So Began the Irish Nation* (Dublin: Talbot Press, 1930).

McCann, M., Ó Síocháin, S. and Ruane, J. (eds), *Irish Travellers: Culture and Ethnicity* (Belfast: Institute of Irish Studies, 1994).

McCarthy, C. *Modernisation: Crisis and Culture in Ireland 1969–1992* (Dublin: Four Courts Press, 2000).

McVeigh, R. 'Ethnicity denial and racism: The case of the government of Ireland against Irish Travellers', *Translocations*, 2, 1 (2007), pp.90–133, www.translocations.ie

McVeigh T. 'Educational disadvantage', in B. Fanning and M. Rush (eds), *Care and Social Change in the Republic of Ireland* (Dublin: University College Dublin Press, 2006).

McWilliams, D. *The Pope's Children* (Dublin: Gill and Macmillan, 2005).

McWilliams, D. *The Generation Game* (Dublin: Gill and Macmillan, 2007).

Maher, S. *The Road to God Knows Where: A Memoir of a Travelling Boyhood* (Dublin: Veritas, 1998).

Matthews, T.J. 'In praise of "Hibernocentrism": Republicanism, Globalisation and Irish Culture', *The Republic*, vol. 4 (2005), pp.7–14.

Modood, T. 'Multiculturalism, secularism and the state', *The Republic*, vol. 4 (2005), pp.15–30.

Mullholland, J. (ed.), *The Soul of Ireland: Issues of Society, Culture and Identity. Essays from the 2006 McGill Summer School* (Dublin: Liffey Press, 2006).

Murphy, C. and Adair, L. (eds), *Untold Stories: Protestants in the Republic of Ireland 1912–2002* (Dublin: Liffey Press, 2002).

Mutwarasibo, F. and Smith, S, *Africans in Ireland: Developing Communities* (Dublin: African Cultural Project, 2000).

National Social and Economic Council, *The Developmental Welfare State* (Dublin: Stationery Office, 2005).

National Economic and Social Council, *Managing Migration in Ireland: A Social and Economic Analysis* (Dublin: Stationery Office, 2006).

Ó Ceallaigh, D. 'Republicanism and nationalism: An imagined conflict', *The Republic*, vol. 2 (2001).

O'Connor, F.M. 'The old age of a poet', *The Bell*, 1, 5 (February 1941), pp.7–9.

Office for Social Inclusion, *Reconciling Mobility and Social Inclusion: The Role of Employment and Social Policy* (Dublin: Stationery Office, 2004).

O'Hearn, D. *The Atlantic Economy: Britain, the US and Ireland* (Manchester: Manchester University Press, 2001).

O'Riordan, M. 'The Sinn Féin tradition of anti-Semitism from Arthur Griffith to Seán South', in P. Feely (ed.), *The Rise and Fall of Irish Anti-Semitism* (Dublin: Labour History Workshop, 1984).

O'Sullivan, D. *Cultural Politics and Irish Education since the 1950s* (Dublin: Institute of Public Administration, 2006).

O'Sullivan, P. *The Irish in the New Communities* (Leicester: Leicester University Press, 1997).

Payrou Shabani, O.A. 'Cosmopolitan justice and immigration: A critical theory perspective', *European Journal of Social Theory*, 10, 1 (2007), pp.87–98.

Pearse, P. 'The Coming Revolution' in S. Regan (ed.) *Irish Writing: An Anthology of Irish Literature in English, 1789–1939* (Oxford: Oxford University Press, 2004).

Penninx, R. and Roosblad, J. (eds), *Trade Unions, Immigration and Immigrants in Europe, 1960–1993* (New York: Berghahn Books, 2000).

Putnam, R.D. *Bowling Alone: The Collapse and Revival of American Community* (New York: Touchstone, 2000).

Putnam, R.D. 'E pluribus unum: Diversity and community in the twenty-first century', *Scandinavian Political Studies* 30, 2 (2007), pp.137–67.

Quinn, E. and Hughes, G. *Illegally Resident Third Country Nationals in Ireland* (Dublin: Economic and Social Research Institute, 2005).

Quadongo, J. *The Color of Welfare* (Oxford: Oxford University Press, 1994).

Rawls, J.A. *A Theory of Justice* (Oxford: Oxford University Press, 1973).

Ritzer, G. *Sociological Theory* (New York: McGraw-Hill, 1992).

Rolston, B. and Shannon, M. *Encounters: How Racism Came to Ireland* (Belfast: Beyond the Pale, 2002).

Rolston, B. 'Bringing it all back home: Irish emigration and racism', *Race and Class*, 45, 2 (2003), pp.39–53, at p.48.

Rorty, R. *Objectivism, Relativism and Truth* (New York: Cambridge, 1994).

Rushanara, A. and Ó Cinnéide, C. *Our House? Race and Representation in British Politics* (London: Institute of Public Policy Research, 2002).

Ryan, J. *Irish Monasticism: Origins and Early Development* (London: Longmans, 1931).

Salter, F.K. 'Estimating ethnic genetic interests: Is it adaptive to resist replacement migration?', *Population and Environment*, 24, 2 (2002), pp.111–40.

Salter, F.K. *Genetic Interests: Family, Ethny and Humanity in an Age of Mass Migration* (Frankfurt: Transaction, 2003).

Salter, F.K. (ed.), *Welfare, Ethnicity and Altruism: New Findings and Evolutionary Theory* (London: Frank Cass, 2004).

Sassen, S. *Guests and Aliens* (New York: The New Press, 1999).

Schmitt, D.E. *The Irony of Irish Democracy* (Lexington: Lexington Books, 1973).

Sen, A. *Identity and Violence: The Illusion of Destiny* (London: Norton, 2006).

Shaw, J. 'EU citizenship and political rights in an evolving European Union', *Fordham Law Review*, vol. 75 (2007), pp.2549–2561.

Shaw, J. *The Transformation of Citizenship in the European Union* (Cambridge: Cambridge University Press, 2007).

Sheehan, E. (ed.), *Travellers Citizens of Ireland* (Dublin: Parish of the Travelling People, 2000).

Siggins, L. *Mary Robinson: The Woman Who Took Power in the Park* (London: Mainstream, 1997).

Solomos, J. and Back, L. *Racism and Society* (London: Routledge, 1996).

Spengler, O. *The Decline of the West: Form and Actuality* (New York: Knoff, 1947).

Spiecker, B. and Steutel, J. 'Multiculturalism, pillarisation and liberal civic education in the Netherlands', *International Journal of*

Educational Research, 35, 3 (2001), pp.293–304, at pp.296–7.

Taguieff, P.E. *The Force of Prejudice: On Racism and its Doubles* (Minneapolis, MN: University of Minnesota Press, 2001).

Taylor, G. 'Hailing with an invisible hand: A "cosy" political dispute amid the rise of neoliberal politics in modern Ireland', *Government and Opposition*, 37, 4 (2002), pp.501–23, at p.521.

Tierney, M. 'Politics and culture: Daniel O'Connell and the Gaelic past', *Studies*, 27, 107 (1938), pp.353–81.

Ugba, A. 'African Pentecostals in Ireland', in B. Fanning (ed.), *Immigration and Social Change in the Republic of Ireland* (Manchester: Manchester University Press, 2007).

Vananen, T. 'Domestic ethnic conflict and ethnic nepotism: A comparative analysis', *Journal of Peace Research*, 36, 1 (1999), pp.55–73.

Walker, C. 'A nation is a nation, is a state, is an ethnic group, is a …' *Ethnic and Racial Studies*, 1, 4 (1988), pp.379–88.

Walsh, C. 'Between rhetoric and reality: Travellers and the unfinished republic', *The Republic*, vol. 2 (2001), pp.82–6.

Whelan, N. *Politics, Elections and the Law* (Dublin: Blackhall, 2000).

White, J. *Minority Report: The Protestant Community in the Irish Republic* (Dublin: Gill and Macmillan, 1975).

Wieseltier, L. *Against Identity* (New York: William Drenttel, 1996).

Wolf, E. *Europe and the People without History* (Berkeley, CA: University of California Press, 1982).

Index